D0758017

Jan Tinbergen

Economic Development and Planning

Essays in Honour of Jan Tinbergen
Edited by
Willy Sellekaerts

 International Arts and Sciences Press, Inc.
White Plains, New York

Editorial matter and selection © Willy Sellekaerts 1974
Chapter 1 © Irma Adelman and Cynthia Taft Morris 1974
Chapter 2 © Bela Balassa 1974
Chapter 3 © V. S. Dadajan 1974
Chapter 4 © John C. H. Fei and Gustav Ranis 1974
Chapter 5 © Karl A. Fox 1974
Chapter 6 © Arnold C. Harberger 1974
Chapter 7 © Harry G. Johnson 1974
Chapter 8 © H. Leibenstein 1974
Chapter 9 © John Letiche 1974
Chapter 10 © Hans W. Singer 1974

Published in Great Britain by
The Macmillan Press Ltd.

First U.S. edition published in 1974 by
International Arts and Sciences Press, Inc.
901 North Broadway, White Plains, N.Y. 10603

Library of Congress Catalog Card Number: 73-92712

International Standard Book Number: 0-87332-055-7

Printed in Great Britain

Contents

Preface

In 1969 Ragnar Frisch and Jan Tinbergen were selected to share the first Nobel Prize in Economics. As former students of Professor Tinbergen my wife and I decided to honour him by compiling and editing a collection of previously unpublished articles, written by leading economists. In order to create a lasting monument to Jan Tinbergen we decided to use the royalties from the volume to create a scholarship fund from which outstanding Dutch students in economics will receive financial assistance during their first year of study in the North American university of their choice. Further details will later be arranged with the Netherlands School of Economics in Rotterdam.

Several North American and European economists were invited to write a paper, preferably focusing on Tinbergen's pathbreaking work in international trade, economic development and planning, econometrics and economic theory. Most invited economists readily accepted the invitation. I thank all the contributors for their continuous interest and spontaneous co-operation during the two years between the mailing of the invitations and the completion of the manuscript.

Although a Nobel Prizewinner does not need to be introduced to the scholars of his discipline, I decided to include in this collection of essays a paper written by Bent Hansen, in which he not only skilfully appraises Professor Tinbergen's contributions to economics, but also pictures Tinbergen the man as a humanitarian idealist, a worthy candidate for the Nobel Peace Prize. I thank the *Swedish Journal of Economics*, and in particular Peter Bohm, for giving me permission to reprint Bent Hansen's paper. As an appendix to each of the three volumes of this Festschrift, a *selected* bibliography of Jan Tinbergen's contributions to economics has been included.

In addition to the contributors, many persons have helped to make the publication of this collection of essays in honour of Jan Tinbergen possible. I thank Professor Dole Anderson, Director of the Institute for International Business and Economic Development of Michigan State University, who supported my idea and made the facilities of the Institute available to invite the contributors. The Faculty of Social Sciences of the University of Ottawa also contributed to the success of this volume. I thank Patrick Meany of The Macmillan Company of Canada for his assistance in the publication of the Festschrift. Above all, my wife, Brigitte made the publication of this Festschrift feasible, by providing invaluable technical and editorial assistance.

WILLY SELLEKAERTS

Ottawa,
November 1971

Introduction

JAN TINBERGEN

An Appraisal of his Contributions to Economics*

By BENT HANSEN

PROFESSOR Jan Tinbergen was born on 12 April 1903. He graduated from Leiden University where he also obtained his doctoral degree. From 1929 to 1945 he was, with certain interruptions, an official of the Netherlands' Central Bureau of Statistics. As from 1933 he has also been a professor of economics at the Netherlands School of Economics at Rotterdam. During the years 1936 to 1938 he served on the staff of the League of Nations at Geneva. At the end of World War II, in 1945, he was appointed Director of the newly created Central Planning Bureau of the Netherlands. He resigned from this position in 1955 and has since then – besides teaching and research – served as an adviser and consultant to numerous governments and international organisations. As from 1966 he is the Chairman of the United Nation's Committee for Development Planning. A considerable number of universities have awarded him honorary degrees.

The message that Professors Ragnar Frisch and Jan Tinbergen were selected to share the first Nobel Prize in Economics was received by the profession with great satisfaction. Few

* Reprinted with the permission of the *Swedish Journal of Economics*. The original reference: Hansen, Bent, 'Jan Tinbergen: An Appraisal of his Contributions to Economics', *Swedish Journal of Economics*, LXXI (1969) 325–36.

contemporary economists are respected as they are. Few, if any, can look back to a stream of pathbreaking contributions to economics comparable to those achieved by these two men. And their work has been so closely related that it was only natural that they should share the prize.

Thus the choice of the Swedish Academy of Science was both wise and correct. It was a happy choice, too, because both Ragnar Frisch and Jan Tinbergen increasingly have turned their attention towards development policy, searching for feasible solutions to the economic policy problems of the poor countries and it is in this capacity that they are best known nowadays outside the profession. It will always remain a matter of subjective judgement what exactly constitutes a great contribution to economics and, more generally, to science. But it would certainly be most natural for the Academy to consider not only the extension of knowledge for knowledge's own sake, but also its applied aspects, its potential benefits to mankind. At a time when funds for civil development aid tend to dry up and developed countries self-righteously begin to 'lose patience' with their earlier possessions and turn their back to the Third World mess, it is gratifying to see the problems of the poor countries recognised – if not explicitly then certainly by implications – as *the* important scientific problem of economics rather than turnpikes, double-switching and other esoteric matters. Frisch and Tinbergen have both contributed to the pure theory of economics and its applications, for developed as well as under-developed economies. The whole range of economists, from the celebrities in the ivory towers and think-tanks of the rich countries to the anonymous people doing the dirty development work in the poor countries, may therefore all of them rightly feel that 'our men' have been chosen for this unique honour. But nobody will probably feel this more strongly and with more justification than the latter category. This makes the choice of the Academy particularly satisfactory.

1. *Tinbergen's stages of development*

It is convenient to divide Tinbergen's activities and contributions to economics into three groups which also happen to represent consecutive periods of his career (see above). During each period he made pioneering contributions to economics and exerted a profound and lasting influence within the field to which he devoted his attention and energy. During each period he helped to set economics on a new track. Each time his contributions opened up new vistas for both economic theory and economic policy. His work paralleled to some extent that of Ragnar Frisch. They were always in close contact and influenced each other on several occasions. In the sequel we shall therefore meet Frisch's name several times.

The *first* period includes the years from the end of the twenties to World War II. This was the period when Professor Tinbergen together with a few other economists and statisticians created econometrics as a science. During the war years Tinbergen was by and large isolated from international contacts, but he used this time in preparing himself for the *second* period, the decade 1945 to 1955 when he, as the Director of the Central Planning Bureau, laid the foundation for modern short-term economic policies. The *third* period, beginning in the middle fifties and, hopefully, continuing many years ahead, Tinbergen has devoted almost exclusively to the methods and practice of planning for long-term development, in particular of under-developed countries, and international economic cooperation.

2. *The establishment of econometrics as a science*
Ragnar Frisch, Jan Tinbergen and Irving Fischer took, in 1930, the initiative in the creation of The Econometric Society. According to the Society's constitution it is 'an international society for the advancement of economic theory in its relation to statistics and mathematics'. Its main objective should 'be to promote studies that aim at a unification of the theoretical-quantitative approach and the empirical-quantitative approach to economic problems and that are penetrated by constructive and rigorous thinking similar to that which has come to dominate in the natural sciences'. The Econometric Society became immediately a success; it obviously satisfied a deeply-felt need. It has served as a stimulating centre of quantitative economic research. I have quoted the words of the constitution of The Econometric Society rather extensively not only because they describe the nature of the direction into which Tinbergen

and the other founders of the Society wanted to develop economics, but also because they characterise so well Tinbergen's own scientific work.

In addition to this organisational achievement Tinbergen made some of the most fundamental early contributions to econometrics. Among them I want in particular to stress the discovery of the so-called cobweb theorem and the related contributions to dynamic theory, and the attempts of statistical testing of business-cycle theories.

In uncontrolled, agricultural markets it is usual to find that prices and quantities fluctuate in opposite directions. This pattern of behaviour is difficult to explain in terms of ordinary demand and supply theory without making rather artificial assumptions of repeated shifts in the demand and/or supply curves. In a celebrated article, 'Bestimmung und Deutung von Angebotskurven: Ein Beispiel,' *Zeitschrif für National ökonomie,* 1930, Tinbergen (simultaneously with, but independent of, two other economists, Hanau and Ricci) pointed out that this phenomenon could be explained on the assumption of fixed demand and supply curves, provided that supply (production) reacts to prices with a time lag of one year. This mechanism is now known as the 'cobweb theorem'. Quite apart from increasing the understanding of price formation in agricultural markets, this innovation in the theory of an isolated market had profound repercussions on economic theory in general. Economic theory at that time ran almost exclusively in static terms. Genuine dynamic economic theory describing a process over time was not entirely unknown; Wicksell's and Robertson's monetary theories are the outstanding examples. But there had been few attempts to formalise dynamic theories; Moore is an example. The cobweb theorem thus became a starting point for modern dynamic theory with the use of difference equations as a characteristic feature. Tinbergen himself applied this mathematical technique to the business cycle problem as early as 1931 in an article on the shipbuilding cycle. By the end of the thirties it had become a standard method of dynamic analysis in economics.

Professor Tinbergen's second great contribution to econometrics was his pioneering work on statistical testing of business-cycle theories. It resulted in the two volumes, *A*

Method and its Application to Investment Activity, and *Business Cycles in the United States of America, 1919–1932*, both published in 1939 by the League of Nations, Geneva. He had already in 1936 ventured upon a model for the Dutch economy, see below, and in 1937 he discussed the question more generally in *An Econometric Approach to Business Cycle Problems*, Paris 1937; the following year he applied his methods in a classical article 'Statistical Evidence on the Acceleration Principle,' *Economica* 1938. But it is the above-mentioned two volumes which stand out as the undisputed monument of early empirical macroeconomic model building and theory testing.

Against the background of the devastating effects of the Great Depression, the League of Nations had, in the middle of the thirties, asked Professor Gottfried Harberler to submit a theoretical study of the business cycle and investigate the differences between various contemporary theories. As a second stage in this research project Tinbergen was then asked 'to confront these various theories with historical facts – to subject them, in so far as those facts can be quantitatively expressed, to statistical analysis'.

In the first volume Tinbergen explained his method and gave three examples of its application. The method was classical multiple regression analysis combined with Frisch's confluence analysis. Tinbergen's contribution was not in statistical methodology, but in the application of existing statistical methods to macroeconomic problems. The methods applied were crude compared with present-day techniques, and the available primary data were highly unsatisfactory for the purpose. Nevertheless, Tinbergen's study of investments yielded results which only recent research has been able to challenge. He showed that whereas residential building is strongly influenced by market rates of interest, the basic determinant of investments in railway rolling stock is the rate of profits. He found little empirical evidence to support the acceleration principle which in contemporary business cycle theory played a predominant role in the discussion of investments. Tinbergen formulated an alternative 'profit principle' which via L. R. Klein became a widely accepted investment theory among econometricians.

In the second volume Jan Tinbergen set up a complete macro model for the United States economy in the form of a system of 48 difference equations, definitional relations, etc. Already the size of the model was a novelty and its details contained a wealth of untraditional ideas concerning economic macro relations. It represented a decisive break with the past in two respects. Old-fashioned business cycle theory had always tended to think in terms of the various phases of the cycle and to search for the 'cause' of each one of these phases. In line with his own early work on the business cycle, Tinbergen demonstrated how the cycle could and should be considered a unified, single phenomenon to be explained by the properties of a complete dynamic model. There was no longer a question of the 'cause' of the business cycle and old-fashioned business cycle theory could at most serve as building blocks for such a complete model. Secondly, he demonstrated the possibility of describing an economy in quantitative terms in such a way that not only may developments of the past be better understood, but also that forecasts of future developments may be made and policies calculated which modify future developments in a desired direction.

It is no exaggeration to say that these two volumes opened up a completely new branch of economics: empirical macro-economics. Keynes' scornful comments branding Tinbergen's work as 'alchemy' fell flat to the ground. Tinbergen's original model for the United States belongs now to history. Economic macro theory has been greatly improved and primary statistical data have been made available in an abundance which nobody could dream about in the thirties. Great progress has, moreover, been made in establishing adequate statistical methods for handling the estimation problems which arise in connection with models of this type. But all these developments were partly triggered off by Tinbergen's pioneering work, and we shall always be in debt to him for initiating this branch of economics.

It has already been mentioned that Jan Tinbergen presented a model for the Dutch economy in 1936. This model is not well known. It was originally published in Dutch and an English translation was not made available until 1959 (in *Selected Papers*, Amsterdam 1959). It deserves to be mentioned, however, not only because it seems to have been the prototype for the later models of the Central Planning Bureau, but also because it is surprisingly modern. The model consists of 24 equations and it explains dynamically both price and volume developments. Money wage changes are explained by a neat Phillips-relation! The rate of change of the money wage rate is a linear function of the rate of change of consumer prices lagged one period, and the level of employment. Prices are thereafter explained by a number of mark-up equations. Consumption is explained (independently of Keynes) by a relatively sophisticated consumption function, and investments are made dependent upon profits. The foreign trade equations, export and import functions, have little to learn from present-day econometric models. World demand and competitiveness determine the volume of exports, while domestic demands and competitiveness determine the various kinds of imports. The main objection to the model, in particular from a policy-making point of view, is that government expenditure and taxation are not integrated properly in the model.

The aim of the 1936 model was partly to discover the dynamic properties of the Dutch economy and partly to construct a basis for economic policy decisions. Tinbergen studied the effects over time of a series of policy measures (the dynamic multipliers in post-Keynesian parlance) but did not at this time formulate the multi-target problem the solution of which should become one of his great postwar achievements.

3. *The foundation of quantitative short-term economic policy planning*

When Professor Tinbergen accepted the directorship of the new Central Planning Bureau he gave macroeconomic model building a new twist. Whilst his pupils and followers, in particular Lawrence R. Klein, for a long time continued to work on the problem originally posed by Tinbergen in his League of Nations work, that is, to explain past developments and test conflicting theories, Tinbergen himself shifted the main emphasis to policy making. His aim was now to build models which would permit reliable forecasts of short-term developments and rational calculation of the policy measures needed for fulfilling given policy targets. As mentioned above, Tinbergen had already tried his hand at this kind of problem in 1936 when he discussed the problem of counteracting the economic consequences of the great depression for the Netherlands by means of econometric methods. A few other countries worked on the same problem, Sweden was one of them, but it goes without saying that nowhere were these efforts pursued so systematically and with so much vigour and progress as in Tinbergen's Central Planning Bureau. It is difficult to pin down exactly what were Tinbergen's personal contributions to 'the Dutch model' and the other achievements of the Central Planning Bureau; its publications are usually anonymous government documents. We have already mentioned, however, that the planning bureau's models seem to have grown out of the 1936 model, and there is plenty of testimony of the pervasive influence he had on all the work done by the bureau. It is in the nature of things that progress in economic prediction must be a slow process extending over many years, a major reason being that until recently prediction has taken place on an annual basis. Nevertheless, already when Tinbergen left the bureau in 1955 it was clear that it had succeeded in building up a model with better predictive capacities than anything else at that time. And, although many of the methods which he originally designed had to be modified and improved upon, partly in response to the experience of other countries, there can be no disagreement about the leading and pioneering role played by Tinbergen's efforts. Most governments in Western countries sponsor now work on these lines. From the very beginning, the Dutch model served as a basis for advice to the government concerning the formulation of the macro-policies of the Netherlands.

Alongside this painstaking work, Tinbergen worked on the theoretical problem of policy making, and in 1952 he made a new breakthrough when he published *The Theory of Economic Policy*, followed in 1954 by *Centralisation and Decentralisation in Economic Policy*, which created a basis for rational thinking and quantitative calculation in economic policy.

In the field of economic policy the tradition had always been to consider various types of economic policy separately and discuss them in relation to particular targets. Fiscal policy, monetary policy, foreign exchange policy, labour market policy, etc., fell apart into so many different policies; policy targets related to the price level, employment, the balance of payments, income distribution, etc., were often dealt with in isolation, subject to one or another of the above-mentioned policies. Even when actual developments forced economists to consider several targets simultaneously, such as the problem of keeping the price level stable during full employment, no method existed for tackling such multi-target problems systematically. Inspired by a memorandum submitted by Ragnar Frisch to the United Nations in 1949 ('Price-Wage-Tax-Subsidy Policies as Instruments in Maintaining Optimal Employment'), Tinbergen gave a precise formulation of the multi-target problem and showed how its solution depended upon the simultaneous, coordinated use of a sufficient number of appropriately chosen instruments. He dealt with both the case of absolute targets and the case of maximising a given social preference function, and solved a number of problems related to the efficiency of policy instruments, centralisation and decentralisation of policy decisions, and other matters. His discussion was confined to so-called quantitative changes in the economy whereas problems related to changes in the economic system as such were left aside. Other authors have continued and extended Professor Tinbergen's basic work which today is considered the obvious starting point for any discussion on general macroeconomic policy problems, although it is a curious fact that it took about fifteen years for the Anglo-Saxon economists to recognise the importance of the Tinbergen theory of economic policy.

It is both interesting and illuminating to compare Tinbergen's theory of economic policy with the so-called modern welfare economics on which the Anglo-Saxon academic economists concentrated during the forties and fifties. The latter was mainly concerned with Pareto-optimal situations in science fiction societies of perfect competition and was developed into an extremely elegant and technically refined body of theorising; it has, however, proved itself rather sterile and difficult to apply to practical policy problems. Tinbergen's theory of economic policy is quite simple, but it is concerned with the actual macro-policy targets of politicians in actually existing economies, and has proved powerful and applicable to current policy problems. This is a characteristic feature of all the scientific work of Tinbergen. He has never been very much interested in esoteric theorising for theory's own sake. His preoccupation has always been quantification and empirical application – an obvious thing in the natural sciences but not in economics – and as soon as a method 'works' empirically he does not waste time on further theoretical refinements, obviously believing that marginal returns are rapidly falling. The *tour de force* which econometrics has taken after his early application of simple least squares methods via complicated statistical methods and back again to improved least squares methods has, therefore, seen little of active participation from the side of Tinbergen. For him the basic economic problems to be tackled have been so many and so large that frontal attacks on a broad scale by means of crude methods look much more rewarding than intensive studies of small isolated problems by means of highly refined methods. In the childhood of the automobile the French engineer Panhard once commented upon the newly invented manual (un-synchronised) gearbox: 'It is brutal, but it works.' Although brutality is the last thing one would associate with Tinbergen, Panhard's comment certainly applies to Tinbergen's economic methods.

In addition to his theoretical studies on economic policy, Professor Tinbergen has also worked on practical problems in line with the principles laid down by the theory. A large number of quantitative policy problems were presented and solved in the volume, *Economic Policy; Principles and Design*, Amsterdam 1956. Many of these problems derived from his work with concrete Dutch policy problems in his capacity as advisor to his government.

4. *Planning for development and economic cooperation*
By the middle of the fifties Professor Tinbergen shifted his field of interest more and more to the problems of economic co-operation and development. His interest in economic co-operation was closely related to the creation of the Benelux and the European Common Market, but with respect to develop-ment it was in particular the problems of poor countries which attracted his attention. These were, of course, the burning issues of the postwar period, but certainly Professor Tinbergen was also led in this direction by his idealistic views on mankind and his deep devotion to humanitarian activities. He has always felt that in working on development problems in poor countries

and devoting his life to improving economic conditions in such countries he would help to repair some of the evils of colonial oppression and pay off some of the debts of the old colonial powers – including his own country.

Tinbergen's scientific contributions to the theory and practices of long-term economic planning for growth are typically Tinbergian in the sense that he has been looking for simple, crude methods that 'work' under the primitive conditions of policy-making in underdeveloped countries. Here again the contrast to contemporary work by mathematical economists, in particular in the United States, is striking. Although he is himself an excellent mathematician, Tinbergen has taken little part in the discussion of topics like optimal growth paths, turnpike theorems and dynamic efficiency. Being essentially an extension of modern welfare theory these theoretical refinements have so far had little practical importance for development planning. Tinbergen's long-term planning models have been designed on the basic assumptions that only a minimum of statistical information is available, and that the skill of planners, administrators and politicians is limited. His contributions are scattered over several books and a large number of memoranda and papers submitted to governments and international organisations, and some of his ideas exist mainly as oral tradition. Three main types of models can, however, be distinguished.

The *first* model can be characterised as 'planning by stages'. A simple macro model of the Keynes and Harrod-Domar type is first used to determine the total investment and savings requirements for the planning period considered. After this follows a sectoral stage where the total volume of investments is distributed by sectors through applications of a small input–output model and sectoral capital-output coefficients. This stage may, depending upon the special circumstances, be followed by a regional stage. The final stage consists of the choice of concrete investment projects within each sector according to investment criteria which depends upon the policy targets of the country. Under favourable circumstances planning can thus follow a recursive chain, but if necessary iteration may lead to a consistent solution. This is probably still the most widely used model for planning in underdeveloped countries.

Its obvious drawbacks are that it does not ensure efficiency in the economic system; and that it does not plan for the implementation in terms of instruments to be used. An otherwise consistent plan may not be possible simply because the necessary instruments (tax and credit policies, for instance) are not available at the given level of development. Moreover, it is not always easy to reach a consistent solution, in particular with respect to foreign trade.

The *second* type of model takes better care of the last mentioned difficulties. Since a growing number of underdeveloped countries now are equipped with computer facilities it becomes possible to work with larger systems of simultaneous equations. Tinbergen has, therefore, designed models where the first and the second stage in the first model are lumped together and where policy instruments are incorporated more explicitly in the solution. This type of model bears close resemblance to the so-called repercussion models upon which Ragnar Frisch worked during the fifties and sixties and is a combination of Harrod-Domar, Keynes and Leontief input–output models. Still, however, this model type does not imply any kind of optimisation with respect to choice of commodities to be produced and/or traded, choice of technique, etc.

The *third* type of model, the so-called semi–input–output method, was designed to overcome all these deficiencies. It differs radically from the other approaches by starting out from the individual projects and simply letting the macro-plan emerge as the sum of micro-plans. The idea here is first of all to let project appraisal be based on shadow prices, and in order to work with observable shadow prices the model centres on the international sectors and international commodity prices, and thus brings the problem of competitiveness at international prices into the planning process right from the beginning. By means of a truncated input–output model, based on engineering data, each investment project in international sectors is converted into an investment block containing the original project and all the necessary complementary investments in domestic sectors. These investment blocks form the basis for investment appraisal. Through concentrating on the investment projects in the international sectors it forces the underdeveloped countries to face the problem of concrete investment projects squarely, and to think in terms of competitiveness in foreign trade, at the same time as it requires a minimum of data about existing conditions in the country.

The semi–input–output method is probably Tinbergen's most ingenious contribution to planning. On the theoretical level it does, however, run into some troubles not only with respect to national sectors where observable shadow prices do not exist, but also with respect to the demand management policies necessary to balance the economy. Attempts to apply the method have run into practical difficulties in determining the international prices needed for the investment block appraisals. The concept of international prices is not a simple one as soon as we leave the basic raw materials and agricultural products and turn to manufactured and semimanufactured goods.

These practical difficulties should not, of course, be taken as an argument against the method as such. Any method of planning which aims at efficiency in production must undertake appraisals of all available investment projects, and for such appraisals appropriate price information is needed. They do, however, have a bearing upon the whole idea of planning for efficiency in resource allocation in underdeveloped countries. Given the production frontier of the country – quite apart from scarcity of capital, shortage of competent engineers and lack of information about technical possibilities may make the frontier lie far inside that of the developed countries – a country may simply not have the specialists (in marketing) needed for finding the optimal point on its frontier. Lack of technical knowledge and inefficiency within the given technical knowledge are both of them characteristics of underdevelopment. To be sure, T. W. Schultz has argued that peasants in underdeveloped countries are highly efficient within their primitive knowledge. He is probably right in that, and his argument extends presumably to all traditional sectors. But it does not apply to development beyond traditional methods in traditional sectors, and this is what matters in development planning.

It goes without saying that what has been said in the last paragraph does not imply that developing countries should pay no attention to the problem of efficiency. On the contrary, there is by far too much unnecessary inefficiency in developing countries which could be removed and thus greatly help to promote growth. But it does imply that one should be careful in condemning such countries for inefficiency, and it raises the question of which planning methods (everything taken into account) are the most efficient ones: the brutal methods that work, or the refined ones that do not work.

This leads us back to the appraisal of Tinbergen's planning methods and his efforts for promoting planning all over the Third World. It is by no means unusual to meet people who maintain that so far, planning by underdeveloped countries in general, and Tinbergen's methods in particular, on balance have done more harm than good. For several reasons this judgement is both unfair and wrong.

People who condemn planning by underdeveloped countries take very often as their basis of comparison an ideal state where both planners and politicians are perfect. This comparison is unfair and overlooks that a basic problem in development policies is exactly that planners and politicians generally are underdeveloped, too. Moreover, governments in underdeveloped countries are usually weak and politically incapable of taking vigorous, rational measures. The relatively disappointing performances of the Third World during the Development Decade have been caused much more by bad internal policies and implementation than by bad planning or external difficulties. Without people like Tinbergen, and their patient, indefatigable efforts things would, however, have been even worse than they are. Those people and their methods should not be blamed for the follies and imperfections of governments and politicians in underdeveloped countries.

Moreover, Tinbergen's crudest model, the stage method, has in most cases been applied to entirely undeveloped or highly underdeveloped countries. In such countries there are often striking natural advantages which have never been exploited, and planners do not need refined optimisation models to understand that such natural advantages should be exploited. It takes only the back of an envelope to figure out that the Euphrates Dam in Syria is a sound economic proposition, and nobody could ever be in doubt that oil drilling was the right thing to embark upon in Abu Dhabi. Some infrastructure is a *conditio sine qua non* for development. If raw materials are available it would be strange if cement, fertilisers and similar products with very high transport costs were not socially profitable. Even without explicit optimisation procedures the possibilities for going seriously wrong at this level of development may therefore be relatively small. The real problems arise when all obvious natural advantages have been exhausted and the most urgent infrastructure is erected. This is the stage of development where advantages have to be created. Even if market forces are strong and the animal spirits of private entrepreneurs are high we may still need planning to take care of externalities. And where private initiative is dormant or ruled out for institutional or ideological reasons the government will have to continue being the primus motor of development. Both the East, the West and the Third World are still waiting for somebody to discover the method which will work at this level of development. Although it certainly is a limitation of Tinbergen's crude planning methods that they apply best, or, perhaps only to highly underdeveloped areas, it should on the other hand be recognised that these are exactly the areas that have been most urgently in need of planning and where the methods actually have been applied.

5. *Other contributions*

Since the thirties Tinbergen has contributed to the solution of many problems other than those now discussed. He has always taken part in the current international debate and has worked on issues such as national accounting, imperfect competition, stability in economic systems, nonlinearities in cyclical models, international factor price equalisation, the theory of interest, international commodity agreements, the empirical determination of demand, supply, and substitution elasticities, problems of education and growth, tariff unions, balance of payments problems, optimum problems in savings and choice of techniques, just to present an unsystematic sample of topics. Since these contributions, brilliant though they very often are, cannot be said to have the quality of outstanding innovation, I mention them here only in passing.

6. *Conclusions*

It must have been quite a problem to select the first Nobel Prize Laureate(s) in Economics. During the last forty years economics have made great progress and are today the only one of the so-called social sciences that begin to deserve the name of a science. A number of contemporary economists have contributed significantly to this development and could have been selected with the full approval of the profession. It would, however, even amongst this group be difficult to find a more worthy candidate than Jan Tinbergen. From the survey given here it appears that on no less than six occasions has he brought economics a large step forward. Thus,

(i) he was a pioneer in modern economic dynamics; (ii) he helped to establish econometrics; (iii) he is the founder of empirical macroeconomics; (iv) he contributed decisively to create the modern techniques of economic forecasting and prediction; (v) he is the founder of the modern theory of economic policy; (vi) he has contributed significantly to modern development planning in backward countries.

Tinbergen is a truly Schumpeterian figure in economics. A man who has triggered off developments in many different directions.

It remains only to be said, that the humanitarian idealism which Nobel wanted to reward has no representative in our profession so fine and noble as Jan Tinbergen. As much as he is respected in the privileged world, he is beloved by the under-privileged, the underdogs. Always at their service, always on their side, always working on improving their conditions, Tinbergen would be an equally worthy candidate for the Nobel Peace Prize.

1 The Derivation of Cardinal Scales from Ordinal Data: An Application of Multidimensional Scaling to Measure Levels of National Development

IRMA ADELMAN AND
CYNTHIA TAFT MORRIS*

1. Introduction

The construction of quantitative measures of national capacity to develop along a broad front is desirable to facilitate investigation of the interactions involved in the development process and to improve the design of development strategies. Broad measures of development capacity provide a better focus than do narrow ones for systematic study of the empirical regularities characterising economic growth and furnish an improved basis for the formulation of comprehensive theories identifying critical interdependencies among economic, social, and political aspects of development. They also facilitate integrated approaches to development planning by making possible quantitative evaluation of the joint impact of social and political as well as economic influences on development.

Progress in the quantification of institutional aspects of modernisation has been gravely impeded by misconceptions regarding the essential characteristics of measurement in the social sciences and confusion concerning the differences between conventional 'quantitative' economic measurements and

* The authors are at the University of Maryland and The American University respectively. We are indebted to J. B. Kruskal for his invaluable assistance and for the computer program with which the calculations were performed and to F. L. Adelman for his comments. The research in this paper was supported by National Science Foundation grant GS–1689.

'qualitative' measurement of institutional phenomena. For this reason, an important part of our recent work has concentrated upon the nature of measurement of social science phenomena and, in particular, upon the problems involved in measurement of qualitative socioeconomic, political, and institutional influences on economic development.

The present paper focuses upon the derivation of comprehensive measures for underdeveloped countries of extent of national progress along a broad front. More specifically, the procedures of multidimensional scaling are applied to the derivation of cardinal measures of the extent of development of nations from ordinal data summarising social, economic, and political characteristics of the national institutions and performance of 74 underdeveloped countries during the 1957–1962 period.[1]

Our focus here contrasts with the common, yet narrow, focus by development economists on the long-term rate of growth of per capita G.N.P. as a primary indicator of development performance. For reasons which are well known, G.N.P. and other single indicators are deficient as measures of both extent of development and development potential.[2] The potential superiority of broad measures derived by multidimensional scaling over single indicators such as G.N.P. will be stressed in the sections which follow.

The approach to measuring development applied in the present paper also contrasts with recent efforts to measure extent of development more broadly by means of ad hoc averages of a small number of economic and noneconomic indicators or weighted averages based on regression studies.[3] This is because, first, our data include a wide range of social, political, and economic characteristics of underdeveloped nations rather than a few easily quantifiable traits; and second, the final representation which we obtain is cardinal rather than ordinal, and thus potentially provides a more precise basis for development planning policies. It should, of course, be stressed that the present effort is exploratory and designed to show the potentiality of the technique; it is not to be expected, therefore,

---

[1] These data are described in [2, chap. II].
[2] See, for example, [13, pp. 51–63], and the references cited therein.
[3] See, for example, the references in Notes 26 and 27 below.

that the results obtained here could be directly applied in program formulation. Considerable improvements in basic data inputs would be necessary in order to obtain results which would be sufficiently reliable and sensitive for policy formulation.

The organisation of the paper is as follows: the next section (Section 2) discusses the nature and different types of measurement. In Section 3 the general principles of multidimensional scaling technique are discussed and in Section 4 the technique is more formally presented. Section 5 reports on our application of the procedures of multidimensional scaling for the construction of a broad measure of extent of development of low-income nations. The final section (Section 6) presents our conclusions.

2. Types of Measurement

Formally viewed, measurement is the assignment of numbers to the properties of empirical objects or events in such a way that a one-to-one correspondence is maintained between the relations among the properties measured and the characteristics of the numbers assigned.[4] Forms of measurement may be differentiated by the type of measurement scale and by the type of link between the numerical scale and the concept measured.

Measurement scales

Four kinds of measurement scales may be distinguished: nominal scales, simple ordinal scales, ordered metric scales, and cardinal scales.[5] Each of these is characterised by a particular set of restrictions on the numbers assigned to represent the relations among the properties of objects or events and, therefore, by a particular set of statistical operations which may legitimately be applied to the numbers assigned.

---

[4] The basic reference for the following discussion is [14, chap. I]. See also, [18, chap. II] and [16, pp. 141–91].

[5] This classification follows Pfanzagl [14]. Stevens in [16] gives the more classic division of scale types into nominal, ordinal, interval, and ratio scales; the last two are treated here in the class of cardinal scales. Clyde H. Coombs introduced the concept of an ordered metric scale in [9]; he makes a finer breakdown between scale types using both the distinction between partially ordered and fully ordered sets of points and between partially ordered and fully ordered distances.

Nominal scales serve to classify a set of objects or their properties into classes within which objects are congruent. The rank order of the classes is not specified so that there are no restrictions on the numerical representation. Typologies having unranked categories and dummy variables are examples of nominal measurement.[6] In recent years, the use of nominal scales has become more common in econometric work because of developments in statistical techniques which permit the use of highly differentiated nominal data in statistical analyses.[7,8]

Ordinal scales must meet both the equivalence requirement for nominal scales and the further requirement that the assignment of numbers preserve the serial order of the properties measured. Numerical representations are restricted to order-preserving transformations of any set of numbers consistent with the serial order of the properties. Permissible statistical manipulations include the calculation of medians and percentiles as well as contingency correlations.[9]

Ordinal scales are widespread in economics since the preponderance of economic composites are ordinal when interpreted as indices of some underlying property or concept. Examples are: price indices interpreted to measure the cost of living, unemployment indices interpreted to represent the economic cost of unemployed labour either to the economy or to the individual, and G.N.P. interpreted to represent either

[6] [4] contains a good deal of political typological data. Paul F. Lazarsfeld and Allen H. Barton [11] cite examples of typological data in social psychology. In economics, nominal measurement is limited largely to the fairly widespread use of dummy variables.

[7] The analysis of hierarchical interactions, for example, is a form of analysis of variance which utilises nominal as well as ordinal independent variables.

[8] All measurement theorists are not agreed that nominal scales constitute a form of 'measurement'. The question, while semantical, is much disputed because to call nominal scales 'measurement' confers on them a status which some would deny. In practice, the validity of using nominal scales is determined in the same manner as the validity of using any measurement scale, i.e. by the extent to which they serve effectively as means to a given end. In econometric work, for example, it is generally accepted that the use of dummy variables can yield meaningful information about the relationships among variables.

[9] See [16] for a discussion of the statistical operations applicable to measurements made with different types of scale.

national economic welfare or national productive capacity.[10]

In practice, economists generally treat widely accepted ordinal economic indices as if they were cardinal. The assumption, rarely stated explicitly, is that the results of statistical analyses are not very sensitive to alternative order-preserving transformations of the input data. This assumption should, of course, be justified case by case through studies of the actual sensitivity of statistical results to reasonable alternative specifications.

Ordered metric scales are the next most refined class of scales after simple ordinal scales. This class of scales must meet the requirement not only that the numbers assigned preserve the rank order of a set of points representing a property, but also that the rank order of distances between all pairs of points be preserved. Ordered metric scales are less familiar to economists than are simple ordinal scales. Psychometricians have used them in the measurement of attitudes where the basic data consist of pair-wise comparisons ranking objects or events. It has been shown that the rankings of distances among pairs of objects can impose sufficient constraints upon the location of the objects to derive a cardinal representation in a space of minimum dimensions.[11]

The final class of measurement scales are *ordered distance or cardinal scales*. These scales must meet the equivalence and order requirements of the simpler scale types and, in addition, the more restrictive requirement that different amounts of a property (or intervals between different amounts) be capable of meaningful combination by addition. The numerical representation of a cardinal scale is restricted to positive linear transformations of any given set of numerical values consistent with the properties measured. The attraction of cardinal scales is that they can, without arbitrariness, be subjected to a wide variety of statistical manipulations including the calculation of standard deviations, product-moment correlations, and so forth.

[10] Economic indices are cardinal only if viewed merely as the result of the mathematical operations involved in the formulae used for their definition. However, when they are viewed cardinally, it is difficult to ascribe meaning to them or to study the relationship between such indices and other variables.

[11] See, for example, [10, pp. 1–27].

In economics, most *elementary* measurements are cardinal; for example, quantities, prices, and measurements based on counting (such as numbers employed in a given occupation) are all represented by cardinal scales.[12] However, these primary measurements are seldom introduced into statistical analyses in their cardinal form. Production and price indices are introduced rather than quantities and prices in order to measure changes in multidimensional properties; ratios or proportions are used to represent the relative importance of underlying properties measured by the classes of objects or events counted, and so forth. As a consequence, the use of cardinal scales in econometric work is relatively rare.[13]

For example, consumers' price indices, commonly used in statistical work rather than cardinal data on consumers' prices, are at best ordered metric representations of the cost of living, interpreted as the cost of maintaining a given level of economic welfare for an average individual; substitution effects induced by price changes, quality changes, and the effects of taste differences among consumers are not reflected in changes in the consumers' price index. Similarly, the unemployment rate is an ordinal scale when viewed either as a measurement of the economic cost of unemployment to the economy or as a measure of the cost of unemployment to the individuals; movement from 1-2% unemployment implies neither the same output foregone nor the same welfare loss as movement from 2-3% unemployment. Of course, both indices are cardinal when viewed merely as the result of the mathematical operations involved in the formulae used for their definition. However, when the aggregate indices are viewed cardinally, it is difficult to ascribe meaning to them, to see the rationale underlying their computation, or to study the relationship between such indices and any other economic aggregates.

The data developed by us in *Society, Politics, and Economic*

[12] For a discussion of the implicit comparison and combination operations involved in measures formed by counting which justify treating them as cardinal measures, see [8, pp. 71-5]. Ratios based on counts are not cardinal, but rather ordinal, when interpreted to represent the relative importance of the underlying property measured by the class of objects or events counted.

[13] The generality of this statement can be seen by examining any typical issue of the *Review of Economics and Statistics* or *Econometrica*.

Development[14] are, without exception, ordinal. Countries are ranked, with ties permitted, into A, B, C, etc. categories with respect to the various social, political, and economic characteristics of their societies. A definitional scheme for each characteristic specifies the particular factual and statistical criteria for grouping countries according to the relevant concept such as, for example, the extent of social mobility or the effectiveness, of financial institutions. Even the conventional 'quantitative' variables such as investment rates and literacy rates are ordinal, since we view them as representing underlying concepts to which they are, at best, monotonely related. Insofar as we have used empirical and theoretical information to determine the spacing of intervals and the distribution of observations between intervals, our data are of the ordered metric variety.[15]

Types of link with underlying concepts
When forms of measurement are classified by type of link between the numerical scale and the property or concept measured, three kinds of measurement may be distinguished: fundamental measurement, derived measurement, and measurement by fiat or definition.

Fundamental or direct measurement is based exclusively on principles relating different amounts of a single property to each other without involving other properties.[16] In establishing a

[14] See [3, chap. II].

[15] The simple linear scale adopted for our factor analyses in effect contained two principles which ranked proximities between categories: first, the proximities between letter categories were wider, the smaller the number of letter categories in terms of which a variable was defined; second, for each variable, the difference between the plus and minus of adjacent categories (e.g. A− and B+) was ranked above the difference between a given letter and its plus or minus (e.g. A and A− or A+).

[16] Fundamental measurement as understood by measurement theorists means that the original construction of a scale depends only on relationships between different amounts of the property measured. Practical procedures for measuring particular objects may, however, be based on an empirical law relating the property measured to another property, even though the scale of measurement for that property has been established fundamentally. When economists speak of 'direct' measurement, they do not mean fundamental measurement. They usually mean that the primary data used in constructing some index has been obtained by direct surveys, census, or questionnaire.

scale for length, for example, the relationships between different 'lengths' can be shown to approximate the 'model' of a cardinal scale by the actual superimposition and combination of objects of various lengths.[17] Originally, physicists conceived fundamental measurement to be applicable only to cardinal ratio scales such as those for length, weight, and electrical resistance.[18] However, psychometricians have established fundamental ordinal scales for subjective sensations such as loudness by tests of the relationships between varying amounts of the sensation measured.[19] In economics, the use of fundamental scales has, to date, been limited primarily to such elementary measurements as weight and length.[20]

Derived measurement is based upon precise functional relationships between the property measured and other fundamentally measured properties. Classic examples in physics are the establishment of ordinal scales for density or force by exact numerical laws relating them to fundamental magnitudes.[21] Derived measurement is rare in economics because economic theories seldom provide exact functional relationships between fundamentally measured magnitudes and concepts or properties not capable of measurement on fundamental scales. By exception, utility under risk has been measured by derivative methods.[22]

Measurement by fiat or definition is a form of indirect measurement by means of operational prescriptions based neither on fundamental procedures nor upon precise functional relationships with fundamental magnitudes.[23] It includes measurement by indices and typologies, and is widespread in the social

---

[17] As Stevens points out [16, p. 147], fundamental scales could be set up without the possibility of physical combination.

[18] See [16, p. 147].

[19] See [18, pp. 35–7 and chap. XIII].

[20] An exception is the measurement of utility under risk by fundamental procedures. See [8, pp. 65ff].

[21] M. R. Cohen and E. Nagel [7, pp. 299–300] describe the construction of a scale for density.

[22] See [8, pp. 65ff.].

[23] Pfanzagl [14, p. 320] writes: 'We speak of measurement by fiat, if the assignment of numbers is defined by some operational prescription which is neither based on homomorphic mapping of an empirical relational system into a numerical relational system (fundamental measurement)

and behavioural sciences for the measurement of multidimensional theoretical concepts for which neither fundamental nor derivative procedures are presently feasible. Measurement by fiat typically yields an ordinal scale for ranking the properties of objects or events with respect to the underlying concepts measured.[24]

Measurement by fiat: indices of economic development
In econometric work, measurement by fiat is the predominant form of measurement. The theoretical concepts important in generalising about economic phenomena – for example, economic welfare, economic development, imperfect competition, capital, income distribution – are complex and multidimensional. Hence, they are not subject to representation by unidimensional, 'primary' cardinal data such as quantities, weights, or counts of events or objects. To represent such complex concepts, it is necessary to define 'empirical constructs' of a relatively low level of abstraction which specify operational rules or criteria for classifying observed behaviour with respect to the relevant concept.[25] Income, investment, and particular indices of unemployment, price, production, capital stock, and output per manhour are examples of 'empirical constructs' or 'operational

---

nor on the functional relationship to fundamental scales (derived measurement)'. Torgerson [18, p. 32] writes: '... *measurement by fiat* ... ordinarily ... depends on *presumed* relationships between observations and the concept of interest. Included in this category are the indices and indicants so often used in the social and behavioural sciences. This sort of measurement is likely to occur whenever we have a prescientific or commonsense concept that on *a priori* grounds seems to be important but which we do not know how to measure directly . . . .'

[24] As indicated above, indices are cardinal only when viewed as sets of formulae; however, when so viewed, their meaning is undefined.

[25] The terminology for discussing the links between concepts important in theorising, 'empirical constructs' which specify rules of correspondence, and 'primary facts' is far from uniform. Richard Stone [17, p. 9] uses the terms 'empirical construct' and 'primary facts'. [Torgerson 18, pp. 4ff.] speaks of 'rules of correspondence' or 'operational definitions' which link together 'observable data' and 'theoretical constructs.' Coombs [9, pp. 4ff.] refers to 'recorded observations' and restricts the word 'data' to that which is analysed, that is, to the output from a scaling 'model'. Torgerson [18, chap. I] was particularly helpful for the discussion in this section.

2

definitions' which provide multidimensional empirical equivalents of abstract economic concepts.

Efforts to measure extent and pace of economic development have resulted in a variety of ordinal indices. Several approaches are practised in constructing these indices. Frequently, a single indicator such as G.N.P. or electric power production per capita is used;[26] sometimes, ad hoc averages of several indicators are constructed;[27] and occasionally, clustering techniques are applied to obtain a statistical aggregate.[28]

There are objections to all three current approaches to the measurement of economic development. The difficulty with single indicators like G.N.P. and electric power capacity is that the ranking they provide is not even ordinal in the presence of major changes in economic structure and income distribution. As for ad hoc averages of selected indictors, they are, at best, ordinal, and in addition, are composed by arbitrary rules which may make it difficult to interpret them. Clustering techniques also yield ordinal indices and are dependent upon the particular variables included in the analysis.

The principal drawback of the ordinality of current measures of extent and pace of economic development is that they do not provide for sufficient discrimination between different 'amounts' of economic progress to satisfy the information requirements of effective development programming. For this reason, the development by psychometricians of methods for deriving cardinal scales from ordinal data is extremely relevant to current efforts to measure growth performance.

3. The Conversion of Ordered Metric Scales into Cardinal Scales

Recent work in psychometrics demonstrates that the ordinal information embodied in ordered metric scales can be sufficient

[26] David McClelland [12, pp. 85ff.] proposes electric power production per capita as a measure of economic development. W. Beckerman and R. Bacon [5, pp. 519–36] develop an index of levels of consumption with weights obtained from a 'best-fitting' regression of real consumption (as measured in national income accounts) on selected items consumed.

[27] See, for example, [6].

[28] An example is the factor analytic study by the present authors of differences in levels of socioeconomic development [3, chap. IV].

to yield unique cardinal scales. That is, the rankings of distances between pairs of objects provided by ordered metric data can impose sufficient constraints upon the spacing of objects to determine uniquely their location in a space of minimum dimensions. To illustrate, consider four points, A, B, C, and D, and consider two alternative rankings of the six interpoint distances AB, AC, AD, BC, BD, and CD. If the distances are ranked in the order BC, CD, AB, AD, BD, and AC, at least a two-dimensional space is required to locate the four points without violating the inequalities expressed by the rank order. However, if the rank order is $BC < CD < AB < BD < AC < AD$, the four points can be represented along a single line as in Figure 1.1.[29] It has been demonstrated, furthermore, that the correlation between the points represented in Figure 1.1 and any other arrangement which satisfies the original inequalities is at least 0.986.[30] These two examples illustrate that, if the number of ranked interpoint distances between n points is large compared with the number of dimensions required to obtain a representation with the initial inequalities, the location of the n points is rigidly determined in a space of minimum dimensions.

$$BC < CD < AB < BD < AC < AD$$

FIG. 1.1 *An Optimum Arrangement of Four Points Satisfying the Stated Inequalities for the Six Inter-Point Distances*

The technique for recovering cardinal scales from ordered metric scales is multidimensional scaling. Objects are rated by some exogenous method with respect to a given property (e.g. tones with respect to loudness, political systems with respect to political participation, economies by extent of development). The ratings may be the result of evaluations by individuals of the similarity of pairs of stimuli or institutions. These evaluations may be either intuitive as in experiments with colour and sound or based on relatively explicit standards of comparison as in our recent work. The scaling problem reduces to finding a spatial

[29] See [15, p. 36].   [30] See [1].

configuration of n objects which meet the requirements, first, that as few as possible of the original inequalities (given by the rank order of the distances between objects) be violated, and second, that the objects be located in a space of as few dimensions as possible. These two requirements tend to conflict since, in general, the fewer the number of dimensions, the larger the number of violations of the initial inequalities. Consequently, the choice of an optimum representation of the original data implies a compromise between (*a*) the extent to which the initial inequalities are not violated (i.e. the goodness of fit), and (*b*) the desideratum of minimising the number of dimensions selected to represent the n objects. The use of these two criteria generally yields a spatial configuration of the points represented which is unique up to a linear transformation provided that the number of ranked distances is large compared to that number of dimensions of the space in which the points can be arranged without violating too many of the original inequalities.

Multidimensional scaling thus accomplishes for nonlinear data structures what factor analysis accomplishes for linear data structures. It finds the representation of n objects in an $r(n)$ dimensional space such that the n objects can be represented without much loss of information as continuous functions of the co-ordinates of the r space. If r is substantially smaller than n, considerable data reduction is accomplished by this process. Furthermore, the data reduction can provide additional insights into the phenomena which generated the data. However, by contrast with factor analysis which aggregates a large number of variables into a small number of dimensions, multidimensional scaling decomposes a single variable into the minimum number of dimensions required to give a consistent and interpretable representation of its meaning.

4. The Technique of Analysis[31]

Multidimensional scaling is a technique for obtaining a spacial configuration having distances between points which represent

---

[31] [10, pp. 1–27]. Kruskal reports an interesting experiment by Shepard in which synthetic data were distorted to obtain a set of dissimilarities which were then subjected to multidimensional scaling. Figure 1.2 portrays the closeness between the original configuration and that recovered by the scaling technique.

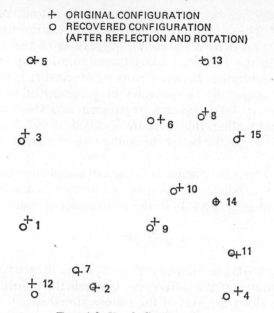

+ ORIGINAL CONFIGURATION
O RECOVERED CONFIGURATION
(AFTER REFLECTION AND ROTATION)

FIG. 1.2 *Kruskal's Experiment*

a statistical 'best fit' for a set of observed similarity comparisons. The data inputs consist of observed ratings of the extents of dissimilarity, δ_{ij}, between all pairs of objects i and j ($i \neq j$) in a set of n objects which can be ranked in order so that

$$\delta_{i_1 j_1} < \delta_{i_2 j_2} < \delta_{i_3 j_3} < \cdots < \delta_{i_M j_M}.^{32} \tag{1}$$

[32] For the moment the possibility of ties will be ignored. Conceptually (though not computationally) the minimum stress configuration is achieved by starting from an arbitrary t dimensional configuration $(X_1, \ldots, X_n)$ computing d_{ij} from (2) and $\hat{d}_{ij}$ by minimising (5) with respect to $\hat{d}_{ij}$ subject to (6), and then moving points X_i and X_j closer together if $\hat{d}_{ij} < d_{ij}$ and apart if the opposite is the case in order to make d_{ij} more like $\hat{d}_{ij}$. Naturally, each point X_i is subject to many partially conflicting requirements. The effect of each particular shift of X_i on S can, however, be calculated. This phase of the process stops when no further movements of points can be found which improve the overall value of S_t. This yields a new starting configuration $(X'_1, \ldots, X'_n)$ from which new sets of values of d_{ij} and $\hat{d}_{ij}$ are computed, leading to new minimum stress values. The process is continued till no further improvements of S_t are possible.

in which the number of dissimilarity comparisons, M, equals $n(n - 1)/2$. The measure of 'goodness of fit' is a residual sum of squares obtained by a monotone regression of the interpoint distances in the estimated spacial configuration upon the observed dissimilarities between pairs of objects. It is thus comparable conceptually to measures of goodness of fit obtained from ordinary least squares regression analyses; in multidimensional scaling, this measure is called 'stress'. Clearly, the smaller the stress, the better the configuration matches the input data.

Let the interpoint distances in the estimated configuration of n points in a t-dimensional space be defined as Euclidian distances between X_i and X_j in the t-dimensional space.

$$d_{ij} = \sqrt{\sum_{s=1}^{t} (X_{is} - X_{js})^2} \qquad (2)$$

That is, the distance from any X_i to X_j is the square root of the sum of squares of the differences between the co-ordinates of X_i and X_j along the axes of the t-dimensional space. A perfect representation of the input data is obtained when the estimated Euclidian distances, arranged in the same rank order as the experimentally obtained dissimilarities, obey the same inequality relationships

$$d_{i_1 j_1} < d_{i_2 j_2} < d_{i_3 j_3} < \cdots < d_{i_M j_M} \qquad (3)$$

To measure the extent of departure from perfect correspondence between the ranking of the Euclidian distances, d_{ij}, and the ranking of the respective observed dissimilarities, δ_{ij} it would be natural to define a residual sum of squares in which the discrepancies between observed and estimated dissimilarities, suitably normalized, are summed and squared

$$T = \sqrt{\frac{\sum_{i<j}^{n} (d_{ij} - \delta_{ij})^2}{\sum_{i<j}^{n} d_{ij}^2}} \qquad (4)$$

This is, however, impossible, since arithmetic cannot be performed with the dissimilarities, δ_{ij}. Instead, therefore, a measure of goodness of fit, called 'stress', is defined in which the observed dissimilarities are replaced by a monotone sequence of numbers,

$\hat{d}_{ij}$, having the same rank order as do the dissimilarities together with the property of being as 'nearly equal' to the Euclidian distances as possible.

$$S = \sqrt{\frac{\sum\limits_{i<j}^{n} (d_{ij} - \hat{d}_{ij})^2}{\sum\limits_{i<j}^{m} d_{ij}^2}} \qquad (5)$$

The selection of the estimated $\hat{d}_{ij}$ for the calculation of the goodness of fit of the Euclidian distances to the observed dissimilarities is designed to obtain a sequence of numbers with the same rank order as the dissimilarities which can be used as a reference to measure arithmetically the degree of non-monotonicity of the Euclidian distances. The numbers $\hat{d}_{ij}$ are obtained by selecting from the full set of numerical sequences having the same rank order as the dissimilarities the one which best fits the estimated Euclidian distances, i.e. the sequence which yields the lowest sum of squares or 'stress'. Specifically, the $\hat{d}_{ij}$ are obtained by minimising S with respect to $\hat{d}_{ij}$ for a given configuration $(X_1, \ldots, X_n)$. The minimisation of S is subject to the monotonicity constraint

$$\hat{d}_{i_1 j_1} \le \hat{d}_{i_2 j_2} \le \hat{d}_{i_3 j_3} \le \cdots < \hat{d}_{i_M j_M} \qquad (6)$$

As the notation in (6) implies, the particular $\hat{d}_{ij}$ which corresponds to a given d_{ij} is defined by the fact that both correspond to a particular dissimilarity, δ_{ikjk}.

Clearly, the configuration which best fits the data in t-dimensions is the one for which the stress in t-dimensions (S_t) is a minimum. The configuration we want is, therefore, that which minimises S_t.[33]

$$S_t = \min_{\substack{\text{all } t\text{-dimensional} \\ \text{configurations}}} S(X_i, \ldots, S_n) \qquad (7)$$

---

[33] Typically, 15–100 interactions are required to achieve $S_t =$ min $\hat{d}_{ij}$, $(X_1, \ldots, X_n)$. In practice, the minimisation of stress is achieved by using an iterative technique for the minimisation of a function of many variables which is standard in numerical analysis: the 'method of gradients', or the 'method of steepest descent'. Practical experience with

The choice of number of dimensions
The discussion up to now has proceeded on the assumption that the number of *t*-dimensions in which the concept being measured should be represented is known. This is, of course, not the case; the experimenter must use his judgment in choosing the number of dimensions. In this choice, he must compromise among several criteria: the first criterion compromises between simplicity and goodness of fit. Of course, goodness of fit decreases with decreases in the number of dimensions, while the fewer the dimensions, the greater the simplicity.[34]

A second criterion for choosing the number of dimensions is the interpretability of the results. If considerations of simplicity and goodness of fit would lead one to choose a larger number of dimensions than that for which satisfying interpretations can be found, it may be advisable to represent the phenomenon in fewer but equally informative dimensions.

A third criterion which can be used relates to the inherent accuracy of the data. The less subject the data is to errors of measurement, the more dimensions can be extracted. With very noisy data the last dimension(s) may merely reflect measurement errors. This is particularly likely to be the case when no straightforward interpretation of the co-ordinates suggests itself.

Uniqueness of the solution
There are two different reasons why multidimensional scaling may not lead to unique results. The first relates to the nature of

---

experimental and synthetic data suggests the following relationships between the magnitude of stress and the goodness of fit.

Stress	Goodness of Fit
20%	Poor
10%	Fair
5%	Good
2·5%	Excellent
0·0%	Perfect

[34] The choice of the appropriate number of dimensions is facilitated by the fact that the rate of decrease of stress is, usually, not uniform. Most often the plot of stress *vs* the number of dimensions exhibits an elbow; the number of dimensions chosen should then generally be one more than the number of dimensions at which the bend occurs.

the input data. The determinancy of the solution clearly decreases as the number of dimensions increases relative to the number of objects (points). This need not concern us much in practical applications since even with as few as ten or fifteen points a reasonably tight (low stress) solution in two or three dimensions usually exists.[35]

Another reason why the scaling might not lead to a unique solution is that the stress function which is minimised may have local minima so that the iterative procedure used to find the minimum may lead to a local rather than a global minimum. In order to guard against this possibility one should perform the scaling computations with several different starting configurations.

In general, one can test for the uniqueness of a solution by performing various experiments with the input data. For example, the dissimilarities can be subjected to monotonic distortion and the results of the scaling compared. If the number of objects in the sample is sufficiently large, the sample can be randomly subdivided keeping certain observations common to both subsamples. The location of the overlapping observations can then be compared. Finally, several different starting configurations can be used to perform each scaling computation.

5. Measurement of Levels of Development of Low-Income Nations

For the present paper, we applied the procedures of multidimensional scaling to construct a measure of the extent of development of low-income nations considerably broader than is offered by per capita G.N.P. or any other single indicator.

Since the use of multidimensional scaling requires a set of intuitively reasonable similarity comparisons as input data,

---

[35] There are some special cases, however, in which no matter how many points are taken, the solution obtained will not represent the true configuration. Consider, for example, points on a semicircular arc; since there will always exist a configuration of points on a straight line for which the rank of the interpoint distances is the same as that on the semicircle, the requirement of minimum dimensionality would force the solution into a single dimension. In practical cases it is, however, unlikely that a sufficiently large set of points would fall on such a special curved subspace. This example is due to Shepard [15].

18   *Economic Development and Planning*

we sought a suitable ranking of differences among nations in the extent of national development. Our starting point was a set of indicators of socioeconomic and political institutions and performance in seventy-four underdeveloped countries for the period 1950–1963, for which the detailed descriptions may be found in *Society, Politics, and Economic Development.*[36] We factor-analysed thirty-eight of these indicators, and obtained in a single factor (accounting for 47% of the total inter-country variance for all thirty-eight characteristics) a cluster of twenty variables representing various aspects of the levels of economic, social, and political development of underdeveloped nations. The economic indicators in this factor were: per capita G.N.P., the size of the traditional agricultural sector, the extent of dualism, the level of modernisation of industry, the level of effectiveness of financial institutions, the level of effectiveness of the tax system, the gross investment rate, the level of adequacy of physical overhead capital, the level of modernisation of techniques in agriculture, the character of agricultural organisation, and the rate of improvement of human resources. The social indicators incorporated were: the character of basic social organisation, the crude fertility rate, the extent of literacy, the importance of the indigenous middle class, the extent of social mobility, the degree of mass communication. In addition, a single measure of political development was included—the extent of political participation.[37]

The factor analysis yielded not only a selection of variables but also a set of weights suitable for constructing a measure of dissimilarity for pairs of countries with respect to the extent of national development. That is, the factor comprising the twenty variables can be viewed as a weighted index of levels of development in which the coefficients or 'loadings' relating the variables to the factor provide the weights. To calculate the extent of dissimilarity for each pair of countries, the difference in country scores on each of the twenty indicators was divided

[36] See [3, chap. II].

[37] This variable is an aggregate of three elements: the extent to which the major socioeconomic and cultural-ethnic groups have their interests represented in national political decisions, the extent of choice among political channels for national representation, and the extent of actual participation in national political processes. The period is 1957–62.

by the variance of that indicator to obtain an inter-country difference in standard units. These differences were then squared and combined in a weighted sum with the appropriate factor loading used to weigh each difference. The square root of this sum of squares provided the final measure of extent of dissimilarity between the two countries in a pair. More specifically, the measure constructed was defined as follows

$$\delta_{ij}\sqrt{\sum_{s=1}^{20} \frac{a_s^2}{\sigma_s^2}(X_{is} - X_{js})^2}$$

where a_s is the factor loading of the sth country attribute in the original factor analysis;[38] σ_s^2 is the variance of the sth country characteristic; and X_{is}, X_{js} are the country scores on the sth attribute of countries i and j respectively. The measure of dissimilarity used is thus analogous to a weighted, normalised, Euclidian distance defined on a space of twenty dimensions.

The 2701 ($74 \times 73 \div 2$) dissimilarities between countries obtained by the procedure just described were subjected to multidimensional scaling. The stress values for the three, two and one dimensional configurations were 5·8%, 7·1%, and 11·3% respectively, indicating that a good fit is obtained in two dimensions, and a fair fit in a single dimension. The two- and one-dimensional representations are presented in Table 1.1; Figure 1.3 plots the location of the seventy-four countries according to the two-dimensional solution. Judged on the joint criteria of fit and interpretability, the two dimensional scaling provides the preferred set of results.[39]

Uniqueness of the representation
As indicated above, sensitivity analyses are necessary to test for the uniqueness of the solution. Three alternative starting configurations used to test whether the solution represented a global rather than a local minimum yielded virtually identical

[38] The maximum value of a_s was 0·89 (for literacy) and its minimum was 0·56 (for the gross investment rate).

[39] The number of iterations required to achieve the minimum stress configurations was 50 for the three dimensional scaling, twenty-seven for the two dimensional scaling, and twenty-two for the one dimensional scaling. The amount of computer time required for convergence was 6 minutes of C.D.C. 6400 time.

TABLE 1.1 *Scaled Measures of Country Levels of Development As of 1960*

		Two Dimensional Scale		One Dimensional Scale
		Horizontal	Vertical	
1	Afghanistan	−0·087	1·246	−1·273
2	Algeria	0·460	0·102	−0·080
3	Argentina	0·125	−1·686	1·746
4	Bolivia	−0·464	0·307	−0·364
5	Brazil	0·226	−0·790	0·845
6	Burma	−0·578	0·291	−0·388
7	Cambodia	−0·128	0·644	−0·665
8	Cameroun	−0·243	0·939	−0·990
9	Ceylon	−0.108	−0.598	0·594
10	Chad	−0·118	1·330	−1·358
11	Chile	0·009	−1·513	1·536
12	Taiwan	0·490	−1·082	1·186
13	Colombia	0·065	−0·804	0·815
14	Costa Rica	0·099	−1·186	1·199
15	Cyprus	−0·131	−1·280	1·307
16	Dahomey	−0·062	1·174	−1·189
17	Dominican Rep.	−0·216	−0·146	0·121
18	Ecuador	−0·113	−0·285	0·258
19	El Salvador	−0·059	−0·239	0·222
20	Ethiopia	−0·279	1·375	−1·418
21	Gabon	−0·252	0·835	−0·893
22	Ghana	0·381	−0·076	0·128
23	Greece	0·177	−1·687	1·752
24	Guatemala	−0·175	0·173	−0·231
25	Guinea	−0·154	1·203	−1·241
26	Honduras	−0·406	0·142	−0·206
27	India	0·111	−0·042	0·032
28	Indonesia	−0·242	0·556	−0·610
29	Iran	−0·024	0·308	−0·342
30	Iraq	0·035	0·303	−0·327
31	Israel	0·402	−2·107	2·212
32	Ivory Coast	0·214	0·757	−0·773
33	Jamaica	0·349	−1·481	1·562
34	Japan	0·302	−1·961	2·048
35	Jordan	0·197	0·134	−0·135
36	Kenya	0·111	0·579	−0·594
37	Korea	−0·564	−0·523	0·524
38	Laos	−0·255	1·172	−1·218
39	Lebanon	0·307	−1·259	1·341

TABLE 1.1 Cont.

		Two Dimensional Scale		One Dimensional Scale
		Horizontal	Vertical	
40	Liberia	0·062	1·049	−1·064
41	Libya	0·013	0·664	−0·713
42	Malagasy	−0·276	0·945	−0·993
43	Malawi	−0·162	1·252	−1·285
44	Mexico	0·255	−1·120	1·152
45	Morocco	−0·073	0·424	−0·466
46	Nepal	−0·193	1·440	−1·474
47	Nicaragua	−0·011	−0·330	0·308
48	Niger	−0·070	1·409	−1·431
49	Nigeria	0·316	0·529	−0·541
50	Pakistan	0·096	0·368	−0·415
51	Panama	−0·193	−0·733	0·719
52	Paraguay	−0·484	−0·089	0·074
53	Peru	0·032	−0·501	0·487
54	Philippines	−0·385	−0·829	0·807
55	Rhodesia	0·573	0·134	−0·091
56	Senegal	−0·085	0·722	−0·750
57	Sierra Leone	−0·076	0·967	−0·997
58	Somalia	−0·297	1·157	−1·209
59	South Africa	0·949	−0·911	1·264
60	Sudan	−0·021	0·858	−0·875
61	Surinam	−0·378	−0·587	0·568
62	Syria	0·109	−0·339	0·349
63	Tanganyika	0·081	0·969	−0·971
64	Thailand	−0·345	−0·021	−0·030
65	Trinidad	0·411	−1·520	1·612
66	Tunisia	0·172	−0·028	0·019
67	Turkey	0·118	−0·694	0·702
68	Uganda	0·042	0·813	−0·833
69	U.A.R.	0·183	−0·362	0·378
70	Uruguay	−0·094	−1·610	1·658
71	Venezuela	0·562	−1·550	1·702
72	Vietnam	−0·231	0·596	−0·636
73	Yemen	−0·188	1·431	−1·468
74	Zambia	0·186	0·678	−0·691

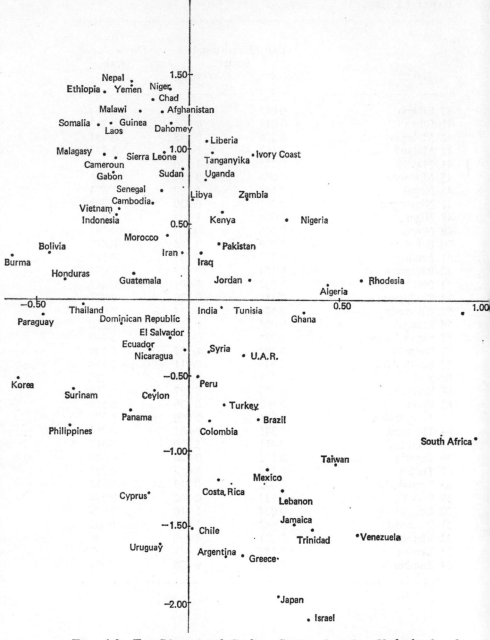

FIG. 1.3 *Two-Dimensional Scaling Scatter Locating Underdeveloped Countries with Respect to Extent of National Development about 1960*

patterns of variation of stress with number of dimensions. The two-dimensional configuration has product moment correlations of 0·977, 0·961, and 0·998 with the configuration in Figure 1.3.

To test the uniqueness of the solution further, the sample was subdivided into two subsamples, chosen in a stratified random

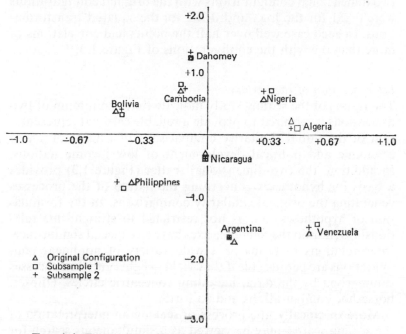

FIG. 1.4 *Comparison of Scaled Configurations for Nine Countries*

manner from the three levels of socio-economic development encompassed by the original sample. Nine countries, three from each level of development, were common to both subsamples; the three countries common to each level of development were chosen so as to span the range of development represented in that portion of the original sample. Figure 1.4 indicates the location of the countries common to the two subsamples.[40]

[40] Since each configuration is invariant only up to a linear transformation, the configurations were subjected to rigid rotation of axes and to shifts of origin to obtain the fits graphed in Figure 1.4.

To test the sensitivity of the results to variations in scoring of the original ordinal data on which the dissimilarities were based,[41] the country scores on the twenty variables were subjected to monotonic distortion. Logs and squares of the original scores were used to calculate dissimilarities and multidimensional scaling applied. The product moment correlation of the new two dimensional configurations with the original configurations were 0·851 for the log., and 0·782 for the squared transformations. In each case well over half the points had correlations of more than 0·9 with the configurations of Figure 1.3.[42]

Interpretation of the results
The results of the scaling study indicate that a minimum of two dimensions is required to provide a reliable cardinal representation of the initial similarity comparisons of extents of socio-economic and political development of low income nations. In addition, the two-dimensional scatter (Figure 1.3) provides a basis for hypotheses concerning the nature of the processes generating the original similarity comparisons. In the formulation of hypotheses, one is not restricted to straight-line relationships; nor do the reference axes have any special significance. Interpretations in terms of a wide variety of nonlinear configurations are permissible if they yield insights into the processes summarised by the data, including concentric circles, ellipses, horseshoe configurations and so forth.

More specifically, the process of seeking an interpretation of the scaling scatter may be viewed as a simultaneous search for variables or other information contributing to a meaningful interpretation of the scatter and for isocontours yielded by plots of relevant variables on the scaling scatter. The isocontours delineate ranges over which a variable has the same values, and may be of any shape, linear or nonlinear. The interpretation of the scaling scatter thus involves an iterative process in which the selection of variables for interpretation and the delineation of configurations of interpretive significance interact. Convergence of the iterative process is achieved by a

---

[41] See [3, pp. 14–15] for a description of the original scoring procedure.
[42] The correlation of two points is measured by the cosine of the angle between rays connecting the two points with the origin.

compromise between several criteria including the simplicity of the contours, the goodness-of-fit of the contours to plots of the relevant variables, and the intuitive appeal of the hypotheses suggested by the iterative process in the light of other knowledge of the phenomena generating the scaling scatter. The interpretations which emerge are not, of course, unique. That is, the same scaling scatter could well suggest different hypotheses to different investigators regarding the nature of the processes engendering the original input data.

To investigate the problem of interpretation, we first regressed the scaled country scores along the two reference axes on country scores for a wide range of indicators, including the twenty variables from which the original comparisons were estimated,[43] scores on a factor representing the level of socioeconomic development,[44] the rate of growth of per capita G.N.P.,[45] and an index of national development potential.[46] In principle, of course, any information of potential relevance could have been used; we selected these particular variables, however, because they covered a wide range of potentially relevant national characteristics, and we had country scores for them which could be plotted on the scaling scatter.

The regression results for country scores on the vertical reference axis yielded a high correlation with measures of levels of national economic and social attainment. We obtained a simple correlation of 0.94 with scores on the factor representing socioeconomic development and an R^2 of 0·90 for the best-fitting relationship between the scores on the vertical axis and the

---

[43] For descriptions of these variables, see [3, chap. II].

[44] These were the country scores on the first factor of a seventy-four-country factor analysis of the inter-relationship between per capita G.N.P and twenty-three social and political variables [3, chap. IV].

[45] Countries were grouped into six categories, A–F, with respect to rates of growth of per capita G.N.P. during the period 1950–51 to 1963–64 [3, chap. II].

[46] This index groups seventy-four underdeveloped countries into three categories according to performance during the 1950–51 to 1963–64 period with respect to rising rates of growth of per capita G.N.P. and to improvements in seven areas of economic institutions and activities [2, p. 261].

factor index.[47] When the factor index was omitted and the remaining variables of potential value introduced in a step-wise regression, the three measures providing the best-fitting statistical 'explanation' of scores on the vertical reference axis were the variables representing the size of the traditional agricultural subsistence sector, the extent of social mobility, and the extent of mass communication.[48] Plots of country scores on the factor representing socioeconomic development and on the measure of the importance of the traditional subsistence sector (Figures 1.5 and 1.6) suggest the presence in the plot of an almost linear configuration which can be summarised quite well by directed lines about 12° to the left of the vertical reference axis. This pattern indicates, not unexpectedly, that an important component of the original inequalities is a single dimensional continuum along which the seventy-four countries can be ranked with respect to the development of such socioeconomic institutions as the spread of the market, the growth of the middle class, and the expansion of social and occupational mobility, as well as per capita G.N.P.

We found country scores on the horizontal axis less well correlated with the original input variables. The three input variables giving the best fit produced an R^2 of only 0.649; they were an index of development potential based upon past dynamic performance along a broad front,[49] the equivalent of a dummy variable stratifying the sample into three groups by

---

[47] The best-fitting relationship between scores on the vertical axis and the factor scores (F) is given by the quadratic relation

$$Y = 0 \cdot 141 + 0 \cdot 917F - 0 \cdot 144F^2 \qquad R^2 = 0 \cdot 903$$

$$(0 \cdot 052) \quad (0 \cdot 036) \quad (0 \cdot 039)$$

[48] The best-fitting regression is given by

$$Y = 0 \cdot 169 + 0 \cdot 014Z_1 - 0 \cdot 011Z_2 - 0 \cdot 009Z_3 \qquad R^2 = 0 \cdot 967$$

$$(0 \cdot 013) \quad (0 \cdot 001) \quad (0 \cdot 001) \quad (0 \cdot 001)$$

where Z_1 is the index of the size of the traditional agricultural subsistence sector; Z_2 is the extent of social mobility; and Z_3, the extent of mass communication.

[49] See Note 46 for a brief description of this variable.

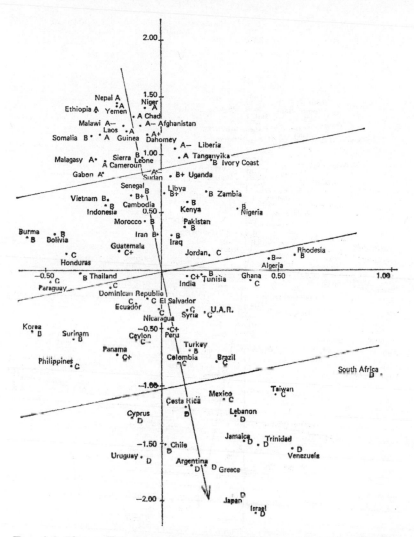

Fig. 1.5 *Plot on Two-Dimensional Scatter of Country Scores on the Size of the Traditional Subsistence Sector about 1960*

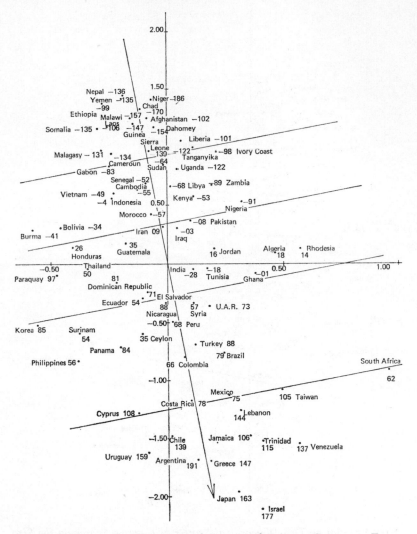

Fig. 1.6 *Plot on Two-Dimensional Scatter of Country Scores on Factor Representing Socioeconomic Development*

degree of differentiation of social organisation,[50] and per capita G.N.P.[51,52] Plots of country scores on the development potential index and on closely related indices such as rates of growth of per capita G.N.P. and improvements in financial institutions suggested a significant nonlinear relationship between levels of socioeconomic development and national capacity to perform economically. Figure 1.7 plots rates of change of per capita G.N.P. during the period 1951–52 to 1963–64, and outlines possible isocontours characterising successive levels of capacity for dynamic economic performance. Our hypothesis is that within each of these isocontours are located countries with institutions and structures having similar capacities to perform economically.

The nonlinearity of the hypothesised relationship is indicated by the shape of the isocontours outlined in Figure 1.7. These show a close relationship between rates and levels of development for countries at very low levels, indicating the small extent to which capacity to perform in the least developed countries can be affected by economic policy in the short run and the large extent to which economic growth is constrained by basic socioeconomic structural and institutional characteristics. In contrast, the isocontours in the middle ranges of the development scale indicate a much wider range of capacities to perform associated with given levels of development and, thus, the greater extent to which development strategies can alter capacity to perform once a given level of social and economic achievement is attained. For underdeveloped countries at the highest level, the isocontours show again a close interconnection between rates and levels, suggesting that, when countries

[50] In countries in the highest-ranking group the predominant form of social organisation is the nuclear family; in countries in the intermediate group the predominant form is the clan or extended family; and in countries with rank lowest on this indicator, tribal social organisation [3, chap. II].

[51] See [3, chap. II]. These data refer to the period 1957–62.

[52] The best-fitting equation is

$$X = -0.296 + 0.0034Z_6 - 0.0054Z_7 + 0.009Z_8 \qquad R^2 = 0.649$$
$$(0.0005)\ (0.0005) \qquad (0.0007) \qquad (0.0002)$$

where Z_6 is the index of development potential, Z_7 is the variable stratifying the sample by degree of differentiation of social structure; and Z_8 is per capita G.N.P.

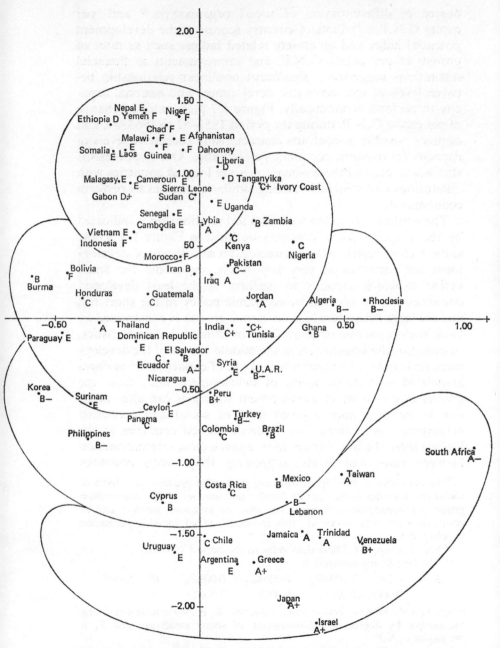

FIG. 1.7 *Plot on Two-Dimensional Scatter of Country Scores on Rates of Change of Per Capita G.N.P.* (1951–52 to 1963–64)

achieve this level of development, their *capacity* for self-sustained growth is established, although ineffective economic policies may result in performance well below capacity.

It will be noted that the plot in Figure 1.7 is of rates of growth of G.N.P., a measure (albeit a narrow one) of *actual* rather than potential performance. Since our interpretation of the isocontours relates to *capacity* to perform while the plot refers to actual growth, we do not expect all countries within a given isocontour to have the same scores. Rather, we expect to find a range of actual changes in average G.N.P. characteristic of each particular level of capacity to perform. For our hypothesis to be reasonable, it should, therefore, be possible to explain the anomalies within each isocontour (i.e. the countries in which by hypothesis actual performance is below or above long-term capacity to perform) by their marked failure or success in exploiting the capacity of their structures and institutions for dynamic economic growth. The anomalies within the highest-level isocontour – Chile, Argentina, and Uruguay – can, indeed, be explained by poor economic performance due to ineffective policy or political orientations unfavorable to growth rather than inadequate socioeconomic and institutional development. Of the B–level anomalies, Colombia has improved its performance considerably since 1963, the terminal date for our data, while Costa Rica may be accounted for by its stress on distribution rather than growth. The mixture of scores within the C–level isocontour can be explained by two phenomena. First, there is the crucial impact of policy upon performance at this level: on the one hand, there are countries in which unusually effective economic policies have resulted in unexpectedly good growth performance for their levels of development (for example, Zambia and Thailand); on the other hand, there are countries in which ineffective policies rather than inadequate capacity have resulted in unusually poor performance (for example, Ceylon, Surinam, Paraguay, and Syria). Second, some of the unexpectedly high scores are accounted for by countries with dualistic structures and export-based growth for which high registered increases in G.N.P. overstate actual country-wide performance (Jordan, Iraq, and Iran). In the lowest-level isocontour with typical scores of D, E, and F, the major anomaly is Libya, a highly dualistic country, for which rates of growth of G.N.P. greatly overstate actual performance.

Thus, the scaling scatter suggests that one should view inter-country differences in socioeconomic attributes by means of a weighted aggregate which combines characterisations by level of socioeconomic development and by capacity for dynamic economic performance. From the resulting two-dimensional characterisation for a given country, one can then infer its other socioeconomic characteristics. Of course, the degree of confidence for such an inference is not 100%, and the relia-bility of the inference varies with the location of the country on the plot.

In explaining inter-country differences in socioeconomic attributes, it is thus meaningful and important to distinguish between levels of socioeconomic development and capacity for dynamic economic performance, particularly once countries have succeeded in raising themselves beyond a critical minimum level of development. This critical minimum is located at about the level of such cash-cropping African countries as the Ivory Coast and Kenya or of such lower-level Latin American coun-tries as Guatemala and Honduras. The analysis suggests that beyond this critical level a rather wide range of actual perform-ance is associated with any given level of capacity to perform due to variations in the effectiveness of economic policies and in political orientations in the individual countries. Finally, it suggests that it is only at the 'highest' level of development characteristic of underdeveloped countries (that typified by the higher-level Latin American countries) that one finds a sub-stantial number of countries whose capacity for growth can sustain a steady high level of actual dynamic per-formance.

The finding of a significant non-linear relationship between levels and rates of development is consistent with the results of our earlier quantitative investigations of the development process. In factor analytic studies of social, political, and eco-nomic influences on rates of growth of per capita G.N.P., the presence of non-linearities required us to stratify our sample of seventy-four underdeveloped countries into subsamples of countries at different levels of development. Factor analyses of data for the subsamples indicated a close interaction between rates and levels of development at the lowest income level, a somewhat greater impact of short-run economic policy on rates of growth at the intermediate income level, and important interconnections for higher-level countries between effective use of the instruments of economic policy and success in raising rates of growth of G.N.P.[53] The present scaling study thus reinforces earlier findings of systematic variations between different levels of development in the relationship between socioeconomic achievement and economic growth rates.

A further search for relationships implicit in the scaling scatter yielded interesting configurations of scores on the character of basic social organisation and on the extent of literacy (Figures 1.8–9). As can be seen in these figures, a good fit for country scores on the social organisation and literacy variables can be obtained along directed lines some 54° to the left of the horizontal reference axis. The angle between the social organisation-literacy scale and the scale representing levels of socioeconomic development (the 'vertical' axis) is about 48°, indicating a correlation between these two aspects of modernisation of about 0.74.[54] This configuration suggests that the extent of national development as measured by the original inputs to the scaling study can be disaggregated into two components which, while significantly correlated, especially at low income levels, are nevertheless distinguishable for higher levels of development.

The finding that extents of social and economic development are increasingly separated as countries achieve higher levels of development is also consistent with the results of our earlier work. The pattern suggested by our factor analytic studies is one in which, at the very lowest level, the primary obstacles to economic growth arise from the all-encompassing nature of tribal social structure; at the intermediate level, there appears a

---

[53] See [3, chaps. V–VII].

[54] The curvature of the isocontours outlined in Figure 1.9 suggests a somewhat nonlinear relationship between the process of social differentiation and the spread of literacy. At lowest levels of development the two aspects of social change are closely inter-related. As would be expected, however, once tribal and clan social structures have been greatly weakened, considerably greater variations in rates of literacy are associated with a given development of social structure.

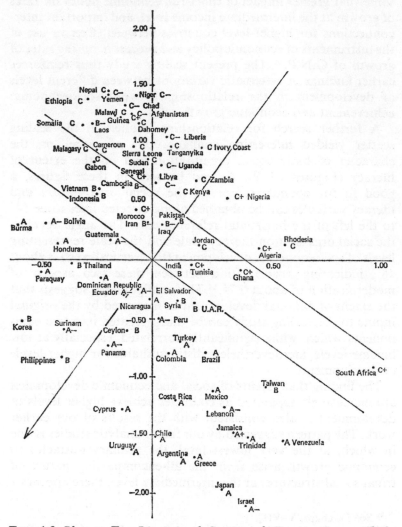

FIG. 1.8 *Plot on Two-Dimensional Scatter of Country Scores of the Character of Basic Social Organisation about 1960*

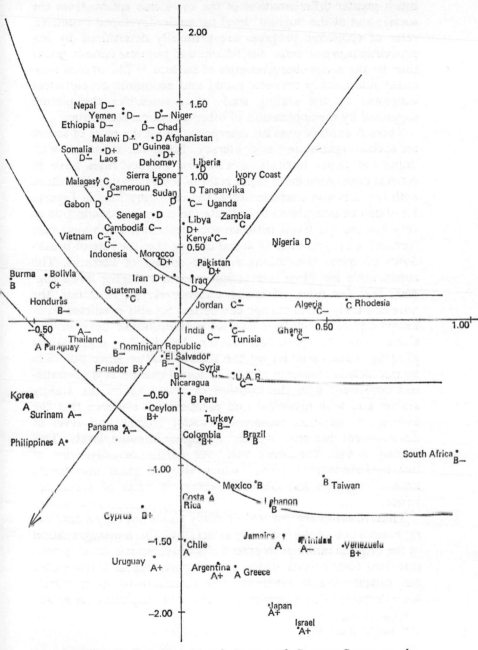

FIG. 1.9 *Plot on Two-Dimensional Scatter of Country Scores on the Extent of Literacy about 1960*

much greater differentiation of the economic sphere from the social; and at the 'highest' level for underdeveloped countries, rates of economic progress are primarily determined by improvements in economic institutions and political climate rather than by the social characteristics of nations.[55] The overall non-linear relationship between social and economic development suggested by the scaling study thus resembles the picture suggested by the application of other statistical techniques.

There is another possible interpretation of the plots of scores on social organisation and literacy. Since the countries with important tribal institutions and low literacy rates have in general undergone more rapid rates of social change than those with the opposite characteristics, the configurations in Figures 1.8–9 can be interpreted to indicate the close interconnection at very low income levels between socioeconomic attainment (the 'vertical' axis) and pace of social change (i.e. the rate of breakdown of tribal institutions and the spread of literacy). The significantly less close interaction evident at higher levels suggests that for more advanced underdeveloped countries, the pace of purely social change can be less reliably predicted from knowledge of a country's level of socioeconomic development alone. This interpretation cannot be directly checked by plotting input variables on the scaling scatter since our data do not include measures of rates of social change. It is nevertheless consistent with the location of countries on the scaling scatter and with historical and comparative evidence that the association between rapidity of social change and level of development becomes weaker at higher income levels. This finding is also consistent with our earlier investigations of intermediate-level countries which showed great unevenness among countries and between sectors in rates of social advance.[56]

Thus, in summary, the scaling study yields not only a cardinal representation of the initial input data but also a disaggregation of the original rankings by extent of socioeconomic development into two components which are interpretable as inter-related but distinguishable continua, one summarising more purely social aspects of development and the other depicting the extent

[55] See [3, chap. VIII].
[56] See [3, chap. VI].

of development of the basic socioeconomic institutions characteristic of modern industrial societies. In addition, the scaling results suggest the presence of a significant nonlinear relationship between actual socioeconomic achievement and capacity for dynamic growth. This relationship is characterised by close interaction between levels and capacity at both very low and relatively 'high' levels of development (for underdeveloped countries) and significant degrees of freedom for countries at intermediate levels to raise their actual performance capacity by the effective application of appropriate economic policies.

6. Conclusion

There are, in principle, two ways of incorporating institutional and attitudinal characteristics of nations in statistical analyses of the process of economic development. One way is to apply to ordinal data summarising these characteristics statistical tools which are not sensitive to the nature of the metric by which the input data are scaled. This is the approach we chose in our earlier applications of analysis-of-variance techniques to country rankings with respect to a wide range of social, economic and political attributes of low-income nations. The other approach is to develop a metric for the various qualitative institutional traits and then apply standard statistical tools of analysis. The present paper employs this latter approach by means of a pilot study designed to show the feasibility of establishing a metric for data inputs which are essentially qualitative. The study simultaneously indicates the potentiality of the scaling technique for yielding insights into the processes involved in the economic development of underdeveloped nations. These insights were found to be consistent with insights resulting from the systematic investigation of the process of economic modernisation by other statistical techniques.

References

[1] ABELSON, R. P. and TUKEY, J. W., 'Efficient Conversion of Nonmetric Information into Metric Information,' Proceedings of the *American Statistical Association Meetings*, Social Statistics Section, 1959, 226–230.

[2] ADELMAN, IRMA and MORRIS, CYNTHIA T., 'Performance Criteria for Evaluating Economic Development Potential: An Operational Approach', *Quarterly Journal of Economics*, LXXXII (May 1968), 260–280.

[3] ADELMAN, IRMA and MORRIS, CYNTHIA T., *Society, Politics and Economic Development*, Baltimore: Johns Hopkins Press, 1967.

[4] BANKS, ARTHUR and TEXTOR, ROBERT, *A Cross-Polity Survey*, Cambridge, Mass.: M.I.T. Press, 1964.

[5] BECKERMAN, W. and BACON, R., 'International Comparisons of Income Levels: A Suggested New Measure', *Economic Journal*, LXXVI (September 1966), 519–536.

[6] BENNETT, M. K., 'International Disparities in Consumption Levels', *American Economic Review*, XLI (September 1951), 632–649

[7] COHEN, M. R. and NAGEL, E., *An Introduction to Logic and Scientific Method*, New York: Harcourt, Brace & World, 1934.

[8] COLEMAN, JAMES S., *Introduction to Mathematical Sociology*, New York: The Free Press of Glencoe, 1964.

[9] COOMBS, CLYDE H., 'A Theory of Psychological Scaling', *Engineering Research Bulletin*, No. 34. Ann Arbor: University of Michigan Press, 1952.

[10] KRUSKAL, J. B., 'Multidimensional Scaling by Optimizing Goodness of Fit to a Nonmetric Hypothesis', *Psychometrica*, XXIX (March 1964), 1–27.

[11] LAZARSFELD, PAUL F. and BARTON, ALLEN H., 'Qualitative Measurement in the Social Sciences: Classification, Typologies, and Indices', *The Policy Sciences*, edited by Daniel Lerner and Harold D. Lasswell, Stanford: Stanford University Press, 1951, 155–192.

[12] McCLELLAND, DAVID C., *The Achieving Society*. Princeton, N.J.: Van Nostrand, 1961.

[13] NUTTER, J. WARREN, 'On Measuring Economic Growth', *Journal of Political Economy*, LXV (February 1957), 51–63.

[14] PFANZAGL, J., *Theory of Measurement*, New York: John Wiley and Sons, 1968.

[15] SHEPARD, R. N., 'Analysis of Proximities as a Technique for the Study of Information Processing in Man', *Human Factors*, 1963.

[16] STEVENS, S. S., 'On the Theory of Scales of Measurement', *Philosophy of Science*, edited by Arthur Danto and Sidney Morgenbesser. New York: Meridian Books, Inc., 1960, 141–149.

[17] STONE, RICHARD, *The Role of Measurement in Economics*, Cambridge, England: The University Press, 1951.

[18] TORGERSON, WARREN S., *Theory and Methods of Scaling*, New York: John Wiley and Sons, 1958.

2 Project Appraisal in Developing Countries

BELA BALASSA*

THE paper deals with some theoretical issues related to project appraisal in developing countries. It examines criteria for project appraisal under alternative policy assumptions: (*a*) optimal policies are applied throughout the economy, (*b*) non-optimal trade policies are applied but these will give place to optimal policies by the time the project is implemented, and (*c*) non-optimal policies will continue to be applied during the lifetime of the project.

In the discussion, consideration is given to the applicability of alternative methods of project appraisal. In particular, comparisons are made between methods involving: (*a*) the use of the rate of return to capital and the domestic cost of foreign exchange criterion, (*b*) the inclusion of direct as against direct plus indirect domestic costs in the calculations, and (*c*) the use of shadow exchange rate and the Little-Mirrlees methods of valuing all goods at world market, (i.e. international prices). Problems relating to the estimation of the shadow wage rate and interest rate and the difficulties of the practical application of project appraisal methods are raised but not discussed.

1. Project Selection under Optimal Policies

Assume initially that there are no external economies or market distortions in a country's economy and that transportation costs in foreign trade are nil. If the country in question

* The author is Professor of Economics, The John Hopkins University, Baltimore, and Research Director, The World Bank, Washington, D.C. This paper was written as part of a consultant arrangement with the World Bank. It should not be deemed, however, to represent the Bank's views. The author acknowledges helpful comments received from G. B. Baldwin, E. Lerdau, S. Reutlinger, and D. M. Schydlowsky.

cannot affect world market (foreign) prices, the adoption of a policy of free trade would entail equating the domestic prices of all products to their foreign prices and this would simultaneously ensure the maximisation of national income and equilibrium in the Balance of Payments. If, however, the country affects foreign prices through trade, domestic prices should be equated to marginal revenue from import substitution or exporting by the use of an appropriate set of import tariffs and export taxes.

Under the stated assumptions, the described policies will be optimal[1] in the Pareto sense and the market prices of primary factors (e.g. labour, capital, and foreign exchange) will equal their opportunity cost or shadow – in Tinbergen's terminology, accounting – prices. Project appraisal will then take the form of comparing returns to a primary factor in the project to its market price; a project will be accepted if the former exceeds the latter when all other primary factors are valued at their market prices. The outcome will be the same irrespective of whether the calculation is made for one or another primary factor. Should returns to a primary factor in a project exceed its market price when the contribution of other factors is evaluated at their market prices, this result will also obtain if comparisons are made in regard to another factor [7].

Nor will it matter whether we evaluate a project on the basis of processing costs at the last stage of fabrication or combine costs at all stages of domestic fabrication. This is because, with the market prices of all primary factors being equal to their shadow prices, the cost of domestically-produced inputs (the sum of payments to primary factors and the cost of imported inputs used in their manufacture) will equal their cost in the world market.

2. Project Selection under Non-Optimal Trade Policies

Consider next the case when the stated assumptions are fulfilled but non-optimal tariffs and export taxes (subsidies) are applied. Market prices of primary factors will now differ from

[1] Additional taxes and subsidies would be needed for attaining a welfare optimum in the presence of interpersonal and intertemporal income-distributional or other non-economic objectives. Notwithstanding their importance, these will not be considered in the paper.

3

the shadow prices corresponding to optimal policies. Tinbergen was among the first to suggest that in such an event projects be evaluated at shadow prices [15]. It will be assumed in the following that shadow prices derive from a general equilibrium model of the economy under the assumption that optimal policies are used in project appraisal.[2]

If primary factors are valued at their shadow prices as defined here, the results will again be the same regardless of whether the calculation is made for one primary factor or another, provided that domestically-produced inputs are valued in the same way. However, the results will now depend on whether we combine costs at all stages of domestic fabrication or consider only the cost of processing at the last stage since the value of domestically-produced inputs will not generally be the same in the two cases. This can be seen if we compare the use of the domestic cost of foreign exchange and the effective protection measures in project appraisal.

The domestic resource cost measure, as originally defined by Bruno [5], involves estimating the value of domestic resources (domestic value added) used directly and indirectly in saving a unit of foreign exchange through import substitution or earning it through exports. If we take foreign prices as given, this measure will equal the combined direct and indirect domestic resource costs incurred at various stages of fabrication, divided by the difference between the foreign price of the product and the foreign exchange cost of its direct and indirect inputs.[3]

The domestic resource cost of foreign exchange is estimated by the use of a full input-output chain until a primary factor or an imported input is reached. Let us denote domestic resource costs (domestic value added) per unit of output at a given stage of fabrication valued at shadow prices (W), the world market price of the commodity (P), the value of imported inputs per unit of output (N), and the elements of the matrix of direct

---

[2] As will be seen below, the use of these prices involves the assumption that optimal policies will be adopted by the time the project is implemented. The implications of the non-fulfillment of this assumption for project evaluation will be discussed subsequently.

[3] In cases when the country can affect foreign prices through trade, the foreign exchange saving should be expressed in terms of marginal revenue. Equations (1) and (2) will need to be reinterpreted accordingly.

and indirect input requirements by r_{ji}. The domestic cost of saving or earning a unit of foreign exchange (B) for commodity i is shown in Equation (1).[4]

$$B_i = \frac{\sum_j W_j r_{ji}}{P_i - \sum_j N_j r_{ji}} \tag{1}$$

In turn, the effective rate of protection (Z) is defined as the percentage excess of domestic value added in processing (W) over foreign value added (V) per unit of output. In the analysis of protection in existing industries, this is derived from data on the nominal rate of protection (T)[5] of the product and its intermediate inputs and the world market (foreign) input-output coefficients for these inputs (M) as in Equation (2).[6]

$$
\begin{aligned}
Z_i &= \frac{W_i - V_i}{V_i} \\
&= \frac{P_i(1 + T_i) - \sum_j M_{ji}(1 + T_j) - (B_i - \sum_j M_{ji})}{P_i - \sum_j M_{ji}} \\
&= \frac{P_i T_i - \sum_j M_{ji} T_j}{P_i - \sum_j M_{ji}}
\end{aligned} \tag{2}
$$

The same formula is used in project evaluation, but for a new industry the nominal rate of protection for the output will now show the difference between domestic and foreign prices that

[4] It is customary to express the denominator in terms of foreign currency. However, for the sake of comparability with the effective protection measure, I will reinterpret the formula by expressing foreign values in terms of domestic currency (i.e. multiplying the denominator by the actual exchange rate). The application to project evaluation of the domestic cost of foreign exchange measure so defined will mean that a project is accepted if B is less than one (i.e. the domestic cost of saving or earning a unit of foreign exchange is less than the shadow exchange rate).

[5] The nominal rate of protection is defined as the percentage excess of domestic over foreign prices; it will equal the rate of tariff if tariffs are the relevant measures of protection.

[6] The formula refers to the case when foreign (world market) input-output coefficients are used in the calculations. A modified formula is applied if we start out from domestic rather than world market coefficients [9, pp. 36–37].

would be necessary to make the project profitable if labour and capital were valued at their shadow prices. The effective rate of protection under this definition will be a social effective rate as contrasted to a private effective rate that obtains when labour and capital are valued at market prices.

It can be shown that the domestic cost of foreign exchange measure equals unity plus a weighted average of effective rates of protection at different stages of fabrication – the weights being the direct and indirect contribution of labour and capital to output under free trade conditions [3]. This is shown in Equation (3).

$$B_i = 1 + \sum_j Z_i \frac{V_j r_{ji}}{\sum_j V_j r_{ji}} \tag{3}$$

It further appears that the two measures will give the same result in project evaluation under optimal policies since in this case inputs will not be produced domestically at greater than world market costs, i.e. the effective rate of protection is nil for all domestic activities. By contrast, the application of non-optimal tariffs and export taxes, permits the domestic production of intermediate inputs that would be imported under optimal policies. The domestic cost of producing these inputs, with labour and capital used in their manufacture valued at shadow prices, will now exceed their world market cost; should this not be the case, the inputs in question would have been produced in the domestic economy under optimal policies.

Under these conditions a project that used inputs produced domestically under protection may be accepted if evaluated by the use of the effective protection measure and rejected if the domestic cost of foreign exchange were the criterion applied. This will be evident if we consider that the former values all domestically produced inputs at their world market cost while the latter values them at their domestic resource cost which exceeds the world market cost in the case of protected inputs. Expressed differently, while the effective protection measure considers only the cost of domestic processing at the final stage of fabrication, the domestic cost of foreign exchange measure also gives expression to the excess costs incurred in the domestic fabrication of intermediate inputs as well.

3. Direct and Indirect Costs

The effective rate of protection can be reinterpreted as a measure of the *direct* domestic cost of foreign exchange[7] while combining costs at all stages of domestic fabrication provides a *total* measure of the cost of foreign exchange. The former will now give the same results in project appraisal as if we calculated the rate of return to capital using the appropriate shadow price for foreign exchange and labour under the assumption that all intermediate inputs are made available to the project at their world market cost. Thus, if the effective rate of protection of a project is less than zero (i.e. the direct domestic resource cost of earning or saving a unit of foreign exchange is less than the shadow exchange rate), the rate of return to capital will exceed its shadow price.

In turn, the (total) domestic cost of foreign exchange measure assumes that inefficiently-produced domestic inputs would be used in the project and values these at their domestic resource costs, measured at shadow prices of labour and capital. Here again, the outcome will be the same as if we calculated the rate of return to capital, including that used in the manufacture of inefficiently-produced domestic inputs. If the domestic resource cost of earning or saving a unit of foreign exchange is less than the shadow exchange rate, the rate of return to capital used in the final stage of processing and in the domestic production of intermediate inputs will exceed its shadow price.

Thus, for project appraisal it will not matter whether the calculation is made for one primary factor or another but under non-optimal policies the result will depend on the number of domestic stages of fabrication considered or, expressed differently, on the valuation of domestically-produced inputs. This can be illustrated by an example. Assume that in a country the manufacturing of precision equipment involves the use of steel produced under protection while the fabrics used by the clothing industry are not protected. Assume further that the production of precision equipment is efficient in the sense that domestic value added equals value added under free trade conditions

[7] More precisely, the effective rate of protection equals the direct domestic cost measure minus one.

while the former exceeds the latter in the case of clothing manufacturing.

Using Equations (1), (2), and (3), we can estimate the domestic cost of foreign exchange and the effective rate of protection for the commodities in question from the data of Table 2.1. The effective rate of protection will be 50% on clothing and nil on precision equipment but the ranking is reversed in terms of the domestic cost of foreign exchange measure that will be 1.2 in the first case and 1.4 in the second. It is apparent that the cost of foreign exchange is lower in clothing manufacturing – a relatively inefficient industry – than in the production of precision equipment because the material input of the former (textile fabrics) is produced at world market costs while the latter is penalised by the protection of the high-cost domestic steel industry.

It follows that the ranking of activities according to the domestic cost of foreign exchange reflects the implicit assumptions that: (*a*) all existing industries will be maintained, (*b*) the expansion of the output of any one industry will bring forth increased output of all domestic industries providing direct and indirect inputs into it (i.e. the direct and indirect marginal input coefficients of domestic resources and of imports taken to equal the corresponding average coefficients), and (*c*) costs in input-producing industries will continue at existing levels. However, the domestic costs of inputs may decline along the learning curve or through the application of large-scale production made possible by increased demand for the product. Also, the country may move closer to optimal policies in which case some of the inefficient industries will have to reduce costs to survive. Finally, even if an inefficient industry is maintained for the sake of non-economic objectives, inputs for new projects can still be imported.

In turn, in using the effective protection measure in project appraisal, each industry is evaluated on its own merits and one will not forgo the establishment of an efficient industry because of high present costs in the domestic production of its inputs. This measure will require adjustments, however, if political pressures would entail the expansion of some inefficient input-producing industries *pari passu* with that of the user industries. But such cases should be judged on their individual

TABLE 2.1 *Evaluation of Clothing and Precision Equipment Projects*
(Pesos)

	Domestic production			Foreign production		
	Processing costs	Foreign exchange	Total	Processing costs	Foreign exchange	Total
Clothing						
Fabrics	6	10	16	6	10	16
Processing costs	6	—	6	4	—	4
Price	12	10	22	10	10	20
Precision instruments						
Steel	10	10	20	6	10	16
Processing costs	4	—	4	4	—	4
Price	14	10	24	10	10	20

$$B_c = \frac{12}{20 - 10} = 1.2$$

$$Z_c = \frac{6-4}{4} = 0.5 (50\%); \quad Z_f = \frac{6-6}{6} = 0$$

$$B_e = 1 + \frac{0.4 \times 0.5 + 0.6 \times 0}{1} = 1.2$$

$$B_p = \frac{14}{20 - 10} = 1.4$$

$$Z_p = \frac{4-4}{4} = 0; \quad Z_s = \frac{10-6}{6} = 0.67 (67\%)$$

$$B_p = 1 + \frac{0.4 \times 0 + 0.6 \times 0.67}{1} = 1.4$$

Source: [3].

merits rather than penalising particular projects on account of all inefficiently-produced domestic inputs.

A related consideration is the definition of the project itself. In cases when two stages of fabrication are closely integrated, the two might be combined for purposes of project appraisal and the effective rate of protection calculated on the combined unit. This will be the case, for example, if the construction of a paper mill is envisaged in order to utilize the output of a previously constructed pulp mill. But such cases too would have to be judged on their individual merits, taking account of possible alternative sources of supply of the major input.

The Treatment of Non-Traded Goods

Removing the assumption of zero transportation costs in foreign trade will entail the introduction of commodities that are not traded internationally. Transportation costs are analogous to tariffs in the sense that both increase the cost of importation and may result in the elimination of particular imports.

From the point of view of project evaluation, however, there is an important difference between tariffs and transportation costs. As was argued before, the production costs of inputs produced domestically under non-optimal tariffs should be considered in judging a project in special circumstances only. By contrast, transportation costs are here to stay and a method has to be found for valuing inputs that are not traded because transportation costs make this prohibitive. Such products, generally including electricity, gas, water, construction, and various services, are customarily called non-traded goods.

Tinbergen was the first to suggest the use of a semi-input-output method in project evaluation in the presence of non-traded inputs [17] while its application in estimating the effective rate of protection was proposed by Corden [8]. This method involves adding traded inputs used directly and indirectly in the production of non-traded inputs to the traded inputs employed directly in the production process and including the sum of direct and indirect value added used in producing non-traded inputs with value added in processing. The rationale of this method is that the cost of non-traded inputs to the national economy equals the cost of the primary factors and traded inputs used in their manufacture.[8]

It should be added, however, that the existence of transportation costs will modify the calculations if a move from non-optimal to optimal trade policies leads to shifts from the import to the export category. If such a commodity is used as an input, it should be valued at the f.o.b. prices applicable under optimal policies rather than at c.i.f. prices. F.o.b. prices should also be used if the commodity in question shifts from the non-traded to the export category whereas in the case of a project that entails both replacement and exports, the amount produced for replacing imports should be valued at c.i.f. import prices and the amount exported at f.o.b. prices.[9] Finally, the evaluation of projects involving the production of commodities which are not traded under optimal policies necessitates taking account of domestic demand conditions in the form of consumer surplus analysis.

4. The Shadow Exchange Rate and the Little–Mirrlees Method

I have assumed so far that shadow prices of primary factors are available from a general equilibrium model of the economy. As this is hardly the case in developing countries, a way has to be found to evaluate projects when the shadow prices are not known. Retaining the assumptions of perfect product and factor markets and no external economies, it may be suggested that if decisions extend to all potential projects and if distortions are due only to the application of non-optimal tariffs and export taxes (subsidies), projects be ranked according to their effective rates of protection, calculated by evaluating labour and capital at their market prices, and available investment funds be used on the higher ranking projects.

[8] In practice, it is rarely necessary to travel back through the input-output chain until a primary factor or a traded input is reached because the absolute magnitudes get smaller at every step. In the case of water, for example, we can estimate value added, the value of traded inputs, and that of non-traded inputs, say electricity, when the latter is further divided into value added, traded and non-traded inputs and the non-traded inputs used in its manufacture allocated on the basis of their approximate value added and traded input content.

[9] In all cases, marginal revenue rather than prices should be used if the country can affect foreign prices through trade.

This alternative is based on the implicit assumption that the application of protective measures does not affect the relative prices of labour and capital. Yet, to the extent that the imposition of non-optimal tariffs and export taxes (subsidies) entails a bias in favour of or against labour-intensive or capital-intensive goods, relative factor prices will change. The extent of this bias could be measured, and adjustment for differences between the market prices and the shadow prices of labour and capital be made, only through a general equilibrium analysis of the national economy. In view of the high levels of protection, and its great variability among industries, as well as the apparent lack of a systematic bias of protection in developing countries, the error due to the neglect of this bias, however, may not be large [1].

Additional problems arise if project appraisal is limited to a single project or, at most, to a few. This is generally the case for an international agency as well as for countries where decision-making by public authorities extends to a small proportion of total investment and/or where public decision-making on projects is decentralised. Project evaluation will now necessitate estimating the shadow exchange rate. This will, however, be subject to considerable error because of the uncertainties related to the values of the relevant elasticities.[10] At the same time, often relatively small differences in the assumed elasticities are sufficient to make or break a project.

To avoid this difficulty, I. M. D. Little and J. A. Mirrlees [13] have suggested that all domestic costs be expressed in terms of world market prices and that the project be judged on the basis of its benefit-cost ratio calculated by using the relevant discount rate. This involves separating non-traded inputs into their direct and indirect labour and traded goods components and valuing the consumption of labour used at the final stage of fabrication and (directly and indirectly) in the production of non-traded inputs at world market prices.[11]

---

[10] The information requirements of the shadow exchange rate include the value of exports and imports; the nominal rates of protection on traded goods; the domestic elasticities of import demand and export supply, as well as the foreign elasticities of export demand and import supply. The method of calculation is described in [2, Appendix A].

[11] The method assumes that labour's income is fully consumed.

The Little–Mirrlees Method thus values the product and its inputs (traded and non-traded) in world market prices while the shadow exchange rate method values them at domestic prices. This is accomplished by expressing labour's consumption in world market prices in the first case and converting the foreign value of traded goods into domestic prices at the shadow exchange rate in the second. The relevant conversion ratios are the average rate of nominal protection (for short, tariffs) on wage goods under the Little-Mirrlees Method and the shadow exchange rate under the shadow exchange rate method.

It follows that the two alternatives will give identical results if the shadow exchange rate equals the average rate of tariff on wage goods. In turn, the shadow exchange rate method will give a more (less) favourable result than the Little–Mirrlees Method in cases when the shadow exchange rate is greater (smaller) than the average tariff on wage goods. This can be seen from the examples of Table 2.2 where, for direct comparability, both project appraisal criteria have been expressed in terms of rates of return.

Assuming a production period of one year and a rate of discount of 9%, the project will be accepted using the Little–Mirrlees criterion in Case A (rate of return of 10% at world market prices) and rejected in Case B (rate of return of 6% under world market prices). The opposite conclusion obtains under the shadow exchange rate method under which the rate of return to capital is 8% in Case A and 11% in Case B.

The differences in the results are explained by the fact that, following customary procedures, in the calculation under the shadow exchange rate method I have not adjusted labour's contribution to the value added either for tariffs on wage goods or for the shadow exchange rate.[13] However, such adjustments

[12] In practice, under the shadow exchange rate method, the adjustment takes place in two steps: (*a*) domestic values of traded goods measured at the existing exchange rate are deflated by the relevant nominal rates of protection, and (*b*) the values thereby obtained are 'reflated' by the percentage difference between the shadow and the existing exchange rate which expresses the extent of overvaluation of the exchange rate as compared to the situation under optimal policies.

[13] D. B. Humphrey [12] makes adjustments for the effects of protection on wages as well as on profits which have been neglected here. But he incorrectly assumes that the resulting increase in money wages would have cumulative effects through higher prices of traded goods.

TABLE 2.2 *Alternative Evaluations of Investment Projects*

	Exchange rate	Investment per unit of output	Price of product	Material Input			Labour			Profit	
				(a)	(b)	(c)	(a)	(b)	(c)	(c) Value	% of investment
Case A											
Observed values in domestic prices under protection (*pesos*) (Tariff rates)	80	100 (25%)	120 (50%)	0·6	110 (37·5%)	66	0·2	110 (37·5%)	22	22	22
Domestic values deflated by tariff (*pesos*)	80	80	80	0·6	80	48	0·2	110	22	2	2·5
Deflated values adjusted for overvaluation (*pesos*) (Shadow exchange rate)	100	100	100	0·6	100	60	0·2	110	22	8	8
Values expressed in world market prices ($) (Little–Mirrlees method)	100	1·00	1·00	0·6	1·00	0·60	0·2	1·00	0·20	0·10	10

Case B

Observed values in domestic prices under protection (*pesos*) (Tariff rates)	80	100 (25%)	120 (50%)	110 (37·5%)	0·6	66	0·24	80 (0%)	19	25	25
Domestic values deflated by tariff (*pesos*)	80	80	80	80	0·6	48	0·24	80	19	5	6·25
Deflated values adjusted for overvaluation (*pesos*). (Shadow exchange rate)	100	100	100	100	0·6	60	0·24	80	19	11	11
Values expressed in world market prices ($). (Little–Mirrlees Method)	100	1·00	1·00	1·00	0·6	0·6	0·24	1·00	24	0·6	6

Notes: (a) world market input–output coefficient
(b) price
(c) value

would need to be made in order to allow for the effects of protection on nominal wages. If this were done, the two methods would give the same result provided that all estimates were without error. The choice between them then becomes a practical question of possible errors in estimation.

I have noted that the adjustment for the shadow exchange rate involves considerable error on account of the difficulties involved in estimating the relevant elasticities. In turn, the application of the Little–Mirrlees Method entails problems in treating the contribution of capital and land to the production of non-traded goods and that of land in producing traded goods; also, labour's consumption of non-traded goods needs to be divided into its labour and traded goods components. It may be suggested, then, that both methods be used in project evaluation and sensitivity analysis be applied to the results.

5. Policy Assumptions in Project Evaluation

In the event of evaluation at shadow prices calculated under the assumption that optimal policies are applied in the economy, a project will be accepted or rejected, depending on whether it would be profitable if optimal policies were adopted by the time of its implementation. As the application of optimal policies is the exception rather than the rule in developing countries, this assumption raises questions as to the eventual adoption of optimal policies and the time pattern of policy changes.[14] These can be looked upon as problems of the second best; i.e. should one use 'first best' shadow prices in one part of the economy if decisions are based on a different set of prices elsewhere?

To begin with, in many developing countries project appraisal at 'first best' shadow prices would mean that industrial projects subject to evaluation by national authorities or international agencies applying such a method (for short, public projects) would be put at a disadvantage as compared to private projects in the industrial sector, which enjoys protection. Now, there may be a welfare loss to the country in question if rejecting a

[14] Identical considerations apply to the application of the Little–Mirrless Method that uses shadow exchange rates implicitly by valuing all commodities, including wage goods, at world market prices.

public project were to lead to private investment in the protected sector of the economy as in the case when the government fails to borrow on the capital market. Similar conclusions apply if an international agency refrained from lending on preferential terms because the project in question did not meet the test at shadow prices.

But even if there is no substitution between private and public projects or loss of preferential credits, the country may suffer a welfare loss if optimal policies are not adopted during the lifetime of the project. Take, for example, the case when the protection of the manufacturing sector entails discrimination against primary activities through high input prices and over-valued exchange rates. Primary exports will now be smaller than under optimal policies and the contribution of a project in the protected sector of the economy will be understated if evaluated at the shadow exchange rate reflecting the application of optimal policies. Correspondingly, the net social benefits of saving or earning foreign exchange will be underestimated.

These considerations suggest that, in making decisions on projects, account would need to be taken of the policies applied and of prospective changes in policies during the lifetime of the project. This would necessitate constructing time series values of marginal social costs and utilities and deriving the shadow prices corresponding to them [10], [14]. If, for example, the alternative to the project is an investment in the private sector, the shadow exchange rate should be defined as the marginal domestic cost of foreign exchange in that sector. In turn, if the alternative is a reduction in investment or an increase in consumption, the marginal utility of foreign exchange will be the appropriate shadow exchange rate [11]. Needless to say, the information requirements of these calculations are formidable.

6. The Meaning of Optimal Policies

I have assumed so far that the agency making decisions on projects adopts a passive stance with regard to policies and that the implementation of the project has no feedback on the policies applied. But implementing a project that would not be viable under optimal policies will make the adoption of such policies more difficult by creating vested interests. Providing incentives to such projects will also tend to increase discrimination against other activities, thus leading further away from optimal policies.

A decision-maker with authority over policies and projects would have to take account of these effects as would, in the case of decentralised decision-making, the policy-making authority that provides policy assumptions to decision-makers on projects. Similar conclusions pertain to an international agency whose acceptance of projects which are not viable under optimal policies may lead to postponing the adoption of such policies. This will be the case *a fortiori* for an international agency with policy-advising responsibilities that could influence policies through the criteria applied in project appraisal.

It follows that decisions on project evaluation will have to depend on the assumptions made concerning the possibilities of effecting policy choices and this may often call for project evaluation under the assumption of optimal policies. The question is then, how can optimal policies be determined? This question will be taken up for the case when there are dynamic external economies in the manufacturing sector, reflecting the skill-producing effects of manufacturing industries, their impact on the modernisation of the economy and the advantages of establishing industries that are connected through input/output type relationships.

Ideally, shadow prices should now be calculated from a general equilibrium model incorporating external economies. But this would increase the data requirements of estimating general equilibrium models and as yet we have little information on the magnitude of the external economies associated with the expansion of the manufacturing sector. In practice, therefore, approximations would have to be used.

I have argued elsewhere that optimal trade policies would involve adopting optimal taxes on primary exports that face market limitations abroad and providing preferential treatment to manufacturing *vis-a-vis* other primary activities through the application of a tariff-export subsidy scheme. Moreover, unless there is evidence that a particular industry brings more (or fewer) benefits to the national economy than do manufacturing industries on the average, identical incentives – i.e. equal rates of effective protection – should be provided within the manufacturing sector [2, chap. V]. This conclusion also applies if the manufacturing sector receives special treatment because of government preference for industry [4].

The question remains at what rate tariffs and export subsidies be provided to the manufacturing sector. The cost of these incentives to the national economy as well as the observed adverse effects of import substitution in developing countries suggest that these rates be kept at moderate levels. While the appropriate norm will differ from country to country depending on the particular circumstances of the situation, it may rarely be outside the range of 10–15% effective protection. Additional incentives could, however, be provided to new industries on infant industry grounds on a temporary basis, preferably on a declining scale.

The described scheme may be implemented by accepting industrial projects that are profitable if their effective protection does not exceed the norm selected for the particular country, with adjustments made in the case of infant industries. In turn, nominal rates of protection for the product would be set so as to make the project profitable for the existing exchange rates and prices which themselves are affected by the system of protection. These nominal rates could be subsequently altered *pari passu* with changes in the system of protection.

Conclusion

I have considered in this paper questions relating to project selection in developing countries under optimal policies and in the event that non-optimal tariffs and export taxes are employed. But the conclusions can be extended to cases where incentives are provided through credit, tax, or expenditure measures rather than through tariffs and export taxes. Also, we can introduce employment or income distribution in the welfare function without affecting the basic conclusions.

Criteria for project appraisal were developed initially by assuming the absence of transportation costs, external economies, and market imperfections. The first two of these assumptions have been subsequently relaxed while the last one has been retained. In developing countries, however, we often observe imperfections in both product and factor prices. In the first eventuality, monopoly or oligopoly positions permit firms to reap above-average profits; in the second, market and shadow prices of primary factors will differ even though trade policies are optimal.

In the case of imperfections in the market for products which are used as inputs in a particular project, an adjustment would need to be made for excess profits. In turn, imperfections in factor markets call for the use of shadow prices which would ideally be derived from a general equilibrium model. Barring this, approximations would have to be used. These have been discussed at length in the literature [13], [18] and will not be taken up here. The problem of using, in the place of a single rate, different discount rates for calculating the present value of future consumption and the opportunity cost of capital, also falls outside the confines of this paper.

It should be emphasised that imperfections in factor markets will not modify the conclusion that a decision on the project is not affected by the choice of the primary factor for which calculations are made provided all other primary factors are valued at their appropriate shadow prices. But as in practice shadow prices are not known without error, it is desirable to use alternative methods of project evaluation and provide a sensitivity analysis of each. This is the more important given the error possibilities of project appraisal which pertain to the determination of shadow prices of primary factors, the comparison of domestic and foreign prices of products, and the treatment of non-traded goods.

References

[1] BALASSA, BELA, 'Effective Protection: A Summary Appraisal', in: *Effective Tariff Protection*, H. G. Grubel and H. G. Johnson, eds. Geneva, 1971, pp. 247–263.

[2] BALASSA, BELA, *The Structure of Protection in Developing Countries*. Baltimore, Md.: Johns Hopkins University Press, 1971.

[3] BALASSA, B. and SCHYDLOWSKY, D. M., 'Effective Tariffs, Domestic Cost of Foreign Exchange, and the

Equilibrium Exchange Rate', *Journal of Political Economy*, LXXVI (May/June 1968), 348–360.

[4] BERTRAND, T. J., 'Decision Rules for Effective Protection in Less Developed Economies', December 1970, (mimeo).

[5] BRUNO, MICHAEL, *Interdependence, Resources Use and Structural Change in Trade*, Jerusalem: Bank of Israel, 1963.

[6] BRUNO, MICHAEL, 'Domestic Resource Costs and Effective Protection: Clarification and Synthesis', *Journal of Political Economy*, (January/February 1972).

[7] CHENERY, HOLLIS B., 'Comparative Advantage and Development Policy', *American Economic Review*, LV (March 1961), 18–51.

[8] CORDEN, W. M., 'The Structure of a Tariff System and the Effective Protective Rate', *Journal of Political Economy*, LXXIV (June 1966), 221–37.

[9] CORDEN, W. M., *The Theory of Protection*, Oxford: Clarendon Press, 1971.

[10] FELDSTEIN, M. S., 'Financing in the Evaluation of Public Expenditure', Harvard Institute of Economic Research, Discussion Paper No. 132, August 1970.

[11] HARBERGER, A. C., 'Survey of Literature on Cost-Benefit Analysis for Industrial Project Evaluation', paper presented at the United Nations Inter-Regional Symposium in Industrial Project Evaluation, Prague, 1965.

[12] HUMPHREY, D. B., 'Measuring the Effective Rate of Protection: Direct and Indirect Effects', *Journal of Political Economy*, LXXVII (September/October 1969), 834–44.

[13] LITTLE, I. M. D. and MIRRLEES, J. A., *Manual of Industrial Project Analysis*, Vol. II, Paris, Development Centre of the Organisation for Economic Cooperation and Development, 1969.

[14] SCHYDLOWSKY, D. M., *On the Choice of a Shadow Price for Foreign Exchange*, Economic Development Report No. 108, Development Advisory Service, Cambridge, Mass., 1968.

[15] TINBERGEN, J., 'The Relevance of Theoretical Criteria in the Selection of Investment Plans', in M. Millikan, ed., *Investment Criteria and Economic Growth*. Cambridge, 1955.

60   *Economic Development and Planning*

[16] TINBERGEN, J., *The Design of Development*, Baltimore, Md.: Johns Hopkins University Press, 1968.
[17] TINBERGEN, J., 'Projections of Economic Data in Development Planning', in *Planning for Economic Development in the Caribbean, Puerto Rico*, Caribbean Organisation, 1963.
[18] U.N.I.D.O., 'Guidelines for Project Evaluation', mimeo, 1 May, 1970.

3 A Long-Term Macroeconomic Forecasting Model of the Soviet Economy

V. S. DADAJAN*

IN the planned economy of the Soviet Union, macroeconomic forecasts have the following main goals:

(1) To determine a general framework of future development;

(2) To find out the degree of influence upon future development of inertial tendencies, which come from the period preceding the forecasted period, taking into consideration possible discontinuities or distortions in otherwise stable trajectories;

(3) To establish some parameters of inter-relations between causes and consequences of economic development;

(4) To analyse opportunities for the realisation of different economic goals through the forecasting period;

(5) To obtain a certain system of macroeconomic variables endogenous to the economy but which could be introduced exogenously into the model as control characteristics and which are used directly at the stage of medium-term planning.

It is possible to realise the goals indicated above by using the following tools.

1. Elaboration of a System of Macroeconomic Indicators which Characterise the General Framework of Long-Term Development

These indicators must be selected so that it would be possible to include them in the system of inter-relations existing within the framework of a quantitative model. Keeping in mind the goals of the forecast described in (5) above, the indicators must

* The author is a member of the Academy of Sciences of the Armenian S.S.R.

be organised as a system of not only horizontal dimension (that is considering one and the same order of variables), but also of a vertical dimension (that is considering at least one stage of disaggregation of those variables which, in the following stages, appear to be exogenously introduced into the model of a medium-term plan).

According to their character, the indicators of every level of aggregation can be absolute (i.e. volumetrical) or relative (i.e. structural). According to their relation to the model they can be either exogenous (i.e. introduced as 'ready-made' from the outside) or endogenous (i.e. determined inside the model). From the point of view of these differences, the indicators of the synthetic level of calculations constitute the following groups:

(i) *Exogenous Indicators*

(a) Structural

1. Uncontrolled macrotechnological parameters:
   Material capacity of G.N.P.;
   Fund capacity of G.N.P. (i.e. capital-output ratio);
   Relation between depreciation and volume of fixed capital;
   Others.
2. Uncontrolled synthetic proportions:
   Share of G.N.I. in G.N.P.;
   Others.
3. Other uncontrolled parameters:
   Share of potential labour force in the total population and the growth of the potential labour force;
   Medium-term price indexes;
   Medium-term indexes of money income and real income;
   Others.

(b) Volumetrical

1. Indicators of the base year:
   the number of people in the total population, including the potential labour force;
   G.N.P.;
   G.N.I.;
   The volume of gross fixed capital;
   Depreciation;
   Accumulation of fixed capital;
   Consumption, including individual consumption;
   Exports;
   Imports;
   Others.

(ii) *Endogenous Variables*

(a) Structural

(b) Volumetrical

1. Alternative control parameters of global effect:
Rate of accumulation;
Relation between consumption and accumulation;
Others.

2. Alternative control parameters of local effect:
Share of housing construction in gross accumulation;
Coefficient of foreign trade balance (relation between exports and imports);
Coefficients of the structure of imports;
Others.

1. Indexes of the forecasted period:
G.N.P.;
G.N.I.;
Volume of fixed capital;
Accumulation;
Consumption;
Exports;
Imports;
Others.

The division of alternative control parameters into the parameters of global and local effect is of little importance. Its only aim is to attract special attention to the great scale of the economic aggregate, which is influenced by the given parameter. It goes without saying that the selection of target values for one of the variables described in (ii)-(a) automatically makes all the other variables uncontrolled parameters, the numerical value of which must be determined exogenously in the framework of (i)-(a)2.

2. Statistical Analysis, Extrapolation and Expert Correction of Stable Trajectories traced out by the Changes in Uncontrolled Structural Parameters (i)–(a)

Statistical analysis, smoothing and subsequent extrapolation of dynamic tendencies of structural parameters of an economic system give us the opportunity to determine pure stable trajectories, the configuration of which is in no way connected with possible changes in worked out tendencies which can take place during the planned period. This extrapolation exhausts the passive element of the forecast. It is immediately followed by the procedure of expert evaluation of worked out stable trajectories which is completed with the definition of possible points of indignation or revolt and – consequently – of discontinuities in the otherwise smooth curves. Since even the most skilled examination does not always permit to give a single answer to the question when and to which extent one or another structural parameter will change over time, simplicity gives place to a great number of variants so that the final result of the examination yields nothing but a variant row of time series of future dynamics of structural parameters. And the starting point of the row is always an extrapolated curve. For example, in elaboration of the forecast of the development of the U.S.S.R. economy for 1971–1985 three hypotheses of the change in the capital-output ratio were introduced in the calculations. One of them was a pessimistic extrapolation, taking into consideration the tendency for the capital-output ratio to increase, which was observed during the period 1959–1965. The other two estimates of the capital-output ratio were based on the assumption of a possible stabilisation of fund capacity beginning from either 1975 or 1980.

3. Construction of a Quantitative Model in which Inter-relations between Structural and Volumetrical Parameters of Economic Growth are Formalised on the Basis of the Level of Synthetic Indicators

The structure of a model which can be used for this purpose will be described below.

4. Introduction into the Model of a Set of Effectiveness Criteria, Built on an Adequate Level of Information

Because of the urgency of speeding up the increase in the production of consumer goods in the U.S.S.R., it is advisable to build a criterion of effectiveness of alternative variants of development on the basis of the indexes of the volume of the annual production of consumer goods. The current effectiveness criterion for consumption can be formed as the weighted sum of past events, which occurred at different moments in time, and it can be written as follows:

$$\sum_{t=1}^{T} (1 + \lambda)^{-t} C_t \Rightarrow \text{Max} \tag{1}$$

where T = a number of years in the forecasted period,

λ = a constant parameter of the weighting function,

C_t = a volume of consumption in year t.

Introduction of the objective function (1) into the model of the forecast inserts an element of optimisation into it, and thus increases the degree of its conditionality: if uncontrolled structural parameters change in accordance with a given combination of hypotheses and if dynamics of control parameters are regulated according to the recommendation, received as a result of the solution to a problem, then general characteristics of future development will form the given, and not any other, system. Thus, the increase in the degree of conditionality of a forecast comes forward as a natural price for having made it active and aim-oriented.

While choosing the duration of the forecasted period mainly considerations of general character are taken into account. This period must be long enough to give us an opportunity to realise effectively a manoeuvre with accumulations for the purpose of the objective function (1), and it must not be too long, so that the exogenous information about hypothetical behaviour of structural parameters is not practically unreliable. And, finally, to comply with condition (5), it is desirable to formulate the forecast for such a number of years which is a multiple of five, the length of time for which medium-term plans are constructed in the U.S.S.R. In accordance with that principle, the period of 15 years was chosen. However, for analytical purposes, the calculations were repeated for different terms ($T = 10, 12, 15, 20$). Thus T appears to be virtually one of the exogenous variables of the model.

As far as the parameter of the weighting function is concerned, we did not manage to find even general factors to protect the selection of its numerical value on whatever level. This fact has already been mentioned in the literature. As a result, this parameter was turned into an exogenous variable. Thus the objective function can be rewritten in a more general way

$$\sum_{t=1}^{T_i} (1 + \lambda_j)^{-t} C_t \Rightarrow \text{Max} \tag{1a}$$

5. Construction of a Greatly Aggregated Inter-industry Dynamic Model Focussing on the Main Branches of the National Economy and Its Co-ordination with the Model of the First Stage Through Iteration

The official classification, adopted by the General Statistical Bureau of the U.S.S.R., recognises six main branches in the national economy of the U.S.S.R.:

(1) Industry;
(2) construction;
(3) agriculture;
(4) transport and communications;
(5) material and technical supply, public trade, state purchases;
(6) other branches.

As far as in the input-output tables each of the last three branches is presented, (as a rule), by one position, i.e. one industry, a corresponding amount of information in the model of the second stage and in the disaggregated model appears to be identical. In other words, the existence of three separate sectors of branches of production services in the model of the second planning stage means that these sectors are not aggregated in the model pertaining to this stage in contrast to large models of the input-output type, on the basis of which the medium-term plan must be calculated. This leads to the conclusion that it is necessary to aggregate these sectors into one, which can be called 'branches of production services'.

Channels of direct and feedback interdependencies between the two models of both planning stages form an iterative loop. Optimal values of the criterion variables which determine the lower limit of changeability of total volumes of consumer goods, performed annually in industry, construction, agriculture and other branches of the model of the first stage represent an input of the four-branch model.[1]

[1] Certainly the procedure of computation must provide for the corrections of its results, received at the top level of calculations, if optimal values of consumption do not satisfy the system of restrictions of the model of the lower stage.

Components of simple formulas according to which medium-term structural parameters are calculated on the basis of four-dimensional vectors and matrices of the second stage enter the model of the first stage from the four-product model through the feedback channel passing through the block of aggregation.

The objective function of the forecast (1a) can also be used at the second stage of calculations if the element structure of the fund of consumption is given.

It is evident that, at this level of aggregation, the requirement of maximisation of the total number of 'macrosets' of consumer goods can be fulfilled without regard for such factors as elasticity of demand for different goods, etc.

The dynamic problem of the second stage solved by means of the linear programming method would provide the four-dimensional vectors of consumption for every predicted period, and – if necessary – vectors of investments and other production characteristics can be introduced as control results into dis-aggregated models of a medium-term plan. Aggregation of the results of medium-term planning and their introduction into the model of the second stage to correct the results closes the second loop of iterations which, together with the first one, constitutes a closed loop framework which has the shape of the number eight. This has been pictured in Figure 3.1.

A model of the first stage of the forecast is constructed under the assumption that it has only one product. That means that any two units of G.N.P., irrespective of their economic role, are characterised by the same structure of costs and are absolutely intersubstitutable.

The following system of symbols will be adopted:

X = G.N.P.;
U = gross intermediate products;
K = volume of fixed capital of the national economy;
C = volume of consumption;
I = accumulation of fixed capital;
E = exports;
D = other elements of final product (depreciation, increase in stocks and reserves, compensation of losses, etc.);
Q = imports, including:
Q_i = imports of fixed capital,

Q_u = imports of intermediate products,

Q_c = imports of consumer goods;

P = population;

L = labour force;

a = coefficient of material capacity of G.N.P.;

b = capital-output ratio;

e = share of exports in G.N.P.;

d = share of other elements in G.N.P.;

s = a coefficient of the foreign trade balance (relation of gross imports to gross exports);

q_u = share of intermediate products in gross imports;

q_i = share of fixed capital in gross imports;

q_c = share of consumer goods and other products' gross imports.

According to the definition, eight structural parameters can be expressed with the help of volumetrical indicators as follows:

$$a_t = \frac{U_t + Q_{ut}}{X_t}; \quad b_t = \frac{K_t}{X_t}; \quad e_t = \frac{E_t}{X_t}; \quad d_t = \frac{D_t}{X_t};$$

$$s_t = \frac{Q_t}{E_t}; \quad q_{ut} = \frac{Q_{ut}}{Q_t}; \quad q_{it} = \frac{Q_{it}}{Q_t}; \quad q_{ct} = \frac{Q_{ct}}{Q_t}$$

Bearing in mind that G.N.P. is used for current needs of production, for accumulation of fixed capital, consumption, exports, and other needs, one can write the following identity

$$U_t + I_t + C_t + E_t + D_t = X_t$$

Substituting U_t for $a_t X_t - Q_{ut}$

E_t for $e_t X_t$

D_t for $d_t X_t$

and using I_t and C_t as independent variables, we find

$$a_t X_t - Q_{ut} + I_t + C_t + e_t X_t + d_t X_t = X_t$$

and

$$a_t X_t - q_{ut} s_t e_t X_t + I_t + C_t + e_t X_t + d_t X_t = X_t$$

Solving the above equation for X_t, yields

$$X_t = \frac{1}{1 - a_t - d_t - e_t(1 - q_{ut} s_t)} (I_t + C_t) \tag{2}$$

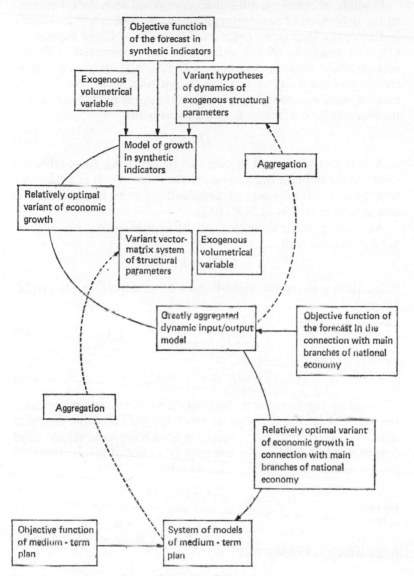

FIG. 3.1 *A Block-Scheme of Outer and Inner Interrelations of a System of Models of a Long-Term Forecast*

Possible information difficulties connected with the estimation of the behaviour of parameters a_t, d_t, e_t, q_{ut} and s_t will inevitably influence the structure of the coefficient $(I_t + C_t)$ in expression (2). For example, if the difficulties are connected with the foreign trade balance parameters (e_t, q_{ut}, s_y), one can estimate the combination $e_t(1 + q_{ut}s_t)$ as a unit parameter. An extreme case of such a modification is the estimation of dynamics of a non-structural coefficient α_t in the expression

$$X_t = \alpha_t(I_t + C_t) \tag{2a}$$

Although the method appears to be artificial, the coefficient α_t will have rather a definite economic meaning; it is a quantity inverse to the total share of accumulated fixed capital (I_t) and consumption (C_t) in G.N.P. (X_t).

According to the definition of the capital-output ratio $(b_t = K_t/X_t)$ one can write:

$$b_t X_t = K_t$$

Substituting X_t for the right-hand side of Equation (2) or (2a) we get:

$$\frac{b_t}{1 - a_t - d_t - e_t(1 - q_{ut}s_t)}(I_t + C_t) = K_t \tag{3}$$

or

$$b_t\alpha_t(I_t + C_t) = K_t \tag{3a}$$

Based on the fact that accumulation of fixed capital increases the value of the existing capital stock for the following year and that the total imports of capital are used for accumulation (and depreciation is held at the expense of national production) we get the following dynamic relationship

$$K_{t+1} = K_t + I_t + Q_{it} \tag{4}$$

In turn

$$Q_{it} = q_{it}Q_t = q_{it}s_t E_t = q_{it}s_t e_t X_t,$$

from which it follows that

$$Q_{it} = \frac{q_{it}s_t e_t}{1 - a_t - d_t - e_t(1 - q_{ut}s_t)}(I_t + C_t) \tag{5}$$

or

$$Q_{it} = q_{it}s_t e_t \alpha_t(I_t + C_t) \tag{5a}$$

Autonomous estimation of the product $q_{it}s_t e_t$ leads to

$$Q_{it} = g_t \alpha_t (I_t + C_t) \tag{5b}$$

where g_t indicates a relation between imports of elements of fixed capital and G.N.P.

Substituting Equation (5a) or (5b) for Q_{it} into Equation (4), and after performing a simple transformation, one obtains:

$$K_{t+1} = K_t + \left\{ 1 + \frac{q_{it}s_t e_t}{1 - a_t - d_t - e_t(1 - q_{ut}s_t)} \right\} I_t$$

$$+ \frac{q_{it}s_t e_t}{1 - a_t - d_t - e_t(1 - q_{ut}s_t)} C_t \tag{6}$$

or

$$K_{t+1} = K_t + (1 + g_t \alpha_t)I_t + g_t \alpha_t C_t \tag{6a}$$

The volume of fixed capital of each year can be expressed as the sum of the quantity available in the base year, K_o, and successive yearly increments

$$K_t = K_o + \sum_{\tau=0}^{t-1} \{(1 + g_\tau \alpha_\tau)I_\tau + g_\tau \alpha_\tau C_\tau\}$$

Introducing this value of K_t into Equation (3a) and bringing the independent variables to the left-hand side, one finds

$$b_t \alpha_t (I_t + C_t) - \sum_{\tau=0}^{t-1} \{(1 + g_\tau \alpha_\tau)I_\tau + g_\tau \alpha_\tau C_\tau\} = K_o,$$

$$(t = 1, 2, \ldots, T) \tag{7}$$

Thus, the system of restrictions of the problem (for a specific combination of hypotheses of the dynamics of the structural parameters) consists of T equations and $2T$ variables. This gives us the opportunity (using T degrees of freedom) to determine an optimal set of values of I_t and C_t, which will maximise the objective function (1). The solution to the problem is chosen from the set of non-negative values of the solution of a linear programming model and has as a specific feature that it represents an optimal regime of the accumulation of fixed capital. This is shown in Figure 3.2.

From an economic point of view this solution appears unacceptable. That is why it is used only as a basis for subsequent calculations, the main task of which consists in the smoothing of the fluctuations in the main economic variables, and first of all in the variable representing the accumulation of fixed capital. Of course, any change in the found solution would lead to a decrease in the value of the objective function. This is shown in curves (1) and (2) of Figure 3.2. In accordance with the considerations which underline the transition from one regime to another, the first solution must be thought of as the technological optimum, the second one must be considered a relative economic optimum.

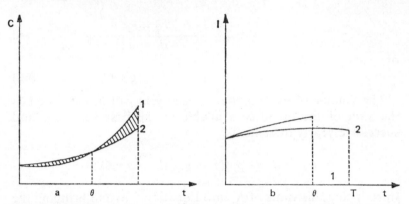

FIG. 3.2 *Increase in the Fund of Consumption (a) and in Accumulation of Fixed Capital (b)*

One of the ways to the final solution is connected with the introduction of a control parameter into the model, and also of a number of additional constraints which restrict both the sphere of determination of optimum values of independent variables and the amplitude of their fluctuations over time.

Let $\qquad r_t = I_t/C_t$

$$R \geq r_t \geq r_{it}$$

where $R =$ the upper limit of variability of r_t, which is established on the basis of additional calculations or expert estimation; $r_{it} =$ the lower limit which can be determined, for example, if $I_{t+1} \geq I_t$ for all t from 0 to $T - 1$. For example, let a 'step' of an annual change in the absolute value of r_t be fixed beforehand

$$|r_{t+1} - r_t| \leq k$$

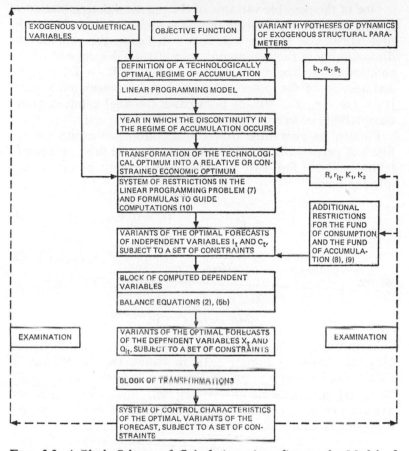

FIG. 3.3 *A Block Scheme of Calculations According to the Model of Economic Growth (in Synthetic Indicators)*

4

One of the possible variants of the practical determination of r_t consists in the calculation of first invariable value of k for the first half-period from $t = 1$ to $t = \theta$, i.e. to the year of 'the discontinuity in the regime of accumulation, determined by the solution of the linear programming problem $[k_1 = (R - r_0/\theta)]$ and second of the other value of k for the remaining years $[k_2 = (R - r_{it}/T - \theta)]$. In both cases the final solution about acceptability of k_1 and k_2 must be made by experts.

Finally, to guarantee that consumption per capita (in the first half period) will not decrease, and that the fund capacity of labour will not fail, two more restrictions must be introduced into the model

$$\frac{C_{t+1}}{P_{t+1}} \geq \frac{C_t}{P_t} \qquad (t = 0, 1, \ldots, \theta) \qquad (8)$$

$$\frac{I_{t+1} + \theta I_{t+1}}{\Delta L_{t+1}} \geq \frac{I_t + \theta I_t}{\Delta L_t} \qquad (t = \theta - 1, \theta, \ldots, T) \quad (9)$$

where

$$\Delta L_{t+1} = L_{t+2} - L_{t+1}$$
$$\Delta L_t = L_{t+1} - L_t$$

Substituting 'relatively optimal' values of r_t into Equation (3a) (as shown in Figure 3.3), in which the dependence is formalised between the possibility of creating the consumption fund and new elements of fixed capital, on the one hand, and available resources of fixed capital on the other hand, we get the following formulae to determine I_t and C_t:

$$I_t = \frac{r_t}{r_t + 1} \cdot \frac{1}{b_i \alpha_t} \cdot K_t$$

$$C_t = \frac{1}{r_t + 1} \cdot \frac{1}{b_i \alpha_t} \cdot K_t \qquad (10)$$

Availability of a circuit of feedback, indicated by a dotted line in Figure 3.3, means that the expert analysis of control characteristics of the forecast (such as the rate of growth of G.N.P. and its components, dynamics of the volume of consumption per capita and other characteristics), can lead to the reconsideration of either the objective or a number of the constraints of the problem.

4 Technological Transfer, Employment and Development

JOHN C. H. FEI AND
GUSTAV RANIS*

IT is generally agreed that one of the most important factors
shaping the course of development in the typical less developed
country (l.d.c.) is its coexistence with developed countries and
the possibility of technological transfers from the latter to the
former, induced by the presence of a so-called technology gap.
In practical terms, such transfers result in a modification of the
ways in which the developing economy's labour force is utilised
and in major changes in its output and employment performance. Our purpose in the present paper is to attempt an analysis
of such technological transfer in the context of a fairly general
growth-theoretic framework.

Such analysis, of course, goes to the heart of the well-known
problem of labour utilisation in the l.d.c.'s. Open unemployment is generally acknowledged to be a significant phenomenon
in the modern sector of these countries.[1] With respect to disguised unemployment, especially in agriculture and the services,
on the other hand, there exists a good deal of controversy on
both theoretical and empirical grounds. Nurkse, Arthur Lewis,
Rosenstein-Rodan and Mellor and Stevens,[2] are among those
who believe that up to 30% of the agricultural labour force is
likely to be disguisedly unemployed in the typical l.d.c. Arrayed
on the other side are Bent Hansen, Jorgenson, Ted Schultz and

* The authors are Professors of Economics, Yale University. We gratefully acknowledge the assistance of Marsha Goldfarb in an earlier version
of this paper.

[1] For Latin America as a whole, for example, it is estimated to have
exceeded 11% for 1965 [10].
[2] See: [14], [12, pp. 139-92], [18], [13].

Viner,[3] among others. While we cannot attempt to deal with the controversy in the context of the present paper,[4] we are willing to stand with Hagen who, after carefully surveying it, concludes that 'there is enough disguised unemployment in various peasant economies so that analyses based on the assumption of its existence merit discussion', [6, p. 302]. Disguised and open unemployment together are clearly important enough to make us concerned about the labour utilisation problem; and increased population pressures are rendering the problem more and more acute.[5] Small wonder that development economists and practitioners alike are becoming increasingly concerned with the problem.[6]

In spite of this concern, the profession has made relatively little progress towards a positive theory of unemployment for the developing world – mainly because it is a relatively complicated phenomenon, centrally related to both capital accumulation and technological change.[7] While capital accumulation can be traced to the conventional sources of saving and investment, the causation behind technological change includes

[3] See: [7], [8], [20], [27].

[4] The issue seems to us to revolve largely around whether or not one insists on the strictly zero marginal product of labour concept or only that a substantial portion of the agricultural labour force is compensated in excess of its marginal product; moreover, on whether or not minor reorganisations among those left behind in agriculture is admitted; finally, on whether the Sen distinction between the marginal product of labour and the marginal product of individual labourers is accepted [21].

[5] For example, A. Lewis [11, p. 78] with respect to Jamaica, and H. A. Turner [25, p. 7] who found unemployment rates rising at an average of 8·5% a year in 14 l.d.c.'s during the 1950s.

[6] Indian planners, for instance, recognise the failure of employment opportunities to keep up with population growth and acknowledge the existence of a 'backlog of unemployment at the beginning of the Fourth Plan of nine to ten million', (*Fourth Five-Year Plan, Draft Outline*, p. 106, Planning Commission of India). The O.E.C.D. Development Center and the I.L.O., among others, have recently launched major research efforts on unemployment.

[7] This contrasts sharply with the highly developed theory of unemployment for the mature economy in the Keynesian Tradition. The essence of the Keynesian theory is that unemployment results from an excess of productive capacity relative to aggregate demand; such a theory is clearly irrelevant to a developing country where unemployment occurs because the productive capacity is too small relative to aggregate demand.

not only the aforementioned transfer of technology from abroad, but also the even more complicated innovative response and learning processes within. In Section 1 we shall discuss the conventional capital accumulation dimensions of the problem and its relationship to unemployment. Sections 2 and 3 will be devoted, respectively, to an analysis of the technological transfer and learning dimensions of the problem. An integration of these facets into a comprehensive deterministic model will be attempted in Section 4. The applications of the model are discussed in Section 5 and its relevance tested against Japanese historical data in Section 6.

1. Capital Accumulation and Unemployment

It is intuitively obvious that unemployment in an l.d.c. can occur simply because of the inadequacy of the capital stock to absorb the available labour force. A rigorous statement of this idea is due to Eckaus [1] who first formulated the concept of 'technical unemployment'. In Figure 4.1 let labour (capital) be plotted on the horizontal (vertical) axis and let the L-shaped production contours be shown with the 'technology line' OT. Then technical unemployment à la Eckaus of U_0 units occurs. This is due to the assumed essentially complementary nature of K and L, i.e. technical unemployment occurs because the existing capital capacity of K_0 units can accommodate only M_0 units of labour. Hence, unemployment is induced by a shortage of capital stock.

Introducing the time dimension, it follows rigorously from the above that technical unemployment can be eliminated through time only when K is growing at a rate faster than L. Let the factor endowment path $E_0, E_1, E_2, \ldots$ be shown in the contour map. It is obvious that the endowment path will bend toward and intersect the technology line at a turning point T (signifying the elimination of technical unemployment) if, and only if, K expands at a faster rate than L.

It is easy to provide an algebraic solution to the above. Let the population grow at a constant rate r, (exogenously determined) and let a Keynesian average propensity to save s be postulated. Let the capital and labour coefficients of the unit ontour (i.e., that contour which produces one unit of output)

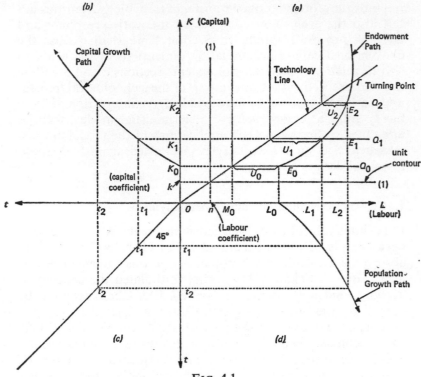

FIG. 4.1

be k and n, respectively, as shown in Figure 4.1. Thus, letting $\eta_x = dx/dt/x$ stand for the rate of growth of x, we have

$\eta_L = r$ (constant population growth rate)   (1a)

$I = sQ$ (saving function)   (1b)

$dK/dt = I$ (investment as the increment to capital stock)   (1c)

$Q = K/k$ (k is the capital-output ratio)   (1d)

$Q = N/n$ (n is the labour coefficient and N the *employed* labour force)   (1e)

$U = L - N$ (technical unemployment)   (1f)

Now suppose we know that the initial endowment point is at E_0 (with L_0 units of labour and K_0 units of capital), below the technology line. Since capital is 'the' bottleneck factor, the Harrod-Domar model applies, i.e. (1b, 1c, 1d). We can then determine the rates of growth ($\eta_x = dx/dt/x$) of K, Q, N, and K/L

$$\eta_K = \eta_Q = \eta_N = s/k \qquad (2a)$$

$$\eta_{K/L} = s/k - r \quad (\text{or } K/L = \frac{K_0}{L_0} e^{(s/k-r)t}) \qquad (2b)$$

Since the slope of the technology line OT is k/n, the turning point (at T) occurs when the K/L (in 2b) is equated to k/n, i.e. when

$$k/n = (K_0/L_0)e^{(s/k-r)t} \qquad (3)$$

and the endowment path intersects the technology line. Solving for t, the time it takes to eliminate technical unemployment, yields

$$t = \frac{1}{s/k - r} \ln (k/K_0/n/L_0) \quad (\text{for } k/n > K_0/L_0) \qquad (4)$$

The logic linking the extent of unemployment to the overall growth performance of the economy is thus clearly established.[8] However, this Eckaus-related formulation undoubtedly exaggerates the extent of technological complementarity between capital and labour. We will now seek to soften this rigidity by introducing technological change.

2. The Transmission of Technology

Most development theorists readily agree that modernisation involves much more than physical resource augmentation *à la* Harrod-Domar but is deeply affected by changes in technology.[9] The basic notion of technological transfer is based on the recognition that a major source of technological change in the developing world derives from the importation of technology from the advanced countries. This basically sound notion of long standing [26] is often paired with the idea that the blessings flowing from such technological transmission are not unmixed; for the so-called 'modern' technology has been developed in the

[8] From (4) we see that a positive solution to t exists if and only if $s/k > r$, i.e. $\eta_K > \eta_L$; and from (1a) and (2a), that continuous increases in per capita income (Q/L) can be achieved only if the same condition holds.

[9] S. Kuznets [9] and R. M. Solow [22], for example.

capital-rich, labour-scarce mature economy and is not necessarily 'appropriate' to the factor endowment of the poor
borrower. Additional unemployment may be created and the
net effect on output is subject to the famous output v employment controversy.[10] Finally, the truly significant aspect of such
borrowing may well lie in its catalytic effect in terms of inducing
domestic innovative processes, illustrated by the case of historical Japan [16]. Let us now proceed to a more rigorous formulation of these intuitive ideas.

First, we introduce the notion of a technology shelf, developed and perfected in the mature economies, from which the
developing countries are free to borrow. We have earlier chosen
to describe a particular technology by an L-shaped unit contour – defined rigorously by a pair of input coefficients (k, n).
A technology shelf may then be represented by a set of unit
activities (k_0, n_0), (k_1, n_1), (k_2, n_2), . . . as represented by the
points A_0, A_1, A_2, . . . forming a smooth envelope curve in
Figure 4.2. An l.d.c. at any point in time is then in a position to
borrow a particular unit activity from the shelf. This view of
technological transfer immediately raises two questions: (*a*) how
does the shelf come about and (*b*) by what rules does an l.d.c.
borrow from it?

With respect to the first question, the technology shelf contains technologies which have been demonstrated to be feasible
in the mature economies either at present or at some historical
point in the past, e.g. A_0 in 1900, A_1 in 1930, and A_2 in 1960, . . .
prevailing, say, in the United States.[11] Thus as we move upward along the shelf, we run into more modern technology, i.e.
that of more recent vintage. This is represented by an ever-
increasing capital per head (k/n) signifying that a typical worker
in the mature world has learned to co-operate with more units
of capital goods in a society with increasing technological

[10] e.g. W. Galenson and H. Leibenstein [4], G. Ranis [17] and J. C. H.
Fei and G. Ranis [2].

[11] In the realistic world, there exist, of course, other technology exporting countries (e.g. western Europe, Japan . . .) whose historical
experience could be summarised on the same shelf. Since there has been
continuous technological transfer among the mature countries it is not
unreasonable to postulate the existence of a single technological shelf for
the entire mature world as a first approximation.

complexity.[12] As we move to the left, labour productivity increases (i.e. n decreases).[13] This is shown by the negatively sloped rectangular hyperbola $(1/n)$ in Figure 4.2b, the height of which indicates labour efficiency (approximated by labour productivity $p = 1/n$) for the corresponding unit technology, vertically lined up with Figure 4.2a. According to this historical view of the technology shelf labour is thus not a homogeneous entity, and the improvement of the quality of labour, through education or learning by doing, is essential for the society to master a more advanced state of technology.

The improvement of the quality of labour through time can also be depicted in Figure 4.2c by the *labour progress function*, given exogenously as a historical reality in the mature economy.[14] Figure 4.2abc thus serves to show that the improvement of labour efficiency through time enables workers to co-operate with more and better capital goods per head, describing a society reaching ever higher levels of technological complexity. When an l.d.c. tries to borrow from the technology shelf it is thus constrained by the education and skill attainment levels of its own economic agents. Consequently, the progress it is capable of making in improving indigenous skill and education levels really constitutes a basic constraint on its rate of progress.

[12] Thus, to us, in an historical sense, a capital deepening process is much more complicated than 'homogeneous labour being equipped with more units of homogeneous capital goods' and is virtually inseparable from increasing technological complexity being mastered by better labour in a learning process. Changes in the quality of both K and N over time are essential facets of growth. This historical interpretation of our unit contour (i.e. the technology shelf) should be sharply distinguished from the unit contour of a static production function as ordinarily encountered in production theory.

[13] The slope of the technology shelf, however, depends on whether or not the capital-output ratio rises or falls in the advanced countries with secular increases in capital intensity and labour productivity. While we concentrate here on the negatively sloped case (rising K/Q) for expositional convenience, the analytical significance of the positively sloped case (falling K/Q) will be explored below (Section 3).

[14] Such a labour progress function could be rendered endogenous via linkage to cultural heritage, accumulated labour performance in the past, learning by doing and/or investment in formal education. While such enrichment is clearly desirable and could easily be accommodated by our present framework, it has not been undertaken in this paper.

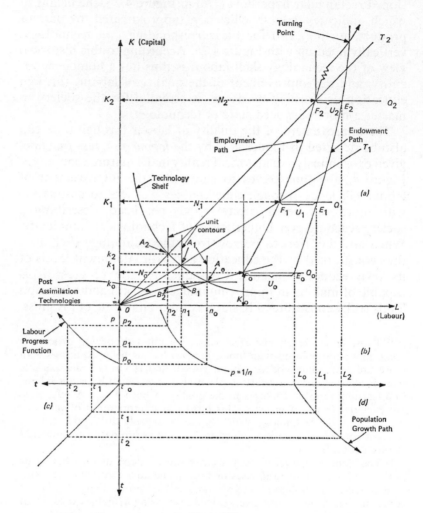

F<small>IG</small>. 4.2

It is with this understanding that we approach an analysis of the rules of borrowing.

3. Education and Technology

When a technology shelf as defined above is postulated, the phenomenon of continuous technological transfer may be depicted as the *climbing upward* by the borrower along the technology shelf so that, through time, the unit technology representative of a more recent vintage A_0, A_1, A_2, ... (Figure 4.2a) is achieved. The historical experience of the mature economy – as analysed in the last section – strongly suggests that the rapidity of technological borrowing is governed by the skill level (broadly interpreted to relate to the level of labour efficiency, and of public and private entrepreneurial ability) necessary for the mastery of an increasingly modern technology.

Proceeding to use Figure 4.2 for a somewhat different purpose, the exogenously given labour progress function of (c) may now be interpreted as that pertaining to the typical l.d.c.[15] It is, in fact, a basic hypothesis of this paper that the rapidity of the development of the domestic human resources in this sense is causally crucial with respect to the rapidity with which foreign technology can be borrowed and, once borrowed, assimilated via the exercise of domestic innovative ingenuity.

In this connection it will prove helpful conceptually to distinguish between the 'pure transplantation case' in which foreign technology is imported without further modification, and the case of 'technological assimilation' in which some domestic innovative effort is made 'on top of' the imported technology. This notion of 'assimilation' refers to that vital indigenous innovative effort through which the initially 'capital using' character of imported technology can be modified and adapted to make it more suitable to the labour-rich and capital-scarce factor endowment condition of the typical l.d.c.[16]

[15] An l.d.c. with a more (less) favourable learning by doing history, cultural inheritance and/or successful education policy over time can be represented by a more (less) steeply rising labour progress function.

[16] Such 'assimilation', taking the form of multiple shifting, machine speed-ups, changes in handling and other peripheral activities, variations in plant size, structure and organisation has been documented for Japan [16], Mexico [23] and the Soviet Union [5].

Using Figure 4.2, let the developing country's labour progress function and the technology shelf available to the l.d.c. be postulated. In the case of 'pure transplantation' the skill level which has been attained at any point in time causally determines the 'vintage' of the unit technology which can be borrowed. Thus at time t_1, t_2, . . . the imported (i.e. borrowed) technology can be represented by technology A_1, A_2, ... This also represents the effective technology which prevails in the l.d.c. at that historical point in time. The underlying justification for this 'rule of borrowing' is that a unit technology of a more recent vintage, or a vintage representing a higher technological complexity, can only be mastered when the pertinent domestic 'skill level' has been achieved.

Turning next to the more general case, i.e. when borrowing is accompanied by technological assimilation, the effective unit technology at time t_1, t_2, . . . in fact turns out to be represented by points B_1, B_2, . . . as shown by the curve labelled 'post-assimilation technologies'. In this general case, the basic hypothesis is that the domestic ingenuity and skill level achieved at a particular point in time (e.g. t_2) enables the country not only to import the technology (e.g. A_2) of the 'correct' vintage but also to 'stretch' the use of that capital, resulting in a reduction of the value of the capital coefficient (e.g. to the level indicated at point B_2). In this case, the ratio of the distance A_2B_2/B_2n_2 in Figure 4.2a may be interpreted as the 'degree of capital stretching' which gives us a quantitative measure of the strength of the indigenous innovative effort aimed at modifying the imported technology. If that effort is weak, the degree of capital stretching may be zero, bringing us back to the special case of 'pure transplantation'.

Notice that a negatively sloped technology shelf, representing pure transplantation, leads to increased labour productivity but only at an increasing capital cost (i.e. rise in the capital-output ratio). In a developing country characterised by capital scarcity, the transfer of technology from abroad may thus actually result in increased technical unemployment and hence a lower value of per capita income (Q/L) – in spite of the fact that labour productivity (Q/N) is raised. This unfavourable unemployment effect can, however, be considerably ameliorated by the domestic capital stretching effort, the effect of which is to enable more

labour to be employed per unit of capital stock. The borrowing
of technology which involves a maximum of domestic innovative effort is thus clearly superior to the pure transplantation
case.[17]

In summary, the rules of technological borrowing as we have
formulated them are based on a one-to-one correspondence
between the 'skill level' attained by a society and the vintage of
the technology which can be borrowed from the international
shelf, and modified. Economies which try to borrow 'ahead' of
their skill level also find it more difficult to assimilate that
technology. This admittedly is only a first approximation to a
fully realistic behaviour pattern underlying the borrowing of
technology by the contemporary developing country. We shall
return to a closer examination of the content of this crucial
assumption after its full significance for growth has been
explored.

4. Technological Transfer and Unemployment

Contemporary growth theory has had a pronounced material
resources orientation and has relied heavily on the accumulation
of capital, as in the Harrod-Domar model of Section 1. On the
other hand, our arguments in the last section have placed considerable emphasis on education, and on technological change
via the transmission from rich to poor. We are now ready to put
these two strands of thought together in order to formulate a
more satisfactory growth model based on our work in Sections 1
and 2.

The deterministic aspects of this model can be easily explained
with the aid of Figure 4.2. Initially at time $t = t_0$, it is the skill
level which determines the effective unit technology (i.e. the
point A_0 and the technology line OT_0) implying the initial
capital-output ratio k_0 in a way described in the last section.
The initial supply of capital stock (K_0) then determines the
scale of operation of the technology (at F_0) the amount of
labour which can be accommodated (N_0) and the output (Q_0).

[17] The successful Japanese growth experience in the nineteenth century,
and the Korean, Taiwanese and Mexican experience in the twentieth, have
provided ample proof of the substantial advantages of the selective
importation of technology coupled with a major domestic innovative
effort.

The initial population (L_0) then serves to determine the volume of unemployment (U_0). The system is thus completely determined statistically. In the next period, (t_1) the skill level (p_1) determines the imported unit technology (A_1) which becomes the effective unit technology (B_1) after capital stretching (measured by the distance $A_1 B_1$). With the aid of the average propensity to save (s) and output (Q_0) we can determine savings and investment $I_0 = sQ_0$ in the second period and hence the new capital stock (K_1). The total population (L_1) is given by the population growth curve. In this way we can determine an *employment path* F_0, F_1, $F_2, \ldots$ as well as an *endowment path* E_0, E_1, $E_2, \ldots$ through time, the horizontal gap between the two curves giving us the time path of technical unemployment U_0, U_1, $U_2, \ldots$. It is apparent that technical unemployment can be eliminated over time when, and only when, the endowment path bends upward fast enough to 'catch up with' and finally intersect the employment path.[18]

For purposes of deduction and statistical implementation, we now proceed with the specification of more precise functional forms for our behaviouristic assumptions. These include the six equations of Section 1 (1(a)–1(f)) which are accepted, with the only proviso that k and n (the capital and labour coefficients) are no longer constant but determined with the aid of the following additional behaviouristic equations

$$\eta_p \equiv i \quad \text{or} \quad p = p_0 e^{it} \qquad (5a)$$

where $p = l/n$ (labour progress function; i is the rate of labour progress)

$$1 = j^\alpha n^{1-\alpha} \quad \text{or} \quad j = p^\theta \quad \text{for} \quad \theta = (1 - \alpha)/\alpha \qquad (5b)$$

(technology shelf; j is the 'imported' pre-assimilation capital-output ratio)

$$m \equiv j/k \quad (m \text{ is the degree of capital stretching}) \qquad (5c)$$

$$m = (p/p_0)^c \qquad (5d)$$

(capital stretching function; c is the capital stretching coefficient)

---

[18] Instead of the fixed technology line of Section 1, the technology line now shifts continuously as technological transfer and assimilation take place.

Taking these one at a time, labour productivity is specified to grow at a constant rate i as described by the labour progress function (5a). The technology shelf available is depicted by the unit contour of a Cobb-Douglas type (Equation (5b)). Notice that in this functional form j is the initial 'imported' capital-output ratio which must be differentiated from the 'effective' post-assimilation capital-output ratio k. In (5c) the degree of domestic capital stretching is measured by $m = j/k$; the higher the value of m, which corresponds to a lower value of k, the higher the degree of capital stretching. Finally, in Equation (5d), we have postulated a capital stretching function which simply states that m is causally determined by the cumulative effect of labour progress (p/p_0), i.e. the multiple by which the current skill level has increased over some initial level. The underlying idea here stresses the importance of education and learning by doing as causal factors determining the amount of capital stretching technological change which can be incorporated in the imported technology.

The reader should note that the continuous change of the post-assimilation capital-output ratio $(k(t))$ through time seems to lead to the presumption that at any point in time $\bar{t}$, there prevails a host of capital output ratios $(k(t)$ for $t < \bar{t})$ that have been adopted in the past. Capital heterogeneity of this type is reminiscent of the 'putty-to-clay' variety of vintage models [15]. We have, instead, opted for a 'putty-to-putty' formulation, according to which, due to the improvement of the quality of of labour, even the old capital can be 'softened up' to the latest standard. Thus the implicit assumption of our model is that the capital-output ratio $k(\bar{t})$ prevailing at $\bar{t}$ will be effective for the entire capital stock in existence.

The three unfamiliar parameters (i, α, c) are all related to the phenomenon of technological change in our model. The rate of labour progress i summarises the cultural heritage and/or the effectiveness of a country's education policy as related to the increase of a nation's technological competence. The elasticity of the Cobb–Douglas function, i.e. the percentage increase of the capital coefficient (dj/j) per unit percentage decrease in the labour coefficient (dn/n), may be defined in terms of α as

$$\theta = (1 - \alpha)/\alpha \quad \text{(pure transplantation cost)} \quad (6)$$

The typical l.d.c. will want θ, which we may call the 'pure transplantation cost', to be as low as possible – for that would mean that a given percentage increase of labour productivity (or decrease in the labour coefficient) can be obtained at a smaller capital cost. Finally, the capital stretching coefficient c (in Equation (5d)) appears to be a crucial behaviouristic parameter since only when it is sufficiently large can domestic innovative efforts be counted on to contribute significantly to alleviating the unemployment and capital shortage impact of the act of importation of new technology.

To solve the entire system, let us now combine the various behavioural assumptions related to technology change. Starting with (5c) we have

$$k = j/m = ap^b \qquad (7a)$$

where

$$a = p_0^c; \quad b = \theta - c; \quad \theta = (1 - \alpha)/\alpha \quad \text{by (5b) and (5d)} \quad (7b)$$

$$Q = Q_0 K^B N^{1-B} \qquad (7c)$$

where

$$B = 1/(1 + b) = \alpha/(1 - c\alpha); \quad Q_0 = p_0^{(1/(1-1/c\alpha))} \cdots \text{by}(7a) \qquad (7d)$$

Notice that (7c) is deduced directly from (7a) and represents the effective 'production function' which turns out to be in a Cobb–Douglas form.[19] However, from (7d) we see that the coefficient B of this Cobb–Douglas function is defined in terms of α and c.

[19] Notice that (7c) is the equation of the post assimilation technology curve OA_0 in Figure 4.2. There are three possible shapes for OA_0 depending upon the relative magnitudes of c and α as seen from (7d): *Case one:* $0 < c < (1/\alpha) - 1$ with OA_0 negatively sloped as in the normal Cobb–Douglas case; *Case two:* $(1/\alpha) - 1 < c < 1/\alpha$, with OA_0 positively sloped and convex as pictured in Figure 2(a); *Case three:* $(1/\alpha) < c$, with OA_0 positively sloped and concave. Given α, the three cases correspond to instances of increasing strength of the domestic capital stretching effort as measured by c. These three cases assume that c is constant through time. There is, of course, the possibility that the value of c itself will increase over time, as the economy gains in experience and becomes more capable, through its capital stretching effort, to overcome the handicaps presented by the technology shelf. In this case the capital-output ratio may first increase and then decline as the country moves from case one, to two, and then to three.

Analogous to (6), the elasticity of K with respect to N in (7c) is

$$b = (1 - B)/B = \theta - c \quad \text{where} \quad \theta = (1 - \alpha)/\alpha \qquad (8)$$

which is the difference between θ, the pure transplantation cost, and c, the capital stretching coefficient. We may think of $-b = c - \theta$ as the 'excess' of the domestic capital stretching effort over the pure transplantation cost attending the importation of technology. The larger this excess, the more favourable the anticipated growth performance of the country in question.

From (7a) and the labour progress function of (5a), we can easily deduce the growth path of the effective capital-output ratio η_k, and – with the aid of the saving function of (1b) – the rate of capital acceleration (η_{η_K}), the growth rate of capital (η_K), and the growth rate of capital per head $(\eta_{K/N})$;

$$\eta_k = b\eta_v = bi \qquad \text{(by (7a); (5a))} \qquad (9a)$$

$$\eta_{\eta_K} = \eta_{(s/k)} = -\eta_k = -bi \quad \text{(by (2a); (9a))} \qquad (9b)$$

$$\eta_K = \eta_0 e^{-bit} \qquad \text{(by (9b))} \qquad (9c)$$

$$K = K_0 J^G, \qquad (9d)$$

where $J = e^{-\eta_0/bi} > 0$ and $G = e^{bit} - 1$

$$\eta_{K/N} = \eta_{(K/Q)(Q/N)} = \eta_{kv} = bi + i$$
$$= i(1 + b) = i(1 + \theta - c) = i(1/\alpha - c) \quad \text{(by (8))} \qquad (9e)$$

From this it is then easy to deduce the rates of growth and the time paths of all the significant economic variables in the system, including output (Q), employment (N), per capita income $(Q^* = Q/L)$, and the extent of employment $(N^* = N/L)$

$$\eta_Q = \eta_{K/k} = \eta_0 e^{-bit} - bi \qquad \text{(by (9a–c))} \qquad (10a)$$

$$\eta_N = \eta_{Q/v} = \eta_0 e^{-bit} - bi - i \qquad \text{(by (10a), (5a))} \qquad (10b)$$

$$\eta_{Q^*} = \eta_{Q/L} = \eta_0 e^{bit} - bi - r \qquad \text{(by (10a), (1a))} \qquad (10c)$$

$$\eta_{N^*} = \eta_{N/L} = \eta_0 e^{-bit} - bi - i - r \quad \text{(by (10b), (1a))} \qquad (10d)$$

In this fashion the system is formally and fully determined.

In summary, the labour progress function (5a) incorporates a basic hypothesis in our paper which describes the improvement of the quality of the labour force. This rate of improvement, proxied by 'labour productivity', is viewed as exogenously given, resulting from informal learning by doing and, possibly, more formal education processes not spelled out in our paper. When combined with the technology shelf and the capital stretching behaviour of (5a–d), our system is formally and fully determined. This system incorporates not only the determination of the trend values of these conventional economic variables but also the effective time path of technology. In other words, the rate of labour improvement resides at the highest level of causal ordering.[20]

Let us now examine the conclusions which flow from an application of this model, before we turn, in the final section, to the matter of empirical verification.

5. Application

To begin with, let us take the raising of per capita income ($Q^* = Q/L$) and the elimination of unemployment (or raising the extent of employment $N^* = N/L$) as the major twin social objectives. In this connection, the well-worn assumption of a necessary conflict between these two objectives, the output and the employment effect often associated with technological transfer, can perhaps be laid to rest. Equations (10c) and (10d), it will be noted, indicate that the rate of growth of both Q^* and N^* are determined by the same term bi, in the sense that the following condition for success is both necessary and sufficient for both η_{Q^*} and η_{N^*} to increase monotonically and without limit in the long run

$$bi < 0 \tag{11}$$

In other words, the employment effect is favourable (i.e. $\eta_{N^*} > 0$) if and only if the output effect is favourable (i.e. $\eta_{Q^*} > 0$) – so that these two crucial welfare criteria are actually never in conflict in the long run.

Moreover, since $i > 0$ (i.e. the rate of labour improvement is positive) (11) really reduces to $b < 0$, i.e.

$$c > \theta \equiv (1 - \alpha)/\alpha \quad \text{(by (11), (8) and } i > 0) \tag{12}$$

[20] In the advanced country growth literature, labour productivity is normally viewed as the consequence of other forces, e.g. capital deepening and technological change. The position of our paper, dealing with the developing country, reverses this causal ordering.

This result represents a conclusion of some importance since it pinpoints the factors related to technological change which make for ultimate success in the development effort. In essence, such success can be achieved in the long run if and only if the domestic innovative capital stretching effort c is sufficiently strong to compensate for the high capital cost (θ) associated with the modern imported technology. What is perhaps surprising about this conclusion is that the question of success seems to depend on technological factors only. The extent of population pressure r, level of austerity s, and even educational performance in terms of labour progress i seems to be irrelevant.

To elaborate on this point, we must note that if (12) is satisfied, the rate of labour progress i does indeed favourably affect the *rapidity* of the increase of Q^* and N^*. Moreover, a lower population pressure (r) and a higher average propensity to save, (S) also contribute favourably to the magnitude of both η_{Q^*} and η_{N^*}, as we would expect.[21]

Finally, a word may be added with respect to the case of pure transplantation analytically defined by $c = 0$, in which case the condition for success is reduced to

$$\theta = (1 - \alpha)/\alpha < 0 \tag{13}$$

(condition for success when $c = 0$)

In this special case 'success' can occur if and only if the unit contour of Figure (2a) is positively sloped.[22] Specifically, this means that, as the process of development in the mature economy unfolds, increasing labour productivity p through time must have been accompanied by a sustained decrease of the capital-output ratio k. Condition (13) permits us to conclude that when a particular l.d.c. fails to develop the ability to engage

---

[21] A closer scrutiny of (10c) shows that when $r > \eta_0 - bi$ and when (11) is satisfied, the value of Q^* decreases at first and then increases monotonically after a finite time span. The same U-shaped characteristic can be established for N^* when the population pressure is relatively high, i.e. when $r > \eta_0 - bi - i$. Notice that the saving parameter s enters into (10) through the initial value of the rate of growth of capital $\eta_0 = s/k_0$ where k_0 is the initial capital-output ratio. Thus, a high saving rate also contributes favourably to the rapidity of the growth of Q^* and N^*.

[22] From (5b) we see that $dj/dp = \theta p^{\theta-1}$ so that the shelf is positively sloped if and only if $\theta < 0$. See Section 2 above for a discussion of what determines the slope of the technology shelf.

in indigenous innovative effort, the only way in which it can still be successful is by being in a position to borrow from a mature economy shelf which itself benefited from secularly declining capital-output ratios.

6. Empirical Analysis

It is, by now, a well accepted fact that the modernisation of Japan since the Meiji Restoration was conspicuous for its emphasis on education and the assimilation of Western technologies.[23] In spite of the soundness of these notions, the relationship between education and the assimilation of technology, on the one hand, and economic development, on the other, have resisted rigorous analysis within the framework of a comprehensive growth model. It is the purpose of this section to fill this gap by implementing our model with the help of historical data for Japan.

The essential task of statistical implementation is to estimate the numerical value of the five parameters (c, i, α, s, r) of our model. Succinctly, the equations which will be used for this purpose are

$$p = \hat{p}_0 e^{\hat{i}t} \qquad \text{(by (5a))} \qquad (14a)$$

$$k = \hat{a} p^{\hat{b}} \qquad \text{(by (7a))} \qquad (14b)$$

$$c = \ln \hat{a}/\ln \hat{p}_0 \qquad \text{(by (7b))} \qquad (14c)$$

$$\alpha = \frac{1}{1 + \hat{b} + c} \qquad \text{(by (7b))} \qquad (14d)$$

$$L = L_0 e^{\hat{r}t} \qquad \text{(by (1a))} \qquad (14e)$$

$$I = \hat{s} Q \qquad \text{(by (1b))} \qquad (14f)$$

where a hat '^' denotes a parameter estimated by the method of least squares. The estimation of (i, r, s) and p_0 is given by $(14a, e, f)$ – for which the time series of output (Q), saving (S), population (L) and labour productivity $p \ (= Q/N)$ for the whole economy are required. If we have, in addition, the time series of capital stock (K), we can estimate a and b in $(14b)$ with the aid of the time series of k (the observed capital output ratio) and p. We can then use $(14c, d)$ to compute c and α. Thus, all the

[23] Cf. Anthony Tang [24]. See also [19].

parameters can be estimated when the time series of Q, N, K, L, and S are available.

The basic data for Japan, for Q, K, L and N for the period 1878–1939, are presented in columns 1–5 of Table 4.1 from which the time series of $p = Q/N$ (column 6), $k = K/Q$ (column 7) and $s = (dK/dt)Q$ (column 8) are derived. The time series of p and k against time and each other yield the following regression coefficients

$$p = \hat{p}_0 e^{tt}, \quad \text{where } \hat{p}_0 = 66 \cdot 86; \ t = 0 \cdot 035 \tag{15a}$$

$$k = \hat{k}_0 e^{bit}, \quad \text{where } \hat{k}_0 = 2 \cdot 57; \ bi = -0 \cdot 0065 \tag{15b}$$

$$k = \hat{a} p^{\hat{b}}, \quad \text{where } \hat{a} = 6 \cdot 006; \ \hat{b} = -0 \cdot 199^{24} \tag{15c}$$

We can then estimate parameters (α, c) in $(14c, d)$ as follows

$$c = \ln \hat{a}/\ln \hat{p}_0 = 0 \cdot 427 \quad (\text{by } (15a, c)) \tag{16a}$$

$$\alpha = \frac{1}{1 + \hat{b} + c} = 0 \cdot 814 \quad (\text{by } (15c, 16a)) \tag{16b}$$

These are the two parameters in terms of which the condition of success of Equation (12) is defined. To see the economic implications of these results, we observe

$$(1 - \alpha)/\alpha < c < 1/\alpha, \quad \text{i.e. } 0 \cdot 229 < 0 \cdot 427 < 1 \cdot 229 \tag{17}$$

This permits us to conclude that the historical experience of Japan represents a case of success, i.e. the domestic effort in the direction of capital stretching was sufficiently strong to compensate for the unfavourable effects of the highly capital-using nature of the imported technology. We can thus explain why the twin criteria $Q*$ and $N*$ increased continuously in the long run in the Japanese case. Moreover from Equation (9e) above, we can see that, if $i > 0$, the development process is characterised by capital shallowing (i.e. declining capital per head) if and only if $c > 1/\alpha$. This would mean that the domestic capital stretching

---

[24] (15b) follows from (9a). We can use (15a) and (15b) to estimate $b = bi/i = -0 \cdot 0065/0 \cdot 035 = -0 \cdot 19$ which is consistent with the estimate of b in (15c).

TABLE 4.1 Basic Japanese Data

Year (1)	Output = Q (2)	Capital = K (3)	Population = L (4)	Employment = N (5)	p = Q/N (6)	k = K/Q (7)	s = I/Q (8)
1878	1152·00	4361	36166	18841	61·14	3·786	0·0391
1879	1519·00	4406	36464	19193	79·14	2·901	0·0362
1880	1664·00	4461	36649	19542	85·15	2·681	0·0325
1881	1533·00	4515	36965	19883	77·10	2·945	0·0274
1882	1473·00	4557	37259	20224	72·83	3·094	0·0597
1883	1420·00	4645	37569	20537	74·01	3·056	0·0368
1884	1561·00	4701	37962	20859	74·84	3·012	0·0442
1885	1877·00	4770	38313	21163	88·69	2·541	0·0378
1886	2245·00	4841	38541	21463	104·60	2·156	0·0272
1887	2116·00	4902	38703	21759	97·25	2·317	0·0766
1888	2140·82	5064	39029	22043	97·12	2·365	0·0411
1889	2012·23	5152	39473	22312	90·19	2·560	0·0462
1890	2379·38	5245	39902	22583	105·36	2·204	0·0416
1891	2270·75	5344	40251	22825	99·49	2·353	0·0484
1892	2381·71	5454	40508	23085	103·17	2·290	0·0714
1893	2665·91	5624	40860	23316	114·34	2·110	0·0476
1894	3139·00	5751	41142	23551	133·29	1·832	0·0484
1895	3072·67	5903	41557	23769	129·27	1·921	0·0778
1896	2867·12	6142	41992	23977	119·58	2·142	0·1071
1897	3134·86	6449	42400	24195	129·57	2·057	0·0683
1898	4141·86	6663	42886	24382	169·87	1·609	0·0311
1899	3512·12	6792	43404	24572	142·93	1·934	0·0661
1900	3753·01	7024	43847	24768	151·53	1·872	0·0397
1901	4108·15	7173	44359	24959	164·60	1·746	0·0343

0·0458	1·982	146·87	25122	44964	7314	3689·79	1902
0·0468	1·826	162·01	25298	45546	7483	4098·57	1903
0·0626	1·899	158·88	25436	46115	7675	4041·31	1904
0·1054	2·240	138·26	25599	46620	7928	3539·43	1905
0·0888	1·981	162·89	25729	47058	8301	4190·94	1906
0·0853	1·936	173·21	25858	47416	8673	4478·78	1907
0·0954	1·929	180·74	25971	47965	9055	4593·88	1908
0·0822	1·994	182·73	26085	48554	9503	4766·62	1909
0·1133	2·168	174·42	26169	49134	9895	4564·51	1910
0·0972	1·943	204·06	26259	49852	10412	5358·37	1911
0·1026	1·866	222·34	26347	50577	10933	5857·93	1912
0·0702	1·927	226·57	26422	51305	11534	5986·46	1913
0·0524	2·047	220·59	26471	52039	11954	5839·37	1914
0·0657	1·910	241·97	26527	52752	12260	6418·65	1915
0·1316	2·225	214·62	26557	53496	12682	5699·78	1916
0·1781	2·257	223·82	26589	54134	13432	5951·24	1917
0·1869	2·161	251·93	26618	54739	14492	6705·74	1918
0·1448	1·936	305·49	26623	55033	15745	8133·19	1919
0·1305	2·599	238·82	27263	55391	16923	6510·99	1920
0·0908	2·287	282·64	27498	56120	17773	7771·99	1921
0·0513	2·293	290·55	27733	56840	18479	8057·82	1922
0·0538	2·250	300·16	27969	57580	18892	8395·31	1923
0·0604	2·180	314·57	28206	58350	19344	8872·71	1924
0·0737	2·081	335·94	28442	59179	19880	9554·87	1925
0·0725	1·978	362·94	28676	60210	20584	10407·79	1926
0·0601	1·961	376·29	28913	61140	21339	10879·71	1927
0·0586	1·995	378·30	29148	62070	21993	11026·76	1928
0·0490	2·003	384·60	29384	62930	22639	11301·21	1929

TABLE 4.7 *Continued*

Year (1)	Output = Q (2)	Capital = K (3)	Population = L (4)	Employment = N (5)	p = Q/N (6)	k = K/Q (7)	s = I/Q (8)
1930	13111·01	23193	63872	29619	442·66	1·769	0·0322
1931	14150·29	23615	64870	28990	488·11	1·669	0·0333
1932	14269·35	24086	65890	29176	489·08	1·688	0·0457
1933	14294·13	24738	66880	29777	480·04	1·731	0·0620
1934	14598·97	25624	67690	30794	474·08	1·755	0·0735
1935	15589·43	26697	68662	31400	499·66	1·702	0·0776
1936	16630·31	27914	69590	30855	538·98	1·679	0·0774
1937	16078·21	29201	70040	31162	515·96	1·816	0·0985
1938	18097·97	30784	70530	31473	575·03	1·701	0·1405
1939	20584·84	33327	70850	31780	647·73	1·619	0·1248

Sources: Output data, in millions of yen, (column 2) are from Ohkawa, *The Growth Rate of the Japanese Economy Since 1878*, Table 3, p. 247, and are deflated by Ohkawa's general price deflator, p. 130, converted to a 1934–36 base. Capital stock estimates, in millions of yen, 1934–36 prices (column 3) are from *Estimates of Long-Term Economic Statistics of Japan Since 1868*, Vol. 3, pp. 149–51, Total Net Capital Stock excluding Residences. Population data, in thousands of persons, (column 4) are from *Hundred-Year Statistics of the Japanese Economy*, published by the Statistics Department of the Bank of Japan. Employment data, in thousands of persons, (column 5) are from Ohkawa, (*op. cit.,*), p. 145 with 'total gainfully occupied population' serving as an approximation to 'total employment'.

effort is so pronounced that it swamps the initial capital deepening effect of imported technology, leading to a net lower effective capital-output ratio. Our results, summarised in the second inequality in (17), however, indicate that the Japanese domestic capital stretching effort was not strong enough to guarantee capital shallowing. This means that for the sixty years taken as a whole Japan developed successfully under conditions of some capital deepening.[25]

The Japanese data moreover reveal that α in (16b) lies between 0 and 1. This depicts the case of a negatively sloping technology shelf (5b), which in turn means that Japan was borrowing technology from a mature world which had shown some tendency for a secularly increasing capital-output ratio.[26] This also means that Japan could not have been successful in its development effort without a major domestic capital stretching effort. This conclusion follows rigorously from the success criterion of (13), i.e. when $c = 0$.

As a second type of empirical verification of our theory, we can compute the 'predicted' values of the growth path of Q^* and N^* based on (10c, d) using the above estimated parameter values. To begin with, we can compute the predicted rate of growth of the capital-output ratio and of the rate of capital

---

[25] From (15c) we have $d(K/N)/dp = d(k \cdot p)/dp - d(ap^{1+b})/dp = a(1 + b)p^b$. Hence, capital deepening occurs when $a > 0$, and $b > -1$, which is our case. This evidence, of course, does not necessarily indicate that capital stretching could not have been sufficiently strong over a more limited period to result in capital shallowing. In Fei and Ranis [2, chap. IV], we, in fact, presented some statistical evidence that, for the industrial sector, capital shallowing gave way to capital deepening around 1917. Since the possibility of 'capital stretching' is greater, the greater the difference between the imported and the indigenous technology, it stands to reason that at the early stages of development (when presumably, the domestic production structure differs more from the foreign technology than at a later stage) the role of capital stretching is greater. This hypothesis can be verified by a more systematic statistical investigation than we have undertaken here, i.e. by placing shorter time periods under examination.

[26] Thus, an examination of purely Japanese data permits us to conclude that the capital-output ratio in the advanced countries must have been increasing during the period 1888–1930. This phenomenon can, of course, be verified by independent evidence. Fellner [3], for example, sees the capital-output ratio for the United States rising slightly between 1870 and 1900, fairly constant between 1900 and 1930, and slightly falling thereafter.

acceleration

$$\eta_k = ib = i(1 - \alpha)/(\alpha - c) = -0{\cdot}00696$$
$$\text{(by (9a), (7b), (15a) and (16a, b))}[27]$$
$$\tag{18a}$$

$$\eta_{n_K} = -ib = 0{\cdot}00696 \tag{18b}$$

While, in our model, the average propensity to save s was assumed to be constant (see 1b), an investigation of the actual time path of s for Japan yields the following

$$s = s_0 e^{gt}, \quad \text{where} \quad g = 0{\cdot}0121 \tag{19}$$

so that the propensity to save in Japan actually shows an annual increase of about one per cent a year. Consequently, our model can be modified by computing the rate of capital acceleration as

$$\eta_{n_K} = \eta_{s/k} = \eta_s - \eta_k = 0{\cdot}0121 + 0{\cdot}00696 = 0{\cdot}019 \tag{20}$$

(by (19) and (18a)). On the other hand, using columns (3) and (8) of Table 4.1, we can calculate the 'observed' rate of capital acceleration

$$\eta_{n_K} = \eta_0 e^{\hat{h}t}, \quad \text{where} \quad \hat{h} = 0{\cdot}019, \tag{21}$$

which is precisely the same as the predicted value above when the more realistic propensity to save is assumed.

We can now, moreover, proceed to compute the time paths of η_{Q^*} and η_{N^*} in (19c, d)

$$\eta_{Q^*} = 0{\cdot}0171 e^{0{\cdot}19t} + 0{\cdot}0075 = \eta_0 e^{ht} + h - r \tag{22a}$$

$$\eta_{N^*} = 0{\cdot}0171 e^{0{\cdot}019t} - 0{\cdot}0275 = \eta_0 e^{ht} + h - i - r \tag{22b}$$

From these equations we see not only that Japan can be predicted to be successful but that the values of the above two welfare indicators can be expected to increase monotonically throughout. This shows that the innovative effort in Japan was sufficiently strong to overcome the relatively modest pressure of population growth. Thus our model coincides with actual Japanese historical experience, with both per capita income and the degree of employment monotonically increasing through time.

[27] The directly observed value of η_k from (15b) is $-0{\cdot}0065$ which is seen to be very close to the predicted value.

The above conclusion leads directly to the last empirical application of our paper, namely the computation of a numerical value for the 'turning point' in Japanese development. Such a 'turning point' is operationally defined as the time when Japan got rid of her technical unemployment, i.e. the employment path and the endowment path finally intersect (see Figure 4.2). From the time path of N^* in (22b) we have

$$N^* = N_0^* \frac{e^u}{e^{\eta_0/h}}, \tag{23a}$$

where

$$u = (\eta_0/h)e^{ht} + (h - i - r)t \tag{23b}$$

for

$$h = 0.019, \quad \eta_0 = 0.0171, \quad i = 0.035, \quad r = 0.0115 \tag{24c}$$

The date when technical unemployment is eliminated can then be obtained by solving for t when $N^* = 1$ in (23a). Unfortunately, we do not have much confidence in the estimates of the initial extent of technical unemployment in 1878, i.e. N_0^*, but we can safely assume that it varied between 10% and 20% of the total labour force. Applying (23a, b), we can then obtain the following results by approximation

Initial degree of employment: (N_0^* in 1878)   0.9   0.8

Duration of unemployment phase, t: (years)   53   58

Calendar Year (1878 + t)   1931   1936

This gives us a 'turning point' in the 1930s which seems to be supported by other independent work on Japan [14a].

Postscript

This paper has sought to demonstrate that a comprehensive theory of development must endeavour to move beyond the factor augmentation emphasis of traditional analysis to encompass technological borrowing and assimilation. Such a more general explanatory framework, of course, should not only be capable of explaining historical experience but also have substantial implications for planning and policy making. In the contemporary world, there exists, of course, a variety of channels, including foreign investment, foreign aid and international trade, through which developed country technology is continuously being transferred to the l.d.c.'s. This phenomenon clearly cannot be viewed as marginal to the development process. Moreover, the heterogeneity of the processes employed and of variations in the motivations of both lender and borrower – which may include a desire to build industrial 'monuments', acquire export markets or pursue some political objective – testifies to the complicated nature of the subject and the need for treatment, at least initially, at a fairly high level of abstraction.

The rules of borrowing advanced in our paper for example, encompass the full range of possible borrowing channels, procedures and policy mixes, by postulating that the rapidity of borrowing (which, to us, is tantamount to achieving higher technological complexity) is governed by the rate of improvement of the economy's human resources base. The rationality of such borrowing rules, moreover, must be examined in conjunction with, and not independent of, the possibility of domestic assimilation. Thus, assuming the initial technology to be at A_0 (Figure 4.2a), the rationality for the country to next accept A_1 (as the skill level advances to p_1) may be precisely based on the expectation that, in spite of the relatively high capital cost and low employment effects of this move, it will ultimately result in the much more advantageous technology B_1, through assimilation. To put the matter more strongly, the introduction of A_1 from abroad may be a prerequisite as a stimulant for breaking domestic technological stagnation and setting off the search for a new intermediate technology which is ultimately responsible for the full exploitation of the indigenous factor supply. In other words, technology A_1 will be imported not only because it *can* be imported (in line with improved labour efficiency) but, more positively, because it is the best means to achieve B_1 – and, hence, it is advantageous and rational to do so.[28]

---

[28] While it is helpful for purposes of exposition to analyse the borrowing and assimilation in terms of two discrete steps, the final effective production method is determined via a highly organic process related to the economy's indigenous human resource base.

Further research in this area might well include a more realistic disaggregation of the human capacity (into entrepreneurial, engineering managerial, etc.), possibly relating each endogenously to differential learning by doing processes or budgetary allocations.[29] Moreover, the relevance, for the borrower, of disparities in the composition (in terms of the relative contribution of innovations and capital deepening) of historical patterns of internal growth within the lending countries requires further exploration.

References

[1] ECKAUS, RICHARD S., 'The Factor Proportions Problem in Underdeveloped Areas', *American Economic Review*, XLV (September 1955), 539–565.

[2] FEI, J. C. H. and RANIS, G., *Development of the Labor Surplus Economy: Theory and Policy*, Homewood, Illinois: R. D. Irwin, 1964.

[3] FELLNER, W. J., *Trends and Cycles in Economic Activity*, New York: Holt, Rinehart and Winston, 1956.

[4] GALENSON, W. and LEIBENSTEIN, H., 'Investment Criteria, Productivity, and Economic Development', *Quarterly Journal of Economics*, LXIX (August 1955), 343–70.

[5] GRANICK, DAVID, 'Economic Development and Productivity Analysis: The Case of Soviet Metalworking', *Quarterly Journal of Economics*, LXXI (May 1957), 205–233.

[6] HAGEN, EVERETT E., *The Economics of Development*, Homewood, Ill.: R. D. Irwin, 1968.

[7] HANSEN, BENT, 'Employment and Wages in Rural Egypt', *American Economic Review*, LIX (June 1969), 298–313.

[8] JORGENSON, DALE, 'Testing Alternative Theories of the Development of a Dual Economy', in *The Theory and Design of Economic Development*, ed. I. Adelman and E. Thorbecke; Baltimore: Johns Hopkins University Press, 1966.

[29] A more refined version of our present model might well also postulate the existence of increasing returns initially and diminishing returns later on, in terms of the strength of the assimilation coefficient as technological borrowing proceeds over time.

[9] KUZNETS, S., *Six Lectures on Economic Growth*, Glencoe, Ill.: Free Press, 1960.

[10] LEDERMAN, E., *Hacia una Politica de los Recursos Humanos en el Desarollo Economica y Social de America Latina*, ILPES Document, Santiago, July 1968.

[11] LEWIS, A., *Development Planning*, New York: Harper and Row, 1966.

[12] LEWIS, A., 'Economic Development with Unlimited Supplies of Labour', *Manchester School of Economic and Social Studies*, XXII (May 1954), 139–192.

[13] MELLOR, JOHN W. and STEVENS, ROBERT D., 'The Average and Marginal Product of Farm Labor in Underdeveloped Economies', *Journal of Farm Economics*, XXXVIII (August 1956), 780–791.

[14] NURKSE, RAGNAR, *Problems of Capital Formation in Underdeveloped Countries*, Fair Lawn, N.J.: Oxford University Press, 1953.

[14a] OHKAWA, K. and ROSOVSKY, H., 'The Role of Agriculture in Modern Japanese Economic Development', *Economic Development and Cultural Change*, IX (October 1960), 43–67.

[15] PHELPS, EDMUND S., 'Substitution, Fixed Proportions, Growth and Distribution', *International Economic Review*, IV (September 1963), 265–288.

[16] RANIS, G., 'Factor Proportions in Japanese Economic Development', *American Economic Review*, XLVII (September 1957), 594–607.

[17] RANIS, G., 'Investment Criteria, Productivity and Economic Development: An Empirical Comment', *Quarterly Journal of Economics*, LXXVI (May 1962), 298–302.

[18] ROSENSTEIN-RODAN, P. N., 'Disguised Unemployment and Underemployment in Agriculture', *Monthly Bulletin of Agricultural Economics and Statistics*, VI (July/August 1957), 1–7.

[19] SAXONHOUSE, GARY, *Basic Determinants of Improvements in the Efficiency of Production in the Japanese Cotton Textile Industry, 1880–1940*, Dissertation in Progress, Yale University.

[20] SCHULTZ, THEODORE W., 'The Doctrine of Agricultural

Labor of Zero Value', in *Transforming Traditional Agriculture*. New Haven, Conn.: Yale University Press, 1964.

[21] SEN, A. K., *Choice of Techniques*, Oxford: B. Blackwell, 1960.

[22] SOLOW, R. M., 'Technical Change and the Aggregate Production Function', *Review of Economics and Statistics*, XXXIX (August 1957), 312–320.

[23] STRASSMAN, P., *Technological Change and Economic Development*, Ithaca, N.Y.: Cornell University Press, 1968.

[24] TANG, ANTHONY, 'Research and Education in Japanese Agricultural Development: 1880–1938', *Economic Studies Quarterly*, XIII (Part I: February 1963; Part II: May 1963).

[25] TURNER, H. A., 'Can Wages be Planned', paper prepared for the *Conference on the Crisis in Planning*, Sussex, June/July 1969.

[26] VEBLEN, THORSTEIN, 'The Opportunity of Japan', in *Essays in Our Changing Order*, New York: The Viking Press, 1934.

[27] VINER, JACOB, 'Some Reflections on the Concept of Disguised Unemployment', *Contribucões a Analise do Desenvolvimento Economico*, Rio de Janeiro: Livraria Ager Editora, 1957. Reprinted under the same title in *Indian Journal of Economics*, XXXVIII (July 1957), 17–23.

5 Combining Economic and Noneconomic Objectives in Development Planning: Problems of Concept and Measurement

KARL A. FOX*

THE Gross National Product is our principal measure of economic progress. It enables us to make reproducible quantitative statements about the same economy at different points in time and about different economies at the same point in time. Operational methods for measuring G.N.P. flow directly from the theory of general economic equilibrium.

G.N.P. describes the performance of an economy. However, political leaders must be concerned about the performance of a society. The absence of accepted measures of societal performance (in addition to G.N.P.) inhibits scientific discussion of social objectives. The current interest in 'social indicators' and measures of 'the quality of life' is directed toward bringing some order into this discussion.

In this paper we suggest the extension of general equilibrium theory to all outputs of a society. This leads us to the concept of a Gross Social Product which includes the G.N.P. and gives symmetrical treatment to economic and noneconomic societal outputs. Such a measure (G.S.P.) would facilitate the task of combining economic and noneconomic objectives in development planning. It would also facilitate intersocietal comparisons at a given time.

The extension from G.N.P. to G.S.P. involves more than a notational exercise. We will introduce some concepts from sociological theory (Talcott Parsons), from individual and

* Iowa State University (Ames). The author is Distinguished Professor in Sciences and Humanities and Professor of Economics.

social psychology (Eric Berne, Harry Levinson and Hadley Cantril), and from ecological psychology (Roger Barker) and comment on some practical problems of measuring the non-economic components of the gross social product.

Introduction

The development problem starts at the world level with three inter-related systems, (*a*) societal, (*b*) technological and (*c*) bio-physical or environmental. These systems correspond roughly to the labour, capital and land of classical economic theory. As factors of (economic) production, elements of the three systems are linked via a set of activities into a world economy. The outputs delivered to final human demand constitute the gross economic product. These outputs are exhaustively allocated to consumers, producers and resource holders, so that gross world (economic) income is identically equal to gross world (economic) product. Under certain well-known assumptions, atomistic competition and free international trade should lead to the maximisation of gross world (economic) product subject to the initial distribution of incomes and resource holdings.

Any functional system can be characterised as a set of inputs, a set of outputs, and a set of relationships for transforming inputs into outputs. Leontief's input/output model clearly fits this description, and the money value of the vector of final outputs in Leontief's model is the Gross Economic Product.

In the United States, some 40% of the population is in the labour force. On the average, members of the labour force devote 35 or 40% of their waking time to 'gainful employment'. Hence, employment directly reflected in the G.N.P. occupies only 15% of the population's total waking time.

Every hour of human behaviour has some value to the participants. The other 85% of total waking time includes the leisure time of workers and all of the waking time of persons not 'gainfully employed'.

It follows from this that the economy is a very open system. Workers enter it in the morning and leave it in the afternoon. Members of the labour force may withdraw from it for protracted periods to become full time students or housewives. The activities of college students may be interpreted in part as a

5

foregoing of current income in order to produce human capital which will raise the income stream in subsequent years. Calculations of the economic value of a housewife reflect some ambivalence about the accounting convention which excludes her unpaid services from the G.N.P. while including the same activities when performed by domestic servants. The boundary between the family and the economy is also unclear in the case of self-supply of food.

The world societal system can, in principle, be characterised in terms of inputs, outputs and transformation functions comprising all human behaviour and occupying total living time. To quantify this system at suitable levels of aggregation, we need exhaustive classifications of inputs, outputs and activities, economic and noneconomic alike. We also need to clarify the formal conditions under which the world society might be able to function as a self-optimising system, maximising world G.S.P. subject to the initial distributions of all relevant resources, including cultural and behavioural resources used in noneconomic activities.

The basic problems of concept and measurement in proceeding from G.N.P. to G.S.P. can best be discussed at the levels of individual human beings and their interactions in 'behaviour settings' (to be defined shortly) and in small relatively self-contained communities. This is the approach we will use.

Talcott Parsons [17] lists eleven 'generalised media of social interchange', one of which is money. All social system outputs are delivered to persons ('personalities'), who perceive them as rewards; all social system inputs are provided by persons ('personalities') who perceive them as contributions. We can adapt Parsons' concepts to our purposes by stating that social system outputs are allocated exhaustively to the members of the society so that the G.S.P. is identically equal to the gross social income (G.S.I.). If we can specify a complete system of prices (equivalent money values in some sense) for all of these outputs we will obtain a measure of the G.S.P. in dollar terms. The G.N.P. will be seamlessly incorporated in the G.S.P.; we can, of course, retrieve the G.N.P. by selecting out those activities, outputs and inputs which are included in the current operational definition of G.N.P.

Eric Berne [4, 5] asserts that people allocate their time

exhaustively among withdrawal, rituals, pastimes, activities, intimacy and 'games'. Roger Barker [3, 1] states that all human behaviour occurs in spatially and temporally bounded entities which he calls behaviour settings. In principle, the total living time of members of a society can be classified in terms of the categories of behaviour settings in which it is spent. From our standpoint, this separates the problem of measuring the G.S.P. into two subproblems, (a) measuring the inputs, outputs and transformation functions of individual behaviour settings and (b) aggregating behaviour settings into appropriate categories analogous, for example, to a Standard Industrial Classification code with its successive levels of detail.

Berne [4] specifically avoids using 'work' as a separate category in structuring time, noting that from the standpoint of social psychiatry many noneconomic activities are also 'work'. Barker applies the same concepts to behaviour settings in schools, churches and government agencies as to those in business firms. Zytowski [22] in reviewing schemes for classifying work satisfactions, lists three main categories of satisfactions (extrinsic, intrinsic and concomitant) each containing several specific values. Thus, 'economic return' is included among the extrinsic values along with security, prestige, achievement, advancement and recognition.

All the authors cited evidently use frames of reference which apply equally to economic and noneconomic settings. They are not inconsistent (for example) with the notion of a generalised input-output model in which deliveries to final demand would include the entire G.S.P. The corresponding set of social accounts maintained over time could also be used as a basis for projecting alternative futures and anticipating social disruptions more clearly and objectively than we now do. Estimates of social costs and benefits could be expressed in terms of G.S.P. rather than of gross economic product (G.N.P.) only.

How far are we from being able to implement G.S.P. measures and models? This depends upon the quality and amount of effort that may be applied to developing them. In this paper, we will juxtapose conceptual frameworks that have been put forward by other social scientists in recent years, make some suggestions toward implementation, and list some problems of concept and measurement that remain to be solved.

1. Talcott Parsons' 'Human Action System'

Talcott Parsons [17] has presented a recent summary statement of his theories. We shall make use of his concepts of organism, personality, society, culture, and generalised media of interchange.

Parsons includes in his conceptualisation of the 'human action system' (*a*) the organism, (*b*) the personality, (*c*) the social system, and (*d*) the cultural system (including beliefs, ideas and symbols that give the action system its primary 'sense of direction'). Our interest here centres on the social system and we will discuss it first.

The social system. Parsons says [17, p. 461]:

... I shall define society as the category of social systems embodying ... the greatest self-sufficiency of any type of social system ...

The core structure of a society I will call the societal community. More specifically, at different levels of evolution, it is called tribe, or 'the people', or, for classical Greece, *polis*, or, for the modern world, *nation*. It is the collective structure in which members are united or ... associated ... The nature of this association is reflected partly in the patterns of *citizenship* (civil-legal, political and social).

The other three primary subsystems of a society are the economy, the polity, and the cultural (or pattern-maintenance) subsystem. Each of the four subsystems of a society is characterised by its own medium of exchange: the societal community by *influence*; the economy by *money*; the polity by political *power*; and the cultural or pattern-maintenance subsystem by *value commitments* or 'generalised commitments to the implementation of cultural values ...' Influence is interchangeable for power, money, and value commitments.

Personality, social system and roles. Parsons states [17, p. 469] that:

The personality, as analytically distinguished from the organism, constitutes the third primary environment of a social system.[1] It interpenetrates with the organism in the

---

[1] The other two are (*a*) the organic-physical environment and (*b*) the cultural environment.

obvious and fundamental sense that the storage facilities of learned content must be organic, as must the physical mechanisms of perception and cognition, of the control of learned behaviour, and of the bases of motivation.

...*the primary goal output of social systems is to the personalities of their members.* Although they interpenetrate crucially with social systems, the personalities of individuals are not core constituents of social systems (nor vice versa) but precisely environments of them...

The unit of interpenetration between a personality and a social system is not the individual but a role or complex of roles. The same personality may participate in several social systems in different roles.

From the viewpoint of the psychology of the personality, the positive outputs from the social system are rewards. Indeed, I would even say that... except for intermediate cases specially involved at the crux of differentiation between organism and personality (notably, erotic pleasure), all rewards arc social system outputs. Conversely, outputs from the personality to the social system are personal goal achievements which, from the viewpoint of the receiving social system, are *contributions* to its functioning...

Generalised media of interchange We have already mentioned the four media of exchange (influence, money, power, and value commitments) which, according to Parsons, are used within the social system proper. In addition, Parsons [17, p. 471] indicates that, 'other generalised media seem to operate in the zones of interpenetration between the social system and the other primary subsystems of action'. These media include erotic pleasure; affect (including recognition and response); technological know-how and skill; ideology; conscience; reputation; and faith.

The concept of media of exchange (in addition to money) 'circulating' in particular subsystems of the social system as a whole is a fruitful one, and we shall make use of it in subsequent sections.

The organism Parsons [17, p. 466] is careful to distinguish between the organism and the personality:

...it should be emphasised that all relations between the social system and the *physical* environment are mediated through the behavioral organism. The perceptual processes of the organism are the source of information about the physical environment ... The organism is also the source of the 'instinctual' components of the motivation of individuals' personalities.

Evidently, the health of the organism places some limits on the behavioural contributions of the associated personality. Barker [1] speaks of five behaviour mechanisms – gross muscular activity, affective behaviour, manipulation, talking, and thinking – all of which draw on capacities of the organism. Gross muscular activity and affective behaviour have a very long evolutionary history; manipulation, talking and thinking are closely interrelated in the most recent phase of human organic evolution which, according to Washburn and Avis [21], was increasingly dominated by the use of tools:

... Increase in brain size resulted from the new selection pressures stemming from tool use. Speech, made possible by the larger brain, was correlated with a complicated technological tradition; and the larger and more complicated society was made possible by the larger food supply. Human hunting depended on tools, and hunting brought about greater mobility ... Increase in brain size was associated with a slowing of the growth rate and a much greater period of dependency. This changed the social life, establishing long term social relations. Thus the hunting life changed man's psychology and the way of life of the human group.

These factors have also determined the general nature of human personality and the process of its development. Personalities, in Parsons' sense, receive the various outputs of the social system and attach values to them as rewards which serve as justifications and incentives for their contributions to the social system.

To what extent can personalities recognise and respond to Parsons' various media of social interchange? We will cite several authors (*a*) on the processes of personality formation and (*b*) on non-economic satisfactions associated with the choice of occupations and specific jobs to indicate that people recognise and respond to these media and that their evaluations of the different media are relatively stable over time.

2. Aspects of Personality Formation

How are human personalities formed? The distinguished neuro-
surgeon Wilder Penfield [16] reported in 1952 some remarkable
findings concerning the nature of human 'memory mechanisms'.
During the course of brain surgery, in treating patients suffering
from focal epilepsy, Penfield conducted a series of experiments
during which he touched the temporal cortex of the brain of a
patient with a weak electric current transmitted through a
galvanic probe. In each case the patient, under local anesthesia,
was fully conscious during the exploration of the cerebral
cortex and was able to talk with Penfield.

Penfield found that the stimulating electrode could force
recollections clearly derived from the patient's memory:

The physical experience thus produced stops when the
electrode is withdrawn and may repeat itself when the electrode is reapplied . . .

The subject feels again the emotion which the situation
originally produced in him, and he is aware of the same interpretations, true or false, which he himself gave to the experience in the first place. Thus, evoked recollection is not the
exact photographic or phonographic reproduction of past
scenes or events. It is reproduction of what the patient saw
and heard and felt and understood . . .

Whenever a normal person is paying conscious attention to
something, he simultaneously is recording it in the temporal
cortex of each hemisphere . . .

The thread of temporal succession seems to link the elements of evoked recollection together. It also appears that
only those sensory elements to which the individual was
paying attention are recorded, not all the sensory impulses
that are forever bombarding the central nervous system.

The demonstration of the existence of cortical 'patterns'
that preserve the detail of current experience, as though in a
library of many volumes, is one of the first steps toward a
physiology of the mind. The nature of the pattern, the mechanism of its formation, the mechanism of its subsequent
utilization, and the integrative processes that form the
substratum of consciousness – these will one day be translated into physiological formulas.

Eric Berne [4, 5] was greatly impressed by Penfield's findings as he developed his own theory of the three components of human personality for which he uses the colloquial terms parent, adult and child. These correspond approximately to the superego, ego and id of Freudian theory.

Harris [15, pp. 17–29] describes Berne's construct as follows:

The Parent is a huge collection of recordings in the brain of unquestioned or imposed external events perceived by a person in his early years, a period which we have designated roughly as the first five years of life . . . The name Parent is most descriptive of these data inasmuch as the most significant 'tapes' are those provided by the example and pronouncements of his own real parents or parent substitutes . . . Parent is specific for every person, being the recording of that set of early experiences unique to him . . .

While external events are being recorded as the body of data we call the Parent, there is another recording being made simultaneously. This is the recording of *internal* events, the responses of the little person to what he sees and hears. . . It is this 'seeing and hearing and feeling and understanding' body of data which we define as the Child. Since the little person has no vocabulary during the most critical of his early experiences, most of his reactions are feelings . . .

At about 10 months of age a remarkable thing begins to happen to the child . . . He begins to experience the power of locomotion. He can manipulate objects and begins to move out, freeing himself from the prison of immobility . . .

The ten-month old has found he is able to do something which grows from his own awareness and original thought. This self-actualization is the beginning of the Adult . . . Adult data accumulate as a result of the child's ability to find out for himself what is different about life from the 'taught concept' of life in his Parent and the 'felt concept' of life in his Child. The Adult develops a 'thought concept' of life based on data gathering and data processing.

Levinson [19] uses Freud's model of personality structure in terms of id, ego and superego and gives considerable emphasis to what he calls the *ego ideal* in connection with personal growth and motivation:

The ego ideal is an internalized image of oneself at his

future best. This image is constructed from the expectations which parents and others hold of the child, from the aspirations the child develops for himself out of his recognition of his capacities and abilities, and from his identification with important figures in his environment . . .

Further, [19 pp. 202–215],

. . . In the course of its development, the ego ideal ultimately incorporates norms, ethics, and social ideals which become part of the person's aspirations . . . When a person meets some of the expectations of his ego ideal, he experiences the applause of the ego ideal with relief, satisfaction, and increased self-respect. The consciousness of deserving this love is felt as pride.

For effective adaptation, the ego ideal must be consolidated [19 pp. 216–218]:

Just as a man is physiologically integrated, so is he psychologically integrated. He must be to function. The quality of his integration will be reflected in the quality of his functioning . . .

Effective adaptation requires the consolidation of a man's life-long experiences into a composite which is internally consistent, structured of complimentary identifications, harmonious values and gratifying avenue for mastery. According to Erik H. Erikson, a psychoanalyst who has given considerable attention to the problems of identity, it also requires finding 'a niche in some section of his society, a niche which is firmly defined and yet seems to be uniquely made for him. In finding it, the young adult gains an assured sense of inner continuity and social sameness which will bridge what he *was* as a child and what he is *about to* become, and will reconcile his *conception of himself* and his *community's recognition of him'*.

Erikson adds that the identity formation of the young man is fostered when those whose activities are significant to him give him a function and a status, and treat him as one whose growth and transformation is important. As his feeling of identity increases, he has the sense of well being, of direction and assuredness that he will be recognized by those whose recognition counts.[2]

[2] See: [9, p. 111].

Hadley Cantril [9] and his associates studied the aspirations and concerns of adults in many walks of life in many contemporary societies. Toward the end of his book Cantril summarises 'the demands human beings everywhere impose on any society or political culture because of their very nature . . .' He lists these demands as follows [9, pp. 315–322]:

1. The satisfaction of survival needs . . .
2. Man needs a sense of both physical and psychological security to protect gains already made and to assure a beachhead from which further advances may be staged. . .
3. Man craves sufficient order and certainty in his life to enable him to judge with fair accuracy what will or will not occur if he does or does not act in certain ways . . .
4. Human beings continuously seek to enlarge the range and to enrich the quality of their satisfactions . . .
5. Human beings are creatures of hope and are not genetically designed to resign themselves . . .
6. Human beings have the capacity to make choices and the desire to exercise this capacity . . .
7. Human beings require freedom to exercise the choices they are capable of making . . .
8. Human beings want to experience their own identity and integrity, more popularly referred to as the need for personal dignity . . .
9. People want to experience a sense of their own worthwhileness . . .
10. Human beings seek some value or system of beliefs to which they can commit themselves . . .
11. Human beings want a sense of surety and confidence that the society of which they are a part holds out a fair degree of hope that their aspirations will be fulfilled . . .

Berne [4, pp. 13–15] speaks of the human infant's need for stroking or stimulation. He cites Spitz's observation that infants deprived of handling over a long period tend at length to sink into an irreversible decline.[3] Berne postulates a biological chain leading 'from emotional and sensory deprivation through apathy to degenerative changes and death'. This *stimulus-hunger*, he says, is later sublimated into *recognition-hunger:*

[3] See: [20].

The *stimulus-hunger*, with its first order sublimation into *recognition-hunger*, is so pervasive that the symbols of recognition become highly prized and are expected to be exchanged at every meeting between people . . . In this country there is a succession of verbal gestures, each step implying more and more recognition and giving more and more gratification. This ritual may be summarized as follows: (a) 'Hello!' (b) 'How are you?' (c) 'Warm enough for you?' (d) 'What's new?' (e) 'What else is new?' The implications are: (a) Someone is there; (b) Someone with feelings is there; (c) Someone with feelings and sensations is there; (d) Someone with feelings, sensations, and a personality is there; (e) Someone with feelings, sensations, a personality, and in whom I have more than a passing interest, is there.

3. Recognition of Noneconomic Rewards Associated with Economic Activities

If Parsons' media are to serve their functions of rewarding current and stimulating future contributions to a social system, the people involved must be able to recognise these media wherever they appear.

There is a great deal of evidence that people recognise and respond to noneconomic media (as well as money) in choosing jobs. For example, Zytowski [22] surveyed some seventy-two references dealing with the concept of 'work values', 'work needs', or 'work satisfactions'. He cites with approval Eli Ginzberg's trichotomisation of work values into intrinsic, extrinsic, and concomitant types. Zytowski compares lists used by several different authors, including from seven to twenty 'values' each, and finds that they cluster rather well into Ginzberg's three categories.

Extrinsic factors, which represent 'the outcomes of work, as contrasted with the means', include security, prestige, economic return, achievement, advancement, and recognition.

Intrinsic factors, which are 'part of the job itself', include independence, altruism, creativity, way of life, intellectual stimulation, variety, and similar terms.

Concomitant factors include surroundings, working conditions, company policy and administration, inter-personal relations (with peers, subordinates, and superiors), dominance, dependence, leadership, authority, and similar terms.

The extrinsic factors can be identified with some of Parsons' media of exchange (money, prestige, recognition, and perhaps influence and political power) plus a survival need, security.

The concomitant factors appear to centre on inter-personal relations. They evidently relate in part to affect (including recognition and response) and to Berne's 'procurement of stroking' [4, p. 19].

Some of the intrinsic factors reflect the use of behaviour mechanisms (thinking, talking, manipulation, gross motor activity, affective behaviour) in line with special abilities and preferences. However, as 'altruism', 'moral values', 'social welfare', 'helpful to others', and 'responsibility' are also classified among the intrinsic factors, it appears that media such as ideology, conscience, faith, and 'generalised commitment to the implementation of cultural values' are involved here as well.

In any event, it is clear that many if not all of Parsons' reward media may be involved in the total satisfactions associated with jobs. Blau and Duncan [8] also point out the close relationship between occupation and social stratification, stating that 'the American occupational structure . . . is the major foundation of the stratification system in our society . . .'.

The occupational structure in modern industrial society not only constitutes an important foundation for the main dimensions of social stratification but also serves as the connecting link between different institutions and spheres of social life, and therein lies its great significance. The hierarchy of prestige strata and the hierarchy of economic classes have their roots in the occupational structure; so does the hierarchy of political power and authority, for political authority in modern society is largely exercised as a full-time occupation . . . The occupational structure also is the link between the economy and the family, through which the economy affects the family's status and the family supplies manpower to the economy.[4] The hierarchy of occupational strata reveals the relationship between the social contributions men make by furnishing various services and the rewards they receive in

[4] See: [13, pp. 51–55 and 70–72].

return, whether or not this relationship expresses some equitable functional adjustment . . .

There is a strong implication here, as well as in Zytowski's study, that people do consider economic and noneconomic media simultaneously in choosing occupations and specific jobs.

4. Roger Barker's Theory of Behaviour Settings

According to Parsons, 'the unit of interpenetration between a personality and a social system is not the individual but a *role* or complex of roles . . . *The primary goal output of social systems is to the personalities of their members*'. Outputs from the social system to personalities are rewards; inputs from personalities to the social system are contributions.

Can we indeed find appropriate units for observing the performance of roles and estimating the rewards and contributions associated with their performance? A highly promising approach to these questions has been pioneered by the psychologist Roger Barker.

4.1 *The concept of a behaviour setting*
Roger Barker spent a good many years observing the behaviour of residents of a small mid-western community of about eight hundred and thirty people. He early addressed himself to the question of how the environment of human behaviour was to be identified, described, and measured. He concluded that the community environment could be divided into parts or units which he called behaviour settings.[5]

Barker says [3, pp. 158–159]:

Behavior settings are units of the environment that have relevance for behavior. They provide the primary data of the study to be reported here. We have dealt only with the settings that occur outside the homes of the community, that is, the public behavior settings. The number of public behavior settings in the town is a measure of the size of the town's public environment.

We must emphasize that a behavior setting coerces people and things to conform to its temporal-spatial pattern. This is not an incidental or accidental characteristic. The person or

[5] See: [4] and [5].

persons who maintain and control the setting (the performers) make a deliberate effort to insure that this is so, and that the setting therefore fulfills its function. This aspect of a setting we call its program. Two settings are said to have the same program when their parts and processes are interchangeable. When this is true, two or more settings belong to the same genotype. Two grocery stores, for example, could exchange stock, personnel, bookkeeping systems, shelving, and so forth, with little interruption in their operation. They belong to the same genotype. A Methodist and a Presbyterian minister could, and sometimes do, exchange pulpits. The number of behavior setting genotypes in a town is a measure of the variety of the town's environment.

Barker identified one hundred and ninty eight genotype settings in his town of eight hundred and thirty people. Examples include grocery stores, hardware stores, ice cream socials, kindergarten classes, business meetings, religion classes, hallways, bus stops, and many others.

When individual grocery stores, churches, and the like were recognised as separate or specific behaviour settings, Barker found eight hundred and eighty four public behaviour settings in his town in 1963–64. He was able to record that the number of daily occurrences of behaviour settings during 1963–64 was 53,258 and that the hours of duration of public behaviour settings in 1963–64 totalled 286,909. Multiplying the hours of duration of each behaviour setting by the number of persons participating in it, Barker obtained a record of 'hours of occupancy' of behaviour settings, totalling 1,129,295 in 1963–64. As there are 8,760 hours in a year, the total hours of 'life lived' during the year by the town's 830 residents was 7,270,800. About 15% of these hours were spent in public behaviour settings; the remaining 'hours of living' were presumably spent in private homes and in transit from one behaviour setting to another.

4.2 *An outline of Barker's system*
In 1968, Barker published a comprehensive statement of his approach in *Ecological Psychology: Concepts and Methods for Studying the Environment of Human Behavior* [1]. We will summarise the main features of his system.

Every behaviour setting has a program. Barker says [1 (pp. 80–81)]:

Organisms of the same genotype have the same coded programs stored in their nuclei, and behavior settings of the same genotype have the same coded programs stored in their most central zones (zone 6 if the most central region has a single inhabitant, zone 5 if it has multiple inhabitants) . . .

. . . When the program of a setting is incorporated within a person, it is one of his relatively permanent attributes, and he is branded with the code name of the program: Attorney, Postmaster, Grocer, etc.

In businesses, government agencies, and schools, the Zone 5–6 performers are usually 'professionals' who receive salaries or proprietary income for operating the behaviour setting. Churches and voluntary associations may have 'professionals' in charge of some behaviour settings and laymen or 'amateurs' in charge of others.

A great deal of higher education is concerned with training individuals to serve (in Barker's terminology) as Zone 5/6 performers in stated genotype behaviour settings.

Each grocery store in a town is a *specific* behaviour setting; 'grocery stores' is a behaviour setting *genotype*. Barker's cutting point for determining whether two specific behaviour settings belong to the same genotype is as follows [1, p. 83]:

Two behavior settings are of the same genotype if, when their zone 5/6 performers are interchanged, they receive and process the same inputs as formerly, in the same way and without delay.

Barker [1, p. 51] uses a diagram consisting of six equally spaced concentric circles to illustrate the six *zones of penetration* of individuals into a behaviour setting. Working from centre to periphery, these zones are (6) single leader, (5) joint leaders, (4) active functionary, (3) member or customer, (2) audience or invited guest, and (1) onlooker.

In general, it appears that an individual in Zone (6) makes a larger contribution to the output of the behaviour setting than an individual in Zones (5), (4), (3), (2) or (1) in descending order. In business firms, the line between Zones (4) and (3) is the boundary between the business and its customers. Occupants of Zone (3) interact to some extent with occupants of Zones (4),

(5) and (6); occupants of Zone (2) evidently play a passive role except for expressing approval or other reactions to the performances of occupants of Zones (6), (5) and (4).

Barker [1, p. 66] also rates behaviour settings on five variables which he calls *behaviour mechanisms*: affective behaviour, gross motor activity, manipulation, talking, and thinking. The three subscales for each of these variables include (*a*) (extent of) participation, (*b*) tempo, and (*c*) intensity.

In addition, Barker [1, p. 52] rates behaviour settings in terms of eleven variables which he calls *action patterns:* Aesthetics, business, education, government, nutrition, personal appearance, physical health, professionalism, recreation, religion, and social contact. Subscales for each of these variables include (*a*) participation, (*b*) supply relationship (if any) to other settings, (*c*) evaluation and appreciation, and (*d*) teaching and learning.

Barker states [1, p. 90] that:

A behavior setting authority system is identified by the controlling setting, e.g., Elementary and High School Board Meeting, Baseball Association Committee Meeting. The controlling setting of an authority system is frequently a committee meeting.

Barker classifies the controlling settings into five *authority systems*, (*a*) business, (*b*) churches, (*c*) government, (*d*) schools, and (*e*) voluntary associations.

Barker [1, p. 76] identifies four decisions regarding the operations of a behaviour setting, namely (*a*) appointment of performers, (*b*) admittance of members, (*c*) determination of fees and prices, and (*d*) establishment of programs and schedules. Each of these decisions may be made (*a*) within the town, (*b*) outside the town but within the school district, (*c*) outside the district but within the county, (*d*) outside the county but within the state, or (*e*) outside the state but within the nation. The loci of these decisions establish the *degree of local autonomy* of the setting.

The demographic characteristics of the occupants of various zones of a behaviour setting are also important data. Barker (pp. 47–48) divides residents of the town into fourteen *population subgroups*, as follows: infants (under 2 years); preschool (2:0–5:11); younger school (6:0–8:11); older school (9:0–11:11); adolescent (12:0–17:11); adult (18:0–64:11); aged

(65:0 and over); male; female; Social Class I; Social Class II; Social Class III; White; Negro. The maximum *degree of penetration* into behaviour settings can be rated for individuals or for population subgroups.

Barker [1, pp. 70–71] recognises seven categories of *pressure* (outside forces bearing upon an individual or a population subgroup) *to approach and enter or to withdraw from and avoid* any specified behaviour setting. For example, with respect to a given behaviour setting, the presence of children may be (*a*) required, (*b*) urged, (*c*) invited, (*d*) neutral, (*e*) tolerated, (*f*) resisted, or (*g*) prohibited.

Barker states [1, p. 75] that the *raison d'être* of a setting with respect to any class of inhabitants is the *welfare attribute*. With respect to children, for example, a specified behaviour setting may be classified as follows: (*a*) not concerned with children; (*b*) serves child members in this setting; (*c*) serves children in other settings (e.g. a meeting of the elementary school board); and (*d*) children serve other members in this setting (e.g. children may provide the program for a P.T.A. meeting).

Barker is definitely concerned with the reproducible measurement of all the aspects of behaviour settings noted above. *Ecological Psychology* [1] is a rich source of ideas which may be useful in the development of social accounts, in measures of output applicable to both market and nonmarket systems, and in the specification of objective functions for both market and nonmarket institutions.

We will need still another of Barker's concepts for use in the last section of this paper, that of homeostasis or equilibrium in the functional level of a behaviour setting.

4.3 *Homeostatic forces operating in and upon behaviour settings*

Barker [1 pp. 161 163] comments on the stability of behaviour settings as follows:

... One source of the stability of behavior settings is a balance between many independent forces that bear upon them. Some of the forces issue from the larger community, some are intrinsic to the setting itself, and some originate within the individuals who populate the setting. Here, for example, are influences pressing a school class toward an increase and toward a decrease in functional level, i.e.,

toward larger and toward smaller enrollment; toward a 'better' and toward a 'poorer' curriculum.
Influences from the larger community:
Toward an increase in functional level
There is a waiting list of applicants for enrollment.
Parents urge a richer curriculum.
Toward a decrease in fuctional level
It is the policy of the school board to limit the number of students per class.
A richer curriculum is expensive, and there is great resistance to higher taxes.
Influences intrinsic to the behavior setting:
Toward an increase in functional level
With a few more pupils, three suitable reading groups arranged on the basis of ability would be possible; with the enrollment as it is, the two groups have ranges of reading ability that are too great.
The classroom is equipped for showing moving pictures.
Toward a decrease in functional level
The room is overcrowded as it is.
The course of study is so full there is no time to use moving pictures.
Influences from individuals within settings:
Toward an increase in functional level
The teacher wants to extend her influence to as many children as possible.
The girls of the class want to have a costume party.
Toward a decrease in functional level
The teacher is dead tired at night as it is, without any more pupils.
The boys of the class refuse to cooperate upon a costume party.
In essence, the functional level of the behaviour setting remains quasi-stationary because increases in functional level which would make some members of the setting better off would make some other members (or supporters) of the setting worse off. If a member puts more into this setting he must, as a rule, reduce his inputs into some other settings. The Zone (6) performer – for example, the teacher in a classroom – controls

the basic program of the setting and must generally take the initiative if the functional level of the setting is to be increased. If membership in the setting for at least some members is maintained by outside pressure, such as compulsory school attendance laws, the setting as such can achieve a local optimum at best. The teacher may be able to restructure the program of the setting so that with no greater demands on her own time and energy the marginal utility of the setting to all or most members is increased (three reading groups instead of two, in Barker's example, might have this effect).

5. Combining the Economic and Noneconomic Outputs of a Society to Form a Measure of the Gross Social Product

Our approach in this section is largely intuitive. However, a number of the concepts presented in previous sections lend themselves to a tentative synthesis.

Parsons' Media of Social Interchange: Parsons' media include influence, money, political power, and value commitments; erotic pleasure; affect (including recognition and response); technological know-how and skill; ideology, conscience, reputation, and faith. Some of these media circulate mainly in specific 'authority systems' (in Barker's sense): money in the economy; political power in the polity; faith in churches; reputation in scientific and professional communities; technological know-how and skill in appropriate occupational groups and labour markets; influence in territorially based communities; erotic pleasure largely in the conjugal family system; and so on.

A number of Parsons' media seem to have 'human capital' aspects. This is clearly true of technological know-how and skill. Higher wages paid to experienced workers imply that human capital is produced on the job as well as in schools. Influence, political power, and reputation usually require considerable application over a period of years – a demonstrated capacity to deliver a specified volume of some desired output per unit of time.

Value commitments may also have to be demonstrated over a period of years to become media of exchange capable of influencing the behaviour of others. According to Churchman [10, p. 58]:

We can say in a very general way what a set of value measurements for a person is: it is a set of numbers that predict the probability that the person will make certain behavior choices in certain environments, given perfect awareness and knowledge on his part.

A long record of (almost always) 'correct' choices from the standpoint of ideology, or conscience, or faith establishes an empirical relative frequency basis for predicting such probabilities.

Levinson's Ego Ideal: Levinson states that a person's ego ideal is his vision of himself at his future best.

As a step toward measurement, the ego ideal might be represented as a vector of desired stocks of Parsons' various media of exchange at each point in a person's life cycle. At each point a shortfall in actual stocks relative to desired stocks would call forth efforts to raise the actual closer to the ideal. This leads to a stock-adjustment equation

$$\mathbf{e} = f(\mathbf{s}^* - \mathbf{s}); \quad \mathbf{e}, \mathbf{s}^*, \mathbf{s}: \ nxll \tag{1}$$

where $\mathbf{e}$ (effort) is a time-and-effort allocation vector and $\mathbf{s}^*$ and $\mathbf{s}$ are vectors of desired stocks and actual stocks respectively. We could rewrite (1) with a time lag as

$$\mathbf{e}_t = f(\mathbf{s}^*_{t+1} - \mathbf{s}_t) \tag{2}$$

to reflect the dynamic flight-and-pursuit nature of the endeavour, with achievement typically lagging behind aspiration.

If his ego ideal is realistic, a person should be able to estimate approximately how much effort will be required to achieve a certain stock (or annual flow) of each medium; he should allocate his effort in such a way that the expected marginal value product of a unit of effort directed at each goal would be the same, measured in terms of his own utility function.

Cantril's ladder-of-life device or Self-Anchoring Striving Scale [9, p. 22] might be used to help a person express the discrepancies he perceives between his ego ideal and his actual condition. The discrepancy for each medium would be stated in numbers of ladder steps on a scale ranging from zero for the worst to ten for the best possible situation he could visualise for himself with respect to that medium. If one step on the money dimension were taken as unity, the person could express the relative importance of one step with respect to any other medium as a fraction or multiple of one. Further, one step on the money dimension might be stated in terms of dollars (of assets or annual income); if so, the other media also could be given dollar values per step.

Barker's Behaviour Settings and Related Concepts: Several of Barker's concepts link up well with those of Parsons.

(1) Barker's five *behaviour mechanisms* (affective behaviour, gross motor activity, manipulation, talking and thinking) occupy most if not all the time in public behaviour settings: these mechanisms have a long evolutionary history. The established equilibrium for an individual at a particular stage of his life cycle would probably involve certain amounts (duration multiplied by intensity) of use of each of these five behaviour mechanisms.

(2) Barker's *authority systems* include business, churches, governments, schools and voluntary associations – these control 'public' behaviour settings. Families could no doubt be added as the authority systems that control behaviour settings in private homes.

(3) Some of Barker's *action patterns* seem to have very nearly a one-to-one correspondence with specified authority systems, namely the action patterns called business, religion, government and education. Professionalism as an action pattern seems to interpenetrate the other four. The remaining six action patterns, nutrition, personal appearance, physical health, aesthetics, recreation and social contact, seem largely independent of authority systems other than families and (in some cases, perhaps) voluntary associations.

(4) Barker's degrees of *local autonomy* (town, school district, county, state, nation) might be generalised into successive levels in an administrative decision-making hierarchy, regardless of whether the successive levels were located in a single building or in a hierarchy of central places which controlled system operations over successively larger geographic territories.

We will make use of Barker's basic concept of behaviour settings shortly in a more formal model.

5.1 *A generalisation of economic theory to all outputs of a social system*

If we extend Barker's system of behaviour settings to include all places of employment and all residences (plus settings occupied by residents of the community when they leave it temporarily on business or personal trips), we can establish an accounting system which is exhaustive with respect to living time, including sleep and private activities.

Each individual in a behaviour setting has a role (student or teacher, grocer or customer, chairman or member, etc.). If two or more persons are involved in a behaviour setting, 'transactions' take place (in the terminology of Berne [4]) involving recognition and response. The utility of a behaviour setting to an individual is a function of the setting as such, his own role in the setting, and his perception of his effectiveness in the role as evidenced by the behaviour of other participants toward him.

We might postulate, then, that a 'rational' personality will allocate his time among behaviour-setting-and-role combinations in such a way as to maximise their (expected) total utility. If a role has a quality dimension, more preparation time may be required to perform it well than to perform it at the threshold of adequacy.

If we assume that a consumer can rate any two arrays of commodities as 'A preferred to B', 'B preferred to A', or 'indifferent as between A and B', it may be equally reasonable to assume that a personality can make similar orderings of two arrays of behaviour setting, role and quality-of-performance-in-role combinations.

In the case of economic transactions, we multiply observed market prices by quantities of the respective goods and services produced in a nation and compute gross national (economic) product, G.N.P. The ratios of market prices are (under certain restrictive assumptions) equal to the ratios of the marginal utilities of the corresponding commodities to each consumer. If the market prices for some base year are used as fixed weights, we can compute changes in 'real' G.N.P. over a period of years.

Would it mean anything to perform the same operation for all of Parsons' media of exchange? Perhaps so, if we visualise a personality as trying to maximise his total utility from a year of living by using his total capacities in the most effective way. If there are s media of exchange, n potential activities representing essentially all forms of human behaviour, and s restrictions limiting the amounts of each medium that a given individual can use ('spend') as inputs into the social system, our model becomes

$$\max U = f(t_1, t_2, \ldots, t_n)$$

subject to

$$\sum_{i=1}^{n} t_i p_i = Y = b_1$$

$$\sum_{i=1}^{n} t_i m_{2i} = M_2 = b_2$$

$$\sum_{i=1}^{n} t_i m_{3i} = M_3 = b_3$$

$$\vdots$$

$$\sum_{i=1}^{n} t_i m_{si} = M_s = b_s$$

$$\sum_{i=1}^{n} t_i = 8760$$

Then

$$\frac{\partial U}{\partial t_i} - \lambda_1 p_i - \lambda_2 m_{2i} - \lambda_3 m_{3i} \cdots - \lambda_s m_{si} - \lambda_t = 0$$

for all

$$i = 1, 2, 3, \ldots, n$$

and

$$\frac{\dfrac{\partial U}{\partial t_i}}{\dfrac{\partial U}{\partial t_j}} = \frac{\lambda_1 p_i + \lambda_2 m_{2i} + \lambda_3 m_{3i} + \cdots + \lambda_s m_{si} + \lambda_t}{\lambda_1 p_j + \lambda_2 m_{2j} + \lambda_3 m_{3j} + \cdots + \lambda_s m_{sj} + \lambda_t}$$

Each unit of activity i uses up some time; many activities use up some money; some use personal influence; some use professional reputation; and so on. Each activity involves occupying a behaviour setting and performing some role in it at a specified quality level. Each medium of exchange corresponds to a goal of activity for some if not all personalities. Some of Parsons' media seem to be *stocks* (for example, professional reputation) which yield a flow of inputs into the social system and bring in a flow of outputs or rewards from the social system. Intense application may increase professional reputation; diversion of effort to politics or gardening may cause it (or permit it) to decline. In measuring the utility enjoyed by a personality during a given year only the *flows* of rewards associated with possession of stock-like media should be included.

Some activities bring in only one or two of the s kinds of rewards from the social system and use only one or a few kinds of the s resources or 'contributions', so there would be many zeros in the n times $s + 1$ 'technology' matrix and hence in the expressions for the $\partial U/\partial t_i$, $i = 1, 2, \ldots, n$. If the individual is free to convert time into money income and into flows of each of the other $s - 1$ resources, the initial b_i's can be adjusted until the marginal utilities of time converted into all other limiting resources are equal.

Consider the following matrix of exchange rates among marginal utilities of the s resources (and time):

$$
\begin{array}{c}
\quad\quad \lambda_1 \quad\ \lambda_2 \quad\ \lambda_3 \quad\ \lambda_4 \quad \cdots \quad \lambda_s \quad\ \lambda_t \\[4pt]
\begin{array}{c}
\lambda_1 \\ \lambda_2 \\ \lambda_3 \\ \lambda_4 \\ \cdot \\ \cdot \\ \cdot \\ \lambda_s \\ \lambda_t
\end{array}
\left[
\begin{array}{ccccccc}
1 & k_{12} & k_{13} & k_{14} & \cdots & k_{1s} & k_{1t} \\
k_{21} & 1 & k_{23} & k_{24} & \cdots & k_{2s} & k_{2t} \\
k_{31} & k_{32} & 1 & k_{34} & \cdots & k_{3s} & k_{3t} \\
k_{41} & k_{42} & k_{43} & 1 & \cdots & k_{4s} & k_{4t} \\
\cdot & \cdot & \cdot & \cdot & & \cdot & \cdot \\
\cdot & \cdot & \cdot & \cdot & & \cdot & \cdot \\
\cdot & \cdot & \cdot & \cdot & & \cdot & \cdot \\
k_{s1} & k_{s2} & k_{s3} & k_{s4} & \cdots & 1 & k_{st} \\
k_{t1} & k_{t2} & k_{t3} & k_{t4} & \cdots & k_{ts} & 1
\end{array}
\right]
\end{array}
$$

The last row (k_{tj}) indicates the marginal rates at which time can be converted into each of the s media; the corresponding element in the last column, k_{jt}, is the reciprocal of k_{tj} (for example, $k_{1t} = 1/k_{t1}$).

If so, we have

$$\lambda_t = k_{t1}\lambda_1$$
$$\lambda_2 = k_{2t}\lambda = k_{2t}k_{t1}\lambda_1$$
$$\lambda_3 = k_{3t}\lambda = k_{3t}k_{t1}\lambda_1$$

$$\vdots$$

$$\lambda_s = k_{st}\lambda = k_{st}k_{t1}\lambda_1$$

In this kind of equilibrium for the individual, we may write

$$\frac{\partial U}{\partial t_i} = \lambda_1\{p_i + k_{t1}(1 + k_{2t}m_{2i} + k_{3t}m_{3i} + \cdots + k_{st}m_{si})\}$$

If we multiply $\partial U/\partial t_i$ by t_i/λ_1 and sum over $i = 1, 2, \ldots, n$, the first term, $\sum_{i=1}^{n} t_i p_i = Y$, is a component of G.N.P.; i.e. the total consumption expenditures of the individual. The remaining terms are also expressed in dollars. The sum of all such terms would be the G.S.P. received by the individual. The corresponding sum over all individuals in a nation would be the G.S.P.

If an individual is making an optimal allocation of his time, the marginal utility of an additional hour per year should be the same in each of the behaviour settings in which he participates. If *cardinal* measures were devised for the s media of exchange and the quantities of each contributed and received per hour in each of $r > s$ behaviour settings were measured, it appears that relative marginal utilities such as $\lambda_2/\lambda_1, \lambda_3/\lambda_1, \ldots, \lambda_s/\lambda_1$ might be estimated by statistical means. Each behaviour setting would yield an observation equation as follows

$$\frac{\partial U}{\partial t_i} = \lambda_1 p_i + \lambda_2 m_{2i} + \lambda_3 m_{3i} + \cdots + \lambda_s m_{si} + \lambda_t$$

However, $\partial U/\partial t_i$ should be the same for all $i = 1, 2, \ldots, r$ and λ_t should be a constant; each observation equation could be rewritten as

$$p_i = \frac{1}{\lambda_1}\left\{\frac{\partial U}{\partial t_i} - \lambda_t\right\} - \frac{\lambda_2}{\lambda_1}m_{2i} - \frac{\lambda_3}{\lambda_1}m_{3i} - \cdots - \frac{\lambda_s}{\lambda_1}m_{si}$$

Now, p_i is the money cost per hour of occupying behaviour setting i. The variance of p_i among the r behaviour settings should be attributable to variations in m_2, m_3, ..., m_s among the r settings. A least squares estimate of $\{-\lambda_2/\lambda_1\}$ would indicate that a unit difference in m_2 per hour between two behaviour settings would offset a difference of $\{-\lambda_2/\lambda_1\}$ dollars per hour in the costs of occupying them. If an hour in each of two alternative settings is regarded as an offer with price and non-price aspects, $\{-\lambda_j/\lambda_1\}$ translates the jth non-price difference into a money equivalent; i.e. a trade-off between a price and a non-price offer variation.

The place of the organism in social system models Parsons states that the outputs of the social system are delivered to personalities and not, except in certain borderline cases (notably erotic pleasure), to organisms.

The model in the preceding section is stated in terms of optimising the flow of rewards to a personality. This model could perhaps be supplemented by a set of constraints relating to the welfare of the organism. Thus, we might specify upper and lower bounds for the amount of use of each behaviour mechanism (affective behaviour, gross motor activity, manipulation, talking, and thinking) to reflect the needs and limitations of the organism. Lower bounds might be specified for sleep, on behalf of the organism. The *social* rationale for these indulgences is that illness or fatigue on the part of the organism will reduce the ability of the personality to make contributions and to earn (and enjoy) rewards. The prevalence of life, accident and health insurance symbolises this dependence of the personality upon the survival and good physical condition of the organism. As Cantril points out [9, p. 315], 'unless the survival needs are satisfied, a person devotes himself almost exclusively to fulfilling them'.

There is a tradition of cost-benefit analysis, damage suits and settlements, and percentage disability estimates on which social accounting measurements might build. In general, it appears that injuries to the organism should be evaluated in terms of reward streams foregone, monetary and nonmonetary, as a consequence. Where population groups are suffering extensively from malnutrition and illness, the difference between actual G.S.P. and potential G.S.P. with adequate nutrition and with illness rates characteristic of higher income groups would be an estimate of the potential *social* value of the necessary health and nutrition programs.

5.2 *Optimising within a behaviour setting*
The concept of optimisation in social transactions is at least implicit in Berne. For example, in describing a simple *pastime* [4, p. 41] he states that 'the transactions are adaptively programmed so that each party will obtain the maximum gains or advantages during the interval. The better his adaptation, the more he will get out of it'. Also, the transactions involved are 'complementary', a word Berne uses quite frequently.

Barker's discussion of the various forces acting in and upon a behaviour setting to maintain its function at a quasi-stationary level is also illuminating. In his classroom example, it appears that any change in functional level which would make some members better off would make others worse off. However, an innovation (such as dividing the class into a number of groups on the basis of proficiency or interest) might lead to a Pareto-better situation in which no student was worse off and most students were better off than before.

A behaviour setting may be regarded as a 'co-operative plant' which has no objective function of its own but should be managed in such a way as to maximise the total net benefits distributed to the members, each member profiting in proportion to the amount he puts into the setting. He tries to allocate his total resources between this setting and all others in such a way as to maximise his expected total utility. If the setting is a classroom, the teacher is responsible for managing the setting for the maximum benefit of the students. The students share in proportion to what they put into the setting; the teacher may get various rewards for good management of the setting in terms of, (a) implicit or explicit feedback from students as to how much they are getting out of the course, (b) self-approval for living up to her ego ideal, and (o) higher salary.

5.3 *Optimisation for sets of inter-related behaviour settings*
The cost to a person of participating in one behaviour setting is the opportunity cost of not participating in the highest-valued alternative setting.

Suppose that all children aged six to eleven in a community are required to be in school for thirty hours a week. If each child has considerable latitude to choose his activities within the school, he may approximate a local optimum and realise most of the complementarities potentially available (from his standpoint) in the school as a whole. Mutually recognised complementarities might lead to near-optimal study groups without external pressure. Each constraint which was thought necessary by teachers or administrators could be evaluated in terms of perceived reductions in the outputs of the settings directly and indirectly affected by it.

As in the theory of general economic equilibrium under perfect competition, it would be possible to *accept* the results of a self-optimising process without attempting to *measure* them. However, if pressures and restrictions have been imposed on the self-optimising process (and the continuance of some restrictions is deemed necessary), measurement of the outputs associated with alternative sets of restrictions is needed for policy guidance.

5.4 *Optimisation for a small community*
The optimising model involved in the theory of consumer behaviour may be expressed as follows

$$\max U = f(q_1, q_2, \ldots, q_n) \qquad (5.4.1)$$

subject to

$$\sum_{i=1}^{n} p_i q_i = Y \qquad (5.4.2)$$

where the q_i are quantities of n consumer goods and services, the p_i are the corresponding market prices, and Y is the consumer's income, assumed fixed; the consumer's utility function, U, depends directly only on the quantities consumed, q_i ($i = 1, 2, \ldots, n$).

This model implies that the weighted average price elasticity of demand for the q_i is -1 and the weighted average income elasticity is 1; if all prices and money income are multiplied by the same scalar, the q_i will be unchanged.

If there are no externalities of consumption, these elasticity properties apply also to an *aggregate* of consumers, such as the eight hundred and thirty residents of Barker's community, provided that each of the eight hundred and thirty incomes is fixed and that consumers pay the same price for any given commodity.

Do these elasticity properties apply to our model of a personality allocating fixed amounts of *s* media among *n* behaviour settings? We assume that his input into any behaviour setting, **i,** is a vector of fixed numbers per hour of occupancy and the output (reward) he gains from that setting is also a vector of fixed numbers per hour of occupancy.

If the money income constraint for this personality is binding, then the price and income elasticity properties must hold with respect to his *economic* transactions. By analogy, it seems that the same properties should hold with respect to each of the other media taken separately. If so, the elasticity properties should also hold for each medium separately over an aggregate of consumers whose resource vectors contain fixed amounts of the *s* media. (These amounts can vary both absolutely and relatively as between different personalities.)

To the extent that each medium circulates within a particular subsystem of the social system as a whole, the rationale for the above conjectures is strengthened. The exchange rates between media could be calculated internally by each personality. However, a programme which improved the health of most members of the community and impaired that of none should alter the exchange rates between health and other media in the same *direction* for every person affected. An increase in the amount of the health medium available should reduce its marginal utility relative to those of other media; the shadow price of a resource falls as its quantity increases.

Competition among behaviour settings for the time of community residents could be conceptualised recognising that the total living time of the residents per year is a fixed number, so an increase in occupancy time for one genotype setting will require a decrease in occupancy time for one or more other genotype settings.

Suppose a resident is allocating his yearly living time among the *n* genotype settings available in the community and receiving a vector of rewards per hour in setting *i* with an equivalent dollar value of r_i. Then, we may write $\mathbf{t} = \mathbf{a} + \mathbf{B}r$ in matrix notation or, the expanded form

$$
\begin{bmatrix} t_1 \\ t_2 \\ \cdot \\ \cdot \\ \cdot \\ t_n \end{bmatrix} = \begin{bmatrix} a_1 \\ a_2 \\ \cdot \\ \cdot \\ \cdot \\ a_n \end{bmatrix} + \begin{bmatrix} b_{11} & b_{12} & \cdots & b_{1n} \\ b_{21} & b_{22} & \cdots & b_{2n} \\ \cdot & \cdot & & \cdot \\ \cdot & \cdot & & \cdot \\ \cdot & \cdot & & \cdot \\ b_{n1} & b_{n2} & \cdots & b_{nn} \end{bmatrix} \begin{bmatrix} r_1 \\ r_2 \\ \cdot \\ \cdot \\ \cdot \\ r_n \end{bmatrix} \tag{1}
$$

and $\sum_{i=1}^{n} t_i = 8760$; the total social income of the resident is $\sum_{i=1}^{n} t_i r_i$. Then the following measure might be taken as a surrogate for his *quality of life:*

$$
\frac{\sum_{i=1}^{n} t_i r_i}{\sum_{i=1}^{n} t_i} = \frac{\sum_{i=1}^{n} t_i r_i}{8760} = \bar{r} \tag{5.4.3}
$$

Now, suppose that the matrix **B** is stated in elasticity form, relating percentage changes in the t_i to percentage changes in the r_i. If every r_i is multiplied by the same scalar, the t_i should not change. Also, if the reward per hour, r_i, for occupying setting i is increased while all r_j's $(j = 1, 2,)$ $i(, \ldots n)$ remain constant, occupancy time in setting i should increase or, at the least, not decrease. Hence the diagonal elements b_{ii} will be non-negative and the off-diagonal elements b_{ij} $(j \neq i)$ will, on the average, be non-positive

$$
b_{ii} \geq 0; \quad b_{ii} + \sum_{\substack{j=1 \\ (j \neq i)}}^{n} b_{ij} = 0; \tag{5.4.4}
$$

therefore,

$$
\sum_{\substack{j=1 \\ (j \neq i)}}^{n} b_{ij} \leq 0. \tag{5.4.5}
$$

The genotype behaviour settings might be grouped according to 'authority systems', in Barker's terminology business, schools, churches, government, and voluntary associations; (also families, since we are including private as well as public behaviour settings in our conceptualisation). Thus, a resident's living time could be allocated exhaustively (for social accounting purposes) among these six authority systems and an average reward per hour calculated for each one; the weighted average of these six quality measures would be the $\bar{r}$ of Equation (5.4.3), a surrogate for the overall quality of the person's life during the specified period.

The quality of life of a resident is improving over time if the value of $\bar{r}$ is rising. If we aggregate over all residents and all genotype settings and divide by total living time of the residents, we obtain

$$\frac{\sum\limits_{k=1}^{N} \sum\limits_{i=1}^{n} t_{ki} r_{ki}}{\sum\limits_{k=1}^{N} \sum\limits_{i=1}^{n} t_{ki}} = \bar{r}_N \tag{5.4.6}$$

$\bar{r}_N$ is the average G.S.P. per hour of living time for all area residents. If $\bar{r}_N$ increases over time, the quality of life in the community is improving.

In addition to the crucial problems of measuring exchange rates between media for a given person and of aggregating 'rewards' over persons, there would remain some more conventional problems such as (*a*) comparing rates of change in $\bar{r}_N$ over time as between different communities and (*b*) comparing absolute levels of $\bar{r}_N$ at a given date across communities.

An increase in the value of output of any behaviour setting per participant hour will tend, *ceteris paribus*, to increase its share of the community's total living time. Some behaviour settings are selective with respect to age or other population subgroups; an improvement in recreational programmes for the aged would have its primary impact on behaviour settings normally occupied by them.

6. Concluding Remarks

Our generalisation of consumption theory to all outputs of a social system is by no means rigorous. Considerable empirical research would be needed to make it operational. A start could be made with Barker's data for the one hundred and ninety eight behaviour setting genotypes in his community of eight hundred and thirty people. Barker specifies two quantitative indexes, the

Ecological Resource Index (E.R.I.) and the General Richness Index (G.R.I.), which are combinations of his ratings on certain of the characteristics of behaviour settings listed earlier. The basic ratings for any setting relate to the setting as a whole as seen by a trained observer and not to the subjective experiences of its participants. One crucial question is whether the outputs perceived by participants in various behaviour settings can be translated into Parsons' media of exchange or some variant of them. Another crucial question is whether participants have reasonably stable exchange rates between money and other media. Would they be willing to pay more money (as taxes, donations, or admission fees) to participate in a behaviour setting if its output per participant hour were increased by specified amounts in terms of other media?

Berne [4, pp. 18–19] evidently takes a simpler view of social system outputs than does Parsons:

The advantages of social contact revolve around somatic and psychic equilibrium. They are related to the following factors: (1) the relief of tension (2) the avoidance of noxious situations (3) the procurement of stroking and (4) the maintenance of an established equilibrium . . .

When one is a member of a social aggregation of two or more people, there are several options for structuring time. In order of complexity, these are: (1) Rituals (2) Pastimes (3) Games (4) Intimacy and (5) Activity, which may form a matrix for any of the others. The goal of each member of the aggregation is to obtain as many satisfactions as possible from his transactions with other members . . .

Berne provides a unit of account for at least one class of rituals, the American greeting rituals; his micro-unit is the 'stroke'. The following exchange of greetings between *A* and *B* would be a 'two-stroke ritual' [4, p. 37]:

A. 'Hi!' (or Hello, or Good Morning).
B. 'Hi!' (or Hello, or Good Morning).

If *A* goes on to ask, 'Warm enough for you?' and *B* responds 'It certainly is', the whole transaction amounts to a 'four-stroke ritual'. Meanwhile, says Berne, '*A* and *B* have improved each other's health slightly'; a bit of recognition-hunger is satisfied.

For more complex exchanges, Berne uses the *transaction* as the unit of social intercourse. He then defines a behavioural entity called a 'simple pastime' [4, p. 41]:

This may be defined as a series of semiritualistic, simple complementary transactions arranged around a single field of material, whose primary object is to structure an interval of time. The beginning and end of the interval are typically signaled by procedures or rituals. The transactions are adaptively programmed so that each party will obtain the maximum gains or advantages during the interval. The better his adaptation, the more he will get out of it.

Pastimes are typically played at parties ('social gatherings') or during the waiting period before a formal group meeting begins . . .

Since Berne refers to informal greeting transactions as consisting of a certain number of 'strokes' and to pastimes as 'a series of semi-ritualistic, simple complementary transactions', it appears that pastimes might also be rated in terms of numbers of 'strokes'. If a 'stroke' in this context is typically a verbal statement implying recognition, approval, agreement, or sympathy, then the tempo of normal conversation under such circumstances may imply a certain average number of 'strokes' per minute. A particularly pleasant or interesting conversation implies more than the average gain per minute, and a dull or halting one implies less.

Berne's concept of recognition-hunger may be translated into several of Parsons' media, including reputation, ideology, conscience, faith and perhaps others. A person enjoys participating in behaviour settings where he is 'liked', 'respected', and 'appreciated'. Once he has identified himself with a group for which (say) faith is the primary medium in its distinctive behaviour settings, his satisfaction per hour of occupancy of these settings may be approximately the same as in settings where the primary medium is reputation (in law, medicine, business or science as the case may be) or ideology or conscience. Thus, behaviour settings sponsored by a wide range of organisations might be lumped together in G.S.P. accounts.

Zytowski's [22] list of 'work satisfactions' suggests that exchange rates between money and other reward media associated with jobs might be estimated on the basis of interviews with

6

individual workers. Also, collective bargaining negotiations between companies and unions must involve many implicit or explicit trade-offs between money and other media. The concept of a time budget for a small community should be useful in discussing socioeconomic policies. Proposed changes in the performance level of any behaviour setting will have some effect on the allocation of time and effort among other behaviour settings in the community. Even if reward vectors and occupancy response coefficients are specified *a priori*, the time budget format will facilitate recognition of probable impacts and stresses on other behaviour settings; the distribution of prospective gains and losses among population groups and authority systems can be anticipated approximately in quantitative terms.

Typically, communities of different population sizes in a country can be characterised as a hierarchy of central places – villages, towns, small cities, regional capitals and so on in ascending order [6, p. 368]. A village is approximately self-sufficient with respect to specified services; a town is self-sufficient with respect to village-level services and to additional ones which require the larger population base of a town plus several nearby villages. The successive levels can be defined in terms of the presence of certain types of retail trade, wholesale distribution, and service establishments – i.e. behaviour settings in the business authority system. However, behaviour settings in other authority systems – government agencies, churches, schools, and voluntary associations – could also be used in defining levels of central places.

Thus, if Barker's community with its one hundred and ninety eight behaviour setting genotypes is a typical American village, a typical American town would contain all or most of these one hundred and ninety eight plus a limited number of additional ones. Distinctive arrays of noneconomic behaviour settings would be closely associated with distinctive arrays of economic behaviour settings at each level. Detailed data for a limited number of actual behaviour settings could be used for estimating multiple regression relationships between occupancy times and behavioural output measures in specified noneconomic and specified economic behaviour settings at each level in the urban (central place) hierarchy. Data from a large scale national sample

Combining Economic and Noneconomic Objectives 139

survey for one year could be used as the bench mark for time series of behaviour setting occupancy derived from smaller current samples and secondary data.

Representative time budgets could be estimated for the populations of successive larger central-place oriented communities. In the United States the regional capitals and their associated commuting fields or functional economic areas (F.E.A.s) are of strategic importance for development planning and socioeconomic policy [7], [12], [13], [14]. An F.E.A. is approximately self-contained as a labour market in the short run and as a retail trade and service area. The matrix equation used in Section VI.4 to represent the effects of changes in performance levels in some behaviour settings upon occupancy times in all behaviour settings in a small community should be equally useful at the F.E.A. level. The leaders of economic and noneconomic behaviour settings in the area are equally engaged in the competition for human time, money and behavioural resources. The rules for maximising G.S.P. in the area should be simple extensions of the rules for maximising G.N.P.

References

[1] BARKER, ROGER G., *Ecological Psychology: Concepts and Methods for Studying the Environment of Human Behavior*, Stanford: Stanford University Press, 1968.
[2] BARKER, ROGER G., 'On the Nature of the Environment', *Journal of Sociological Issues*, XIX (April 1963), 17–38.
[3] BARKER, ROGER G., LOUISE S. BARKER, and DAN D. M. RAGLE, 'The churches of Midwest, Kansas and Yoredale, Yorkshire: Their contributions to the Environments of the Towns', in W. J. Gore and L. C. Hodapp (eds.), *Change in the Small Community: An Interdisciplinary Survey*. New York: Friendship Press, 1967, 155–189.
[4] BERNE, ERIC, *Games People Play: The Psychology of Human Relationships*, New York: Grove Press, Inc., 1964.
[5] BERNE, ERIC, *Transactional Analysis in Psychotherapy*, New York: Grove Press, Inc., 1961.
[6] BERRY, BRIAN J. L., and CHAUNCY D. HARRIS, 'Central place', in *International Encyclopedia of the Social*

Sciences, New York: The Macmillan Company and the Free Press, 1968, Vol. II, 365–370.

[7] BERRY, BRIAN J. L., *et al.*, *Metropolitan Area Definition: A Re-evaluation of Concept and Statistical Practice*, U.S. Department of Commerce, Bureau of the Census, Working Paper 28, June 1968.

[8] BLAU, PETER M. and OTIS DUDLEY DUNCAN, *The American Occupational Structure*, New York: John Wiley and Sons, Inc., 1967.

[9] CANTRIL, HADLEY, *The Pattern of Human Concerns*, New Brunswick: Rutgers University Press, 1965.

[10] CHURCHMAN, C. W., 'Problems of value measurement for a theory of induction and decisions', in J. Neyman (ed.), *Proceedings of the Third Berkeley Symposium on Mathematical Statistics and Probability*, Vol. V. Berkeley: University of California Press, 1956, 35–59.

[11] ERIKSON, ERIK H., 'Identity and the Life Cycle', *Psychological Issues*, I (January 1959), 111.

[12] FOX, KARL A., 'The new synthesis of rural and urban society in the United States', Chapter 28 in Ugo Papi and Charles Nunn (editors), *Economic Problems of Agriculture in Industrial Societies* (proceedings of a conference sponsored by the International Economic Association). London: Macmillan and New York: St. Martin's Press, 1969, 606–628.

[13] FOX, KARL A., 'Strategies for area delimitation in a national system of regional accounts'. Paper prepared at the request of Charles L. Leven, Director, Institute for Urban and Regional Studies, Washington University, St. Louis, Missouri, November 1967. 48 pp., plus seventeen Figures. Most of this material appears in pp. 105–125 and 138–147 of Charles L. Leven, J. B. Legler and P. Shapiro, *An Analytical Framework for Regional Development Policy*, Cambridge: M.I.T. Press, 1970.

[14] FOX, KARL A. and T. K. KUMAR, 'The Functional Economic Area: Delineation and Implications for Economic Analysis and Policy', *Regional Science Association Papers*, XV (1965) 57–85.

[15] HARRIS, THOMAS A., *I'm O.K. – You're O.K.: A Practical Guide to Transactional Analysis*, New York: Harper and Row, 1969.

[16] PENFIELD, W., 'Memory Mechanisms', *A.M.A. Archives of Neurology and Psychiatry*, LXVII (1952) 178–198, with discussion by L. S. Kubie *et al.*

[17] PARSONS, TALCOTT, 'Systems analysis: Social systems', in *International Encyclopedia of the Social Sciences*, New York: The Macmillan Company and the Free Press, 1968, Vol. XV, 458–473.

[18] PARSONS, TALCOTT and SMELSER, NEIL J., *Economy and Society*, Glencoe Free Press, 1956.

[19] LEVINSON, HARRY, *The Exceptional Executive: A Psychological Conception*, Cambridge: Harvard University Press, 1968.

[20] SPITZ, R., 'Hospitalism: Genesis of Psychiatric Conditions in Early Childhood', *Psychoanalytic Study of the Child*, I (1945), 53–74.

[21] WASHBURN, S. L. and VIRGINIA AVIS, 'Evolution of human behavior', in Roe, Anne and George Gaylord Simpson (eds.), *Behavior and Evolution*. New Haven: Yale University Press, 1958, pp. 421–436.

[22] ZYTOWSKI, DONALD G., 'The concept of work values', *Vocational Guidance Quarterly*, (March 1970) 176–186.

6 The Case of the Three Numeraires

ARNOLD C. HARBERGER*

THIS paper is concerned, at a theoretical level, with that wide class of general-equilibrium models with which the word numeraire is associated: models whose 'reduced forms' expressing real endogenous variables as functions of real and nominal exogenous variables are homogeneous of degree zero with respect to the latter set, and whose 'reduced forms' expressing nominal endogenous variables as functions of real and nominal exogenous variables are homogeneous of degree one with respect to the latter set. Traditionally, in models of this type there has been only one exogenous variable expressed in nominal terms (usually the quantity of money) and movements in this variable therefore determined movements in the general level of prices. The case in which money is the nominal exogenous variable is not the only one represented in the literature, however; there is also the traditional Gold Standard case in which the exchange rate is assumed to be exogenously fixed while the money supply is endogenous, and the Keynesian case in which (at least in the original variant and in some models subsequently constructed) the wage level is taken as exogenous.

So long as in the basic equations of such a model nominal variables enter only as ratios to each other, the equilibrium values of the real variables will remain unchanged as a consequence of any equiproportional change in all nominal variables. Moreover, so long as the equilibrium associated with any set of exogenous variables is unique, then an equi-proportional movement of all nominal exogenous variables, keeping the real exogenous variables constant, will leave the equilibrium values of all real endogenous variables unchanged, while moving all

* University of Chicago

nominal endogenous variables in the same proportion with the nominal exogenous ones.

This paper explores the case in which there are three nominal exogenous variables – the money supply M, the exchange rate X, and the wage rate W. In the background of the paper's development are the problems of countries – such as Brazil, Argentina, and Chile – suffering from continual inflationary pressures. In all of these cases, the money supply is a significant policy variable, and the exchange rate as well. Moreover, wages are at least to some extent under policy control, as the Government frequently establishes more or less mandatory patterns of wage readjustment within the inflationary setting.

As compared with the traditional general-equilibrium models, a model with three exogenous nominal variables must permit additional disequilibria. In brief, although a movement of M, X, and W in the same proportion should leave the real magnitudes determined by the model unchanged, their movement in different proportions should have real effects. Likewise, although a proportional increase of M, X, and W should increase all prices in the system in the same proportion, the movement of any one of these keeping the others constant should not in general lead to a proportionate rise in the level of all prices and (as stated above) should have real effects as well. In particular, it is to be expected that under independent and exogenous movements of M, X, and W, even the most well-behaved general-equilibrium model will produce equilibria at less than full employment on occasions, and will not be able to maintain equilibrium in the Balance of Trade.

Let the reduced form of such a general-equilibrium model be, in differential form

$$d \log. P = R_{PM} \, d \log. M + R_{PX} \, d \log. X$$
$$+ R_{PW} \, d \log. W + \ldots \quad (1)$$
$$dy = R_{YM} \, d \log. M + R_{YX} \, d \log. X$$
$$+ R_{YW} \, d \log. W + \ldots \quad (2)$$
$$dB = R_{BM} \, d \log. M + R_{BX} \, d \log. X$$
$$+ R_{BW} \, d \log. W + \ldots, \quad (3)$$

where P represents the price level, y the level of real output or employment and B the Balance of Trade expressed in foreign currency (a *real* magnitude), and where the omitted terms are the changes in the real exogenous variables of the system times their respective reduced form coefficients. Since we will throughout be exploring the reactions of the system to changes in the nominal exogenous variables holding the real ones constant, nothing is lost in this omission.

The properties of the R's in (1) derive from the basic homogeneity conditions of the class of models which we are considering. They are

$$R_{PM} + R_{PX} + R_{PW} = 1 \qquad (4)$$

$$R_{YM} + R_{YX} + R_{YW} = 0 \qquad (5)$$

$$R_{BM} + R_{BX} + R_{BW} = 0 \qquad (6)$$

This model collapses to a traditional general-equilibrium model when two of the three nominal exogenous variables are shifted to the endogenous category, and when at the same time a full-employment equilibrium condition ($d \log. y = 0$) and a balance of trade equilibrium condition ($d \log. B = 0$) are imposed. One can also think of this shift of variables to the endogenous category as a process in which the policy-makers who control the variables in question are assigned the specific tasks of using these instruments to achieve equilibrium in particular markets.

Thus, if policy instruments X and W are assigned to the tasks of maintaining equilibrium in the y and B markets, we set $d \log. y$ and $d \log. B$ equal to zero and obtain

$$-R_{YM} \, d \log. M = R_{YX} \, d \log. X + R_{YW} \, d \log. W$$

$$-R_{BM} \, d \log. M = R_{BX} \, d \log. X + R_{BW} \, d \log. W,$$

from which

$$d \log. W = \begin{bmatrix} R_{YX} - R_{YM} \, d \log. M \\ \dfrac{R_{BX} - R_{BM} \, d \log. M}{R_{YX} \quad R_{YW}} \\ R_{BX} \quad R_{BW} \end{bmatrix}$$

$$= \frac{(-R_{BM}R_{YX} + R_{YM}R_{BX}) \, d \log. M}{R_{YX}R_{BW} - R_{BX}R_{YW}} \qquad (7)$$

and

$$d \log. X = \begin{bmatrix} -R_{YM} \, d\log. M & R_{YW} \\ -R_{BM} \, d\log. M & R_{BW} \\ R_{YX} & R_{YW} \\ R_{BX} & R_{BW} \end{bmatrix}$$

$$= \frac{(-R_{YM}R_{BW} + R_{BM}R_{YW}) \, d\log. M}{R_{YX}R_{BW} - R_{BX}R_{YW}} \tag{8}$$

Substituting $-R_{BM} = R_{BX} + R_{BW}$ [from (6)] and $R_{YM} = -R_{YX} - R_{YW}$ [from (5)] into (7) we obtain

$$d \log. W = \frac{\begin{pmatrix} R_{BX}R_{YX} + R_{BW}R_{YX} \\ - R_{YX}R_{BX} - R_{YW}R_{BX} \end{pmatrix}}{R_{YX}R_{BW} - R_{BX}R_{YW}} \, d\log. M = d\log. M \tag{9}$$

and similar substitutions for R_{YM} and R_{BM} in (8) produce $d\log. X = d\log. M$. Substituting for $d\log. X$ and $d\log. W$ in (1) produces:

$$d \log. P = (R_{PM} + R_{PX} + R_{PW}) \, d\log. M = d\log. M$$

Similarly it can be shown that when $d\log. B$ and $d\log. Y$ are set equal to zero and X and W considered to be endogenous, the new reduced form coefficients relating $d\log. Y$ and $d\log. B$ to $d\log. M$ are both zero.

In the same way, we can derive that when M and W are assigned the tasks of maintaining $dy = dB = 0$, the reduced form of the system reduces to $d\log. P = d\log. X$, and when M and X are assigned the same jobs, $d\log. P = d\log. W$.

We have now considered the cases in which all three 'numeraires' are genuinely exogenous, and those in which only one of the three is in this category. We now turn to the more interesting class of cases, in which one of the three variables – M, X, or W is assigned to a particular task, while the other two remain genuinely exogenous. It is indeed plausible that situations of this kind arise. When a country has ample foreign-exchange reserves, the authorities simply feel no pressure to bring about foreign trade equilibrium. Yet there may be signs of abnormal unemployment in the country, and the authorities may be intensely interested in alleviating it. They may pursue this objective by an 'incomes policy', attempting to limit wage increases and thus absorb the unemployment, or by monetary policy, or by an exchange rate policy of 'beggar my neighbour' devaluation, or by a combination of these measures. We shall examine here only the 'pure' cases in which one policy instrument is assigned the job of maintaining full employment.

In other circumstances, a country may be operating under extreme Balance of Payments pressure, and the authorities may react by using one of the policy instruments at their disposal to prevent any further deterioration of the trade balance. This could, most plausibly, be either M or X, as both monetary and exchange rate policy have been traditionally used as instruments to influence the trade balance. But it is conceivable that wage rate policy might also be adopted for this purpose – as the recent use of incomes policy in the United Kingdom suggests.

We thus have six cases to examine – three in which W, M, and X, respectively, are assigned the task of maintaining full employment, and three in which one of these variables is assigned the job of keeping the balance of trade at some desired level.

Let us call S_{PM} and S_{PX} the reduced form coefficients that result when W is assigned the task of maintaining full employment and is thus converted to the endogenous category. Setting (2) equal to zero and solving for $d\log. W$ we obtain

$$d\log. W = -\frac{R_{YM}}{R_{YW}} d\log. M - \frac{R_{YX}}{R_{YW}} d\log. X$$

Substituting in (1) we get

$$d\log. P = \left[R_{PM} - \frac{R_{YM}R_{PW}}{R_{YW}} \right] d\log. M$$
$$+ \left[R_{PX} - \frac{R_{YX}R_{PW}}{R_{YW}} \right] d\log. X$$

This is the reduced form equation for $d\log. P$ in the revised system, and therefore

$$S_{PM} = R_{PM} - \frac{R_{YM}R_{PW}}{R_{YW}}$$
$$S_{PX} = R_{PX} - \frac{R_{YX}R_{PW}}{R_{YW}}.$$

If we call T_{PX} and T_{PW} the reduced form coefficients which emerge when M is assigned the task of maintaining full employment we find, by an analogous procedure

$$T_{PX} = R_{PX} - \frac{R_{YX}R_{PM}}{R_{YM}}$$

$$T_{PW} = R_{PW} - \frac{R_{YW}R_{PM}}{R_{YM}}$$

Similarly, defining U_{PM} and U_{PW} as the reduced form coefficients which result when X is assigned the job of maintaining full employment, we have

$$U_{PM} = R_{PM} - \frac{R_{YM}R_{PX}}{R_{YX}}$$

$$U_{PW} = R_{PW} - \frac{R_{YW}R_{PX}}{R_{YX}}$$

To establish indications of the orders of magnitude of the coefficients S, T, and U, we can work with the presumptive signs of the R's in Equations (1) to (3). These are
    Greater than zero $R_{PM}, R_{PX}, R_{PW}, R_{YM}, R_{YX}, R_{BX}$
    Less than zero R_{YW}, R_{BM}, R_{BW}
On this basis and using the properties (4), (5), and (6) we establish the following inequalities:

$$R_{PM} < S_{PM} < (R_{PM} + R_{PW})$$
$$R_{PX} < S_{PX} < (R_{PX} + R_{PW})$$
$$T_{PX} < R_{PX}$$
$$(R_{PW} + R_{PM}) < T_{PW}$$
$$U_{PM} < R_{PM}$$
$$(R_{PW} + R_{PX}) < U_{PW}$$

Note also that U_{PM} is > 0 when $R_{PM}R_{YX} > R_{YM}R_{PX}$, and that T_{PX} is > 0 when $R_{PX}R_{YM} > R_{YX}R_{PM}$. Hence one of these two coefficients must necessarily be less than, and the other greater than zero. Correspondingly, because $U_{PM} + U_{PW} = 1$, and $T_{PX} + T_{PW} = 1$, either U_{PW} or T_{PW} must be greater than unity.

There is no general answer as to which of U_{PM} or T_{PX} is less than zero, but for a particular model (which is quite relevant for the smaller, less developed countries) an unambiguous answer can be obtained. Assume that

(1) There are two classes of goods – domestic, H, and international, I;

(2) the country in question has no influence over the world prices (in foreign currency) of international goods, with the result that their prices within the country are simply the given world prices multiplied by the exchange rate;

(3) we are concerned with a short to middle run situation in which labour is the only relevant variable factor of production, and in which the output of domestic goods is therefore a positive function of (P/W), where P is now the price level of domestic goods, and output of international goods a positive function of (X/W), where X represents the internal price of international goods (this implicitly chooses units of international goods so that their foreign-currency prices are equal to unity).

When, under these assumptions, we seek to isolate the value of T_{PX}, we postulate a hypothetical situation in which wages are held constant, the exchange rate is increased, and the money supply is so adjusted as to maintain full employment. The increase of the exchange rate will draw resources, at the given wage level, into the production of international goods. Maintaining total employment will therefore require release of resources from the domestic goods sector. To accomplish this, monetary policy must operate to reduce demand to the point where domestic goods output (and the price level of such output) are lower than before, with wages remaining constant throughout the exercise. In this case, therefore, we have

$$T_{PX} < 0$$
$$1 < T_{PW}$$
$$0 < U_{PM} < R_{PM}$$
$$(R_{PW} + R_{PX}) < U_{PW} < 1$$

We now turn to the three cases in which, respectively, X, M, and W are assigned the task of maintaining the balance of trade at a given level. Let E_{PM} and E_{PW} be the reduced form coefficients that result when X is assigned the task of controlling the balance of trade. Setting (3) equal to zero and solving for

$d \log. X$, we obtain

$$d \log. X = - \frac{R_{BM}}{R_{BX}} d \log. M - \frac{R_{BW}}{R_{BX}} d \log. W$$

Substituting this expression into (1) we get

$$d \log. P = \left[R_{PM} - \frac{R_{BM}R_{PX}}{R_{BX}} \right] d \log. M$$

$$+ \left[R_{PW} - \frac{R_{BW}R_{PX}}{R_{BX}} \right] d \log. W$$

The expressions in brackets are E_{PM} and E_{PW}, respectively. Proceeding analogously, and letting F_{PX} and F_{PW} represent the reduced form coefficients when M is used to control the Balance of Trade, we have

$$F_{PX} = R_{PX} - \frac{R_{BX}R_{PM}}{R_{BM}}$$

$$F_{PW} = R_{PW} - \frac{R_{BW}R_{PM}}{R_{BM}}$$

Finally, when W is used to control the Balance of Trade, the reduced-form coefficients are

$$G_{PM} = R_{PM} - \frac{R_{BM}R_{PW}}{R_{BW}}$$

$$G_{PX} = R_{PX} - \frac{R_{BX}R_{PW}}{R_{BW}}$$

Once again applying the presumptive signs of the R's, and using the homogeneity properties (4), (5), and (6), we can establish

$$R_{PM} < E_{PM} < (R_{PM} + R_{PX})$$
$$R_{PW} < E_{PW} < (R_{PW} + R_{PX})$$
$$(R_{PX} + R_{PM}) < F_{PX}$$
$$F_{PW} < R_{PW}$$
$$G_{PM} < R_{PM}$$
$$(R_{PX} + R_{PW}) < G_{PX}$$

Just as in the case of T_{PX} and U_{PM}, it is necessary that F_{PW} and G_{PM} have opposite signs, since the condition for the former being positive is $(R_{PW}/R_{PM}) > (R_{BW}/R_{BM})$, and that for G_{PM} being positive is $(R_{PW}/R_{PM}) < (R_{BW}/R_{BM})$. By the same token, either F_{PX} or G_{PX}, but not both, must be greater than unity.

Again, to see which of F_{PW} or G_{PM} is likely to be negative, we must resort to a somewhat tighter specification of the model. Let us build on assumptions 1–3 above, and assume additionally that the elasticity of supply of international goods (at a given wage rate) is smaller than that of domestic goods. This is plausible because a high elasticity of supply of international goods would enable a country quite easily to overcome any Balance of Payments difficulties by a small effective devaluation – something we do not observe in the types of countries whose problems motivated this analysis. Similarly, we shall assume that the price elasticity of demand for domestic goods is smaller than that for international goods. This last assumption is rendered plausible by the fact that the substitution-effect in a two-good model produces own-price elasticities which are inversely proportional to the importance of the commodities in the consumer's budget. International goods (including the domestically produced and consumed counterparts of imports and exports) rarely account for as much as a third of total expenditures in any country; hence on this score the elasticity of demand for international goods should be at least twice that for domestic goods.

Working with these assumptions, we can explore the case in which wages are assigned the job of equilibrating the balance of trade as M changes, while the exchange rate is held fixed.

In Figure 6.1 there is initial equilibrium at price level P_0 in the domestic goods market, and at the exchange rate X_0 in the international goods market. There is an initial increase in the demand for both classes of goods, caused by an autonomous increase in the money supply from M_0 to M_1. The initial shifts in demand are not depicted in the diagrams, for we are operating under the requirement that wages adjust so as to leave the Balance of Trade unchanged. The height of the supply curve (assumed to reflect marginal costs) will accordingly move in proportion to movements in the wage rate, producing perhaps further reactions of demand. The ultimate equilibrium in the international goods market will be of the type depicted, with

$S(W_1)$ crossing $D(M_1, W_1)$ at the price X_0, the equality of S and D reflecting equilibrium in the Balance of Trade.

In the domestic goods market, the supply function will be displaced vertically by the same proportion as was the supply function for international goods, as a consequence of the change in wages from W_0 to W_1. We cannot make any similarly exact assertion about the shift of the demand curve for domestic goods. But it is clear that the demand for domestic goods is responding to the same general forces as the demand for international goods. If the response were in the same proportion as

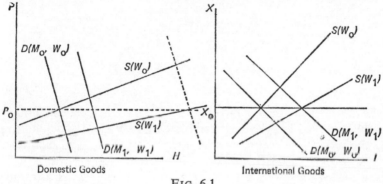

Domestic Goods   International Goods

FIG. 6.1

that for international goods, it is clear that, under the assumptions stated and reflected in the diagram, the price level of domestic goods would fall. Indeed, the domestic goods demand curve could shift to any position short of the dotted curve, and still produce a fall in the domestic price. (A little experimentation will reveal that the key factors in determining the wide range of outcomes compatible with a fall in the domestic price level are the assumptions concerning relative elasticities of supply and demand in the two markets.)

Thus while we have no theoretical necessity that G_{PM} be negative, a plausible case can be made that this is so. On this basis we have

$$G_{PM} < 0$$
$$1 < G_{PX}$$
$$0 < F_{PW} < R_{PW}$$
$$(R_{PX} + R_{PM}) < F_{PX} < 1$$

We are now in a position to summarise how the reduced-form coefficients of M, X, and W can change as the assumptions regarding the uses of particular policy instruments are altered. For the money supply, we have

$$G_{PM} < 0 < U_{PM} < R_{PM} \begin{array}{l} < E_{PM} < (R_{PM} + R_{PX}) < 1 \\ \\ < S_{PM} < (R_{PM} + R_{PW}) < 1 \end{array}$$

For the exchange rate we have

$$T_{PX} < 0 < R_{PX} \begin{array}{l} < (R_{PX} + R_{PM}) < F_{PX} < 1 < G_{PX} \\ \\ < S_{PX} < (R_{PX} + R_{PW}) \end{array}$$

And for the wage rate we have

$$0 < F_{PW} < R_{PW} < E_{PW} < (R_{PW} + R_{PX})$$
$$< U_{PW} < 1 < T_{PW}$$

In all cases the degree of reaction of the price level to changes in the specified exogenous variable can vary greatly depending on the policy environment prevailing at the time. For example, if the money supply is varied, while the exchange rate is held fixed and while wages are (endogenously) varied so as to maintain equilibrium in the Balance of Trade the reaction of the price level is likely to be in the opposite direction to the change in money supply. If on the other hand, the money supply is varied, while both wages and the exchange rate operate endogenously to equilibrate the labour market and the Balance of Trade, then the price level will move in the same direction with and in proportion to the change in money supply. The other cases examined, represented by U_{PM}, R_{PM}, E_{PM}, and S_{PM} fall between these extremes, but even here there are significant inequalities among the various reaction coefficients of the price level to changes in the quantity of money.

The following conclusions appear to emerge from the present exercise:

(1) In econometric work designed to explain variations over time in the rate of inflation of a country, the effort should be made to introduce M, X, and W as independent explanatory variables. This is tantamount to sticking to the 'basic' reduced form and estimating the R's in Equations

(1), (2), and (3). Once the R's are obtained the other coefficients that we have derived from particular policy assumptions can be obtained by algebraic manipulation of the R's.

(2) as a corollary of the above, simple econometric relationships relating d log. P to one other variable such as d log. M or d log. W should be avoided as far as possible, as these relationships are not likely to be very stable. Where, as is often the case in less developed countries, adequate wage data are not available, such information as is available on wage movements should at least be used in interpreting observed changes in the relationship between, say, d log. P and d log. M. The same goes for the exchange rate, in cases where, because of multiple rates and other currency practices, no series appropriate for econometric work can be obtained.

(3) The types of reactions explored in this paper, for cases in which particular policy variables are assigned to particular 'tasks', may also be relevant for certain cases in which the relevant market is freely functioning. For example, a country in which the money supply and the wage rate are subject to erratic ('exogenous') variations, and in which a genuinely freely-fluctuating exchange rate maintains reasonably continuous equilibrium in the Balance of Payments is in a situation quite analogous to that postulated above in deriving E_{PM} and E_{PW}, the only difference being that the 'task' assigned in the text to exchange rate policy in the case examined in the text is here accomplished by the 'policy' of reliance on market forces.

(4) The principal conclusion, as is to be expected from an essentially theoretical exercise, is in the realm of theory. The underlying class of models, as described at the outset, is traditional to the point of being almost 'standard' in the literature. When set out in the standard way, that is, with full-employment and Balance of Trade constraints imposed and with only one nominal exogenous variable, the response of prices is proportional to changes in that exogenous variable. In particular, when M is the only nominal exogenous variable, the (class of) models we are concerned with all produce the quantity theory of money in its most rigid form for

changes in M holding all exogenous real variables constant.
Yet what seems to be a comparatively minor modification of
the assumptions underlying this traditional model – by
relaxing one or both of the full-employment and Balance
of Trade constraints – leads to a drastic alteration of the
ways in which changes in the nominal exogenous variables
influence the level of prices. The principal motivation of
this paper, in fact, derives from the surprise with which I
and a number of others reacted to the results. The principal
message, in turn, is that the surprise should be overcome,
and our professional intuitions adjusted to recognise that
results of the type obtained in this paper are in no sense
implausible and are, on the contrary implied by highly
traditional assumptions.

Finally, a *caveat*. In an attempt to put some flesh on the bare
bones of the models under discussion, I have referred to the
problem of explaining price level movements in countries like
Argentina, Brazil, and Chile. In so doing, I do not mean to
imply that the simple fitting of a relationship like Equation (1)
would adequately cope with the complex problems of dynamic
adjustment that are involved in these real-world cases. Rather
I am thinking in the following terms. A number of attempts to
explain price level changes in inflationary countries have started
from a basic quantity-theory framework and fitted equations in
which changes in the supply of money together with some real
variables were taken as the independent variables of the exercise. In these attempts, dynamic factors have been grafted on
to the basic quantity-theory framework, typically by the introduction of distributed lags. The analysis of the present paper
suggests that it would be preferable to start with an equation in
which price level changes were related not only to changes in the
money supply but also to changes in wage levels and exchange
rates, and then to modify this relationship so as to incorporate
the relevant dynamic factors.

In a similar vein it should be noted that the signs attributed to
the R's are presumptive but not necessary. For example, it is
possible to construct models meeting the homogeneity conditions of Equations (4)–(6) in which for certain not implausible
values of the basic behaviour parameters (supply and demand
elasticities, etc.) the price level of domestic goods would fall

TABLE 6.1 *Summary Table of Reduced Form Coefficients*

Constraints	Instruments used to achieve constraints	Coefficient (underlined) of reduced form under given constraint(s)		
		d log. M	d log. X	d log. W
None	None	$\underline{P_{PM}}$	$\underline{R_{PX}}$	$\underline{R_{PW}}$
$dy = 0$	W	$R_{PM} < \underline{S_{PM}} < (R_{PM} + R_{PW})$	$R_{PX} < \underline{S_{PX}} < (R_{PX} + R_{PW})$	—
$dy = 0$	M	—	$\underline{T_{PX}} < 0$	$1 < \underline{T_{PW}} < (R_{PW} + R_{PX})$
$dy = 0$	X	$0 < \underline{U_{PM}} < R_{PM}$	—	$\underline{U_{PW}} < 1$
$dB = 0$	X	$R_{PM} < \underline{E_{PM}} < (R_{PM} + R_{PX})$	—	$R_{PW} < \underline{E_{PW}} < (R_{PW} + R_{PX})$
$dB = 0$	M	—	$(R_{PX} + R_{PM}) < \underline{F_{PX}} < 1$	$0 < \underline{F_{PW}} < R_{PW}$
$dB = 0$	W	$\underline{G_{PM}} < 0$	$1 < \underline{G_{PX}}$	—
$dB = 0$	X, W	—	—	—
$dy = 0$ $dB = 0$	X, W	$\underline{1}$	—	—
$dy = 0$ $dB = 0$	M, W	—	$\underline{1}$	—
$dy = 0$ $dB = 0$	X, M	—	—	$\underline{1}$

as a consequence of an independent rise of the exchange rate holding money supply and the wage rate constant. But in general it is only a relatively small subset of the space of plausible parameter values which leads to this result. Hence, the pattern of signs which we have assumed for the R's should be considered as the normal case. And it should be noted that while changing the sign of one or another of the R's would change the inequalities summarised in the table shown on p. 155, it would not change the basic conclusion of this paper that the reduced form coefficients relating the change in domestic prices to changes in a given policy variable change greatly as one alters the tasks assigned to other policy variables.

7 An Informal Classical Model of the Current Economic Development Problem

HARRY G. JOHNSON*

THROUGHOUT most of the period since the end of the Second World War, one of Jan Tinbergen's prime professional interests has been with the promotion of the economic development of the poorer parts of the world, and particularly with the development and application of models for the projection and planning of manpower utilisation. Recently, the Pearson Report has called attention, among other things, to a range of serious problems confronting the global development effort in the next decade. These include the population explosion, the growing problem of urban unemployment, a concern about the inappropriateness of western industrial technology to the conditions of relative abundance of labour and scarcity of capital in the developing countries and a complementary emphasis on the need to develop more appropriate technologies, and the judgment that the promotion of economic development as so far practiced has produced increasing, or at least no lessening, inequality in the distribution of income and wealth, with serious effects, actual in some cases and potentially ominous in many others, on the political stability necessary for modernisation and orderly economic development.

The purpose of the present paper, written in tribute to Jan Tinbergen, is to suggest that these phenomena are logically connected and can be explained by a rather simple theoretical model. This model draws heavily on the early classic article of Arthur Lewis, on 'Economic Development with Unlimited Supplies of Labour' [1], but goes beyond that model in

* Professor of Economics, London School of Economics and Political Science and the University of Chicago

developing an analysis of its implications for unemployment
and inequality of income distribution, and also in pointing to
alternatives to Lewis's proposed solution of the poverty problem
through increasing productivity in the subsistence sector. In
so doing, it employs ideas derived from a still earlier and unduly
neglected paper by R. F. Kahn [2]. The model is described as
'classical' for two reasons: its foundation on the Lewis model,
whose approach is classical in the history-of-thought meaning
of the term, and its assumption of rationality in behavioural
responses to economic incentives. The particular form given to
the latter I owe to the work of my colleague at the University
of Chicago, Arnold C. Harberger. The model is described as
'informal' because I do not on this occasion attempt to develop
a fully explicit dynamic general equilibrium model of the development process, but only to indicate the key elements of such
a model – though I shall try to indicate the points at which the
more elaborate model would need to be closed.

The starting point of the model is Lewis's two assumptions
that there is an unlimited supply of labour available at a certain
wage in the subsistence sector, and that the wage rate in the
industrial sector exceeds the subsistence sector wage by a conventional margin greater than the excess costs of urban as
compared with subsistence-sector living. In contrast to the
general tenor of Lewis's work, however, it is emphasised that
the assumption of unlimited labour availability presumes a
dynamics of population growth according to which labour
breeds to the level of subsistence. This has the important implication that an increase in the subsistence wage cannot be
obtained simply by improving the technology of production in
the subsistence sector. Any such improvement by itself will
merely enlarge the population in the subsistence sector, the
benefits most plausibly being assumed to accrue to the owners
of land, or natural resources in general, which may be assumed
to be the factor of production in inelastic supply in that sector.
The fact that on the assumption of unlimited labour supply at a
constant subsistence wage the benefits of technical progress
will accrue entirely to landowners implies, given the usual
circumstances of unequal initial shares of land ownership and
differential propensities to refrain from consumption in order
to accumulate land holdings, that such technical progress will

produce a growing inequality in the distribution of income from agricultural activity, and consequently growing political unrest and agitation for land reform. This part of the story, however, will not be developed further here. The point relevant to the present analysis is that an increase in the real subsistence wage requires a constriction of the population, either absolutely in relation to the available natural resources in the absence of technical progress, or relatively in relation to the rate of technical progress in the subsistence sector. The problem is that, except in the case of a purely peasant agriculture, the social gain from population restraint (in terms of average standard of living) is not reflected in private incentives to population limitation, since by assumption reduction of procreativity by any individual family will simply permit the survival of more children born to other families. A further interesting possibility is also neglected, though its implications in the model can easily be worked out – that improved medical care provided at public expense will reduce the level of the subsistence wage to which the population breeds.

Lewis's second assumption is the existence of a conventional margin of urban industrial wages over farm earnings. Part of the observed margin represents the higher real costs of urban as compared with rural life; this margin will be ignored in what follows. The artificial part of the margin can be explained in two major ways. The first is that rural labour obtains an average share of agricultural or subsistence sector output, including a share of the part attributable to the rent on natural resources. This explanation is dependent on the supplementary hypothesis either of a landowning peasant with an equalitarian family structure or of social restrictions on landlords requiring them to share some part of their rents with their tenants, and in either case is implausible as an approximation to the typical land-holding situation of the developing countries. Hence it will be ignored in what follows. The alternative explanation is that for various reasons the industrial sector finds it profitable to pay wages above the alternative opportunity cost of the relevant labour in the rural sector.

There are three types of reasons that may be mentioned, each having somewhat different implications. The first is that industry finds it worthwhile to pay a premium wage in order to have its pick of the available labour force to ensure maximum physical and mental efficiency of those workers it hires – the traditional 'economy of high wages' argument – or in order to maintain community and political goodwill, or to ensure the availability of a labour force large enough to satisfy its peak demands. These motivations are common enough in the industrial history of the western countries – witness labour practices on the docks and more recently in the automotive industry – not to occasion surprise in the less developed countries, where a reliable labour force is likely to be a far more economically advantageous industrial asset than in the advanced industrial countries given the comparatively much less reliable quality of the labour force in those countries. On this explanation, the industrial wage differential over the subsistence sector wage is a necessary economic cost of industrial efficiency in a backward environment, and its incidental effects in causing income inequality and unemployment are part of the price of economic development.

The second explanation is that some combination of the political power of organised labour and socialist ideas favouring trade unionism, 'fair' industrial wages, and social security insists that industrial labour be paid a wage (including fringe benefits in the form of 'decent' working conditions, and social security rights) above the alternative opportunity cost of labour from the subsistence sector. In this case the wage differential is not an economic cost of doing business in an underdeveloped economy, but a tax imposed by the political environment on the process of economic development.

The third explanation is that, as a legacy of past colonial rule, Civil Service pay scales and, in line with them, industrial pay scales, continue to be set at levels designed to attract educated Westerners into an uncomfortable expatriate existence. This case also involves a political tax on industrial development, but in this case a tax favouring the educated rather than the organised, one with more serious social and economic implications than the ones previously described. For the key to entry into this kind of pay system is education attainment, which involves a much smaller investment of resources for natives than for foreigners but nevertheless a substantial investment in local terms. The investment required places a demand on relatively scarce local capital resources that manifests itself politically as a demand both for free or subsidised provision of higher education on a level above the capacity of the economy to absorb its products, and for deterioration of educational standards to permit more candidates to obtain the formal qualifications demanded of job applicants, with the result that the educational product is excessive in quantity and on average deficient in quality, reflecting a misallocation of national resources. (By contrast, the monopoly privileges for acceptable members of the labour force discussed in the previous two cases involve discrimination among individuals and inequity of income distribution but not necessarily significant waste of resources in the determination of who deserves to belong to the restricted group of beneficiaries.) Further, both the sharp discrimination in income and social status between those who are marginal educational successes and obtain the high-paid jobs and those who are marginal educational failures and have to make do with inferior careers, and the presence in the society of both a body of students temporarily pampered by society but deeply worried about whether they will succeed or not, and in this state of mind critical and envious of those who have successfully passed the crucial educational test, and a body of educational failures educated beyond their necessary eventual status in life, is a potent source of political unrest. Even in advanced industrial societies, which have far more capacity to absorb and use people of diverse standards of university-level educational achievement, it has been evident that the combination of control of access to the better jobs by educational requirements with a 'democratic' provision of subsidised university education to those possessing the prior qualification for it makes the student body (or at least a substantial minority of it) a potential source of disruptive political activity. Whatever the reason for the conventional wage differential and hereafter I abstract from the higher costs of urban life, the real elements in the 'economy of high wages', and the cost of acquiring economically necessary educational qualifications – its effects are predictable from conventional economic theory, along two lines.

First, the conventional theory of production implies that entrepreneurs will choose a more capital-intensive and technology-intensive method of production than is appropriate to the true social alternative opportunity cost of labour. (An alternative way of putting this point, favoured by Harberger and explained below, is to say that the wage rate does, in fact, measure the alternative opportunity cost of labour in the economy, because of the unemployment the wage differential generates.) In consequence of this rational choice by entrepreneurs, there will naturally be dissatisfaction over the failure of industrial growth and investment in industrial capital to generate as much employment as expected, and complaints that the technology employed is inappropriate to local relative factor prices and demands that it be modified by one means or another so as to become more labour-intensive. In the popular mind, the entrepreneur's choice of technology is typically regarded as the result of a wilful slavishness to Western methods, on which he should be forced by political pressure to recant for the public good; at a more sophisticated level new technology is recognised to require an investment by someone which must somehow be paid for, and the obvious candidate (*vide* the Pearson Report) is Western development assistance. In neither case has the influence of labour pricing policies in choice of techniques been adequately appreciated.

Second, and more important because more subtle, the standard theory of choice under conditions of uncertainty implies that the conventional wage differential will necessarily create urban unemployment. Faced with a choice between a career in the subsistence sector, with a certain but low real income, and a chance of high-paid industrial employment carrying a risk of initial or recurrent unemployment, labour will tend to move from the subsistence sector into the industrial sector until the probability of unemployment in the latter sector rises to the point at which the average prospective net advantages of urban existence are no more attractive than those of existence in the subsistence sector. The equilibrium rate of unemployment required for this will depend on two factors. First, as the theory of choice under uncertainty has made clear, if the average labourer is a risk-averter, prepared to sacrifice prospective average income for the sake of security, the average expectation of income in the industrial sector, allowing for unemployment, must be higher than the subsistence wage; conversely, if the average labourer is a risk-lover, prepared to sacrifice expected income for the sake of a gamble on the chances of a high income, the average expectation of income in the industrial sector, allowing for unemployment, will be lower than the subsistence wage. One might venture the conjecture on the basis of the casual evidence of the literature on young men (and women) who leave the farm to seek their futures in the city, that in developing economies with a relatively small urban-industrial sector the industrial sector will be dominated by the risk-lovers. Second, the recently emerging theory of public goods suggests that occupational and locational choices are influenced not merely by private income opportunities but also by the availability of costless utility-yielding amenities and entertainments. Since the typical individual in a developing country cannot afford possession of the instruments of instant communication and mass transport – the telephone, the radio, television, and the private automobile – that enable people in the advanced countries to remain in touch with each other and with civilization while living remotely from each other, the attractions of urban life, in the form of availability of public contacts and entertainments of various kinds, are presumably much stronger in such a country than in the advanced countries. A further consideration in this respect is that city life offers a far more extended range of private choice in the expenditure of income than does life in the traditional subsistence sector, so that more utility may be derived from a smaller measured income than is obtainable in the subsistence sector. The implication of both these factors is that an industrial wage differential will generate far more urban unemployment in a developing country than it would in an industrially advanced country.

The central point in the foregoing analysis is the positive functional relationship between the industrial-subsistence sectoral wage differential and the unemployment rate. This has a direct implication for the question of inequality of income distribution, especially if one identifies politically relevant inequality with inequality as perceived by the urban population. The higher the wage differential, the larger the proportion of the urban population that is living on the strength of frustrated expectations of a relatively high income: the higher the wage differential, both the larger the number of the unemployed and the higher the income that they could have but do not – and also, the higher the cost to them of the luxury goods of industrial life.

There are other and more indirect, but still important, connections between the wage differential and the perceived inequality of income distribution. In order to construct a model of these, it is necessary to make further assumptions about industrial competition and industrial pricing. The simplest assumption to make is that government policy with respect to the protection and stimulation of industrial activity guarantees prices for industrial products sufficiently high to provide a certain minimum real return in the form of goods and services per unit of capital employed in the industrial sector. Both capitalists and workers in the industrial sector may be assumed to spend their incomes partly on industrial products, and partly on the direct or indirect products of the subsistence sector. (Note that this implicitly ignores the problem of subsistence sector demand for industrial goods.) The indirect products of the subsistence sector are conceived of as the services and product rendered within the urban sector by people who migrate from the rural sector and are prepared to work for regular wages at the subsistence sector level. The existence of these people involves a kind of multiplier relationship between the industrial labour force, employed and unemployed together, and the total urban labour force. More specifically, there is at any point of time a given stock of capital guaranteed its minimum rate of return in real terms; an employed industrial labour force, the number of which is determined by the capital stock and the industrial wage level (or the wage differential); an unemployed industrial labour force, determined by the wage differential and the labour supply preference factors previously discussed; and a service and handicraft urban sector determined by the proportions in which industrial capitalists and labour distribute the expenditure of industrial income among industrial products, urban non-industrial products and services, and subsistence sector goods. A higher wage differential implies no change in the real income of the capitalists; an increase in the real income but a reduction of the numbers of the industrially employed; an increase in the ratio of the industrially unemployed to the industrially employed; and through a shift of demand towards non-industrial goods and services induced by the rise in the price of industrial products consequent on the higher cost of industrial labour without a compensating reduction in capitalists' profits, an increase in the ratio of the non-industrial to the industrial urban labour force. The result must be, on most definitions of inequality, an increase in the perceived inequality of urban income distribution, because not only are capitalists' incomes unchanged and the incomes of the industrially employed increased but the ratio of the industrially unemployed and the urban non industrial subsistence wage labour force to the industrially employed increased. (The exceptional possibility is that because of a high elasticity of substitution between labour and capital in production in the industrial sector and a low elasticity of substitution between industrial and urban non-industrial goods in the consumption of capitalists and the industrially employed, the total numbers of unemployed workers and of these plus non-industrial urban workers falls.)

The foregoing analysis is couched in comparative static terms. The outline of an analysis of the effects of economic growth on technology, unemployment, and income inequality are, however, already clear, and can be briefly indicated. Sheer accumulation of capital, at a constant rate of return, technology and the wage differential remaining unchanged, will merely expand the industrial and urban sectors of the economy (and possibly also the subsistence sector, to the extent that its size depends on the urban demand for its products in exchange for industrial goods). However, what happens to the personal distribution of income and its inequality will depend on whether the accumulation of capital is the result of saving by existing capitalists or the emergence of new capitalists. The presumption in developing countries is that much of the accumulation of capital will be conducted by existing capitalists, so that economic development will involve mounting perceived disparities in the distribution of industrial income and income in general between capitalists and workers. On the assumptions that capital accumulation requires a rising income for capitalists per unit of capital invested, in order to induce them to undertake the increasing risks of investment in more ambitious industrial ventures, income inequality will increase unless the number of capitalists increases sufficiently faster than the amount of capital. On the assumption that capitalists enjoy a constant real income per unit of capital invested but that over time the wage differential is steadily increased, the result must be increasing inequality of income distribution, with the possible two exceptions previously mentioned, which involve either a high elasticity of substitution between labour and capital in the industrial sector or a low elasticity of substitution between industrial and subsistence urban goods, or third, a steady reduction in the average capital of the individual capitalist.

Technical progress of a general kind, on the assumption of a fixed wage differential and income per unit of capital invested, would tend to reduce inequality of income distribution in the urban sector in two ways; by increasing employment per unit of capital (though the unemployment ratio would remain constant) and by reducing the ratio of non-industrial urban labour to the industrial labour force through a reduction of the relative price of industrial goods as compared with the goods and services provided by the urban subsistence sector. At the other extreme, if industrial wages rose proportionately with technical progress, and industrial prices remained constant in terms of subsistence sector prices, the percentage of industrial unemployment would steadily rise, while the ratio of the urban non-industrial to the urban industrial labour force would remain constant, so that inequality would increase. More detailed examination of the effects of technical progress obviously requires a more precise examination of its nature, which is beyond the scope of the present essay.

The main conclusions that emerge from the analysis of this paper, with respect to the current problems of economic development, are as follows. First, contrary to the recommendations of Arthur Lewis, improvement in the technology of the subsistence sector is no solution, unless by 'improvement of productivity' is meant both an improvement in technology and the application of a population control policy sufficiently effective to translate that improvement into an increase in subsistence sector wages. In terms of greater equality of income distribution, subsistence sector wages must rise relative to industrial sector wages. Second, the recommendation of Raùl Prebisch and many others for an accelerated programme of industrialisation to provide more urban industrial employment will not solve the problem so long as population breeds to the level of subsistence. The only hope for a crash programme of industrialisation to succeed is that by temporarily raising subsistence sector incomes it will raise the long-run real supply of population (the minimum real wage in the subsistence sector), by inducing more stringent population control practices. Third, a determined effort to reduce the conventional industrial subsistence wage differential – which would require a reversal of important and deep-rooted political attitudes and industrial practices – could do much to mitigate the problems of urban unemployment and inequality of income distribution that currently trouble the developing world.

References

[1] LEWIS, W. ARTHUR, 'Economic Development with Un-limited Supplies of Labour', *The Manchester School*, XXII (May 1954), 139–91.

[2] KAHN, R. F., 'The Pace of Development', *The Challenge of Development* (Eliezer Kaplan School of Economics and Social Sciences, The Hebrew University of Jerusalem, 1958), 163–198.

8 Efficiency Wages, X-Efficiency, and Urban Unemployment

HARVEY LEIBENSTEIN*

Introduction

There is a basic asymmetry between returns to human and non human inputs. The essence of the asymmetry is that the wage *can* affect the efficiency of labour while the return to the owners of non human inputs, such as machines, buildings, or land, has no influence on the inputs' physical contributions. This distinction has a number of implications – some of which will be examined in this paper. The implication to be considered is the possibility that the effect of the rate of return of an input, on efficiency, may imply a lower boundary below which the return to the input owner cannot go, and as a consequence this limits the effectiveness of such a variable as a means of clearing a market. For instance, if there is a minimum wage then it is possible for that labour market never to come into 'equilibrium' because the wage cannot get low enough to equate the demand and supply for labour. This is similar to the idea of the liquidity trap when there is a floor to the interest rate. 'Efficiency wages' can operate in a similar manner.

The basic problem to be treated is the explanation of the pervasiveness of urban unemployment is developing countries. To use Kaldor's felicitous phrase, the following are the 'stylised facts' that we presume to hold: (*a*) there is a persistent positive rate of income growth in the country in question; (*b*) the wage rate in the urban sector is significantly higher than the wage in

* The author is Professor of Economics, Harvard University, Cambridge, Massachusetts. Research for this paper was done under N.S.F. grant No. GS–2400. The author is indebted to his research assistant, Mr Raul Schkolnick, for many helpful suggestions, and also to members of a seminar at the University of Toronto where an earlier version of this paper was presented. All errors and shortcomings are, of course, the author's responsibility.

the agricultural sector; (c) the degree of urban unemployment is considerable, say more than 10%; (d) there exists a moderate to high rate of population growth, say between 1.5–3% per annum. (e) the percentage of the labour force in agriculture is high, usually between 50–80%.

From the viewpoint of the textbook version of neoclassical theory this is a difficult set of circumstances to explain. Nor does Keynesian theory help. As far as one can judge, unemployment is not a consequence of a lack of aggregate demand. In fact, heavy rates of unemployment frequently persist side by side with high, if not quite galloping, rates of inflation. Nor is the kernel of an explanation found in a lack of significant rates of consumption. The lack of adequate rates of savings is probably one of the major causes of the inflation without seeming to contribute to the reduction of unemployment. The neoclassical theory would suggest that the unemployment would induce a reduction in the urban wage rate to the degree necessary (a) to move labour in the direction where employment expands and (b) to substitute more labour-using for less labour-using capital so that the end result is to wipe out unemployment. But this process does not appear to take place.

In reality, the causes of urban unemployment are complex, and the character of the problem differs to some extent from country to country. I shall treat only what appears to me to be a few of the salient features in most developing countries. It is hoped that the speculations and results that emerge may suggest hypotheses that are critical to the situation, and hopefully to suggest some of the important relations and conclusions that should be subjected to empirical investigation. This paper suggests the kernel of two possible explanations. Only empirical research can determine whether these explanations have any bearing on the real problem.

1. Efficiency Effects of Higher Wages

The terms 'wages' and 'labour' are used in a formal sense. By wages we have in mind the returns to all types of human inputs, whether or not these are normally classified as labour, management, or entrepreneurship.

The essential idea is that an increase (or decrease) in the wage may change some physical or psychological qualities of an individual or group of individuals so that his or their efficiency increases (or decreases). A clear-cut example is the relation between wages, diet, and labour productivity. An increase in wages may increase consumption, which in turn increases the calorie intake and physical strength. In occupations where strength is a significant quality in determining efficiency a relation between wages and productivity will exist. This relationship has been developed by the author elsewhere [2, chap. 6] and has been developed further by a number of other investigators. There are some obvious limits to this relation: (a) beyond a relatively low level of calories consumed an increase in calories will have relatively little influence on strength, and (b) beyond some level an increase in strength will have little or no effect on efficiency in most occupations. In this paper the physical basis of the wage/efficiency relationship will not be used. Instead, a psychological/attitudinal hypothesis will be posited.

In the X-efficiency theory developed elsewhere by the author [3] it was suggested that there are considerable variations of responses of individuals within different work settings. Hiring individuals and getting productivity out of them are two different things. Productivity per worker depends, in part, on the incentive elements within the work setting to which individuals respond. Part of these incentive elements is the payment system. Thus we may contrast at one extreme a payment system and employment setting which has no influence on productivity irrespective of the wage per worker. The tacit neoclassical assumption is that tasks are completely and clearly specified. The worker agrees to carry out predetermined and specified tasks at some given pace and the only aspects of choice are (a) whether or not the individual will be hired, and (b) at what wage. Since the tasks are presumed to be well specified the individuals's physical productivity is presumed to be clear-cut and determined. In equilibrium the labour market is cleared and the wage is equal to the value of the marginal product of labour. The point to note in the conventional theory is that the wage rate and productivity are independent of each other.

Labour economists and management specialists have examined the economics of various wage incentive schemes. But the labour economists' work has had no impact on economic theory. This may be because incentive wage systems can be interpreted as influencing only the unit on which the wage is made. If *A* produces twice as much as *B* per week, and *A* receives twice as much as *B*, the wage rate may be presumed to be the same in both cases. The significant unit is not labour per unit of time but *per piece of work*. There is no necessary presumption in this model that *A* would produce even more if his wage *per week* was increased. It is not that this possibility is not considered – it simply has not been the focus of attention. But this is an unduly limited interpretation of incentive wage systems.

At the other extreme we might consider a payments system in which there is a range of wages such that when we consider moving from some lower wage to a higher one the output increases more than proportionately. The significance of this possibility is that within the range, as wages increase, the cost per unit of output per worker actually declines. Even if we presume that both the worker and the employer fully understood the nature of this situation and were able to control the variables, they might still agree on a set of potential bargains so that this type of wage/productivity relation would result. In essence, it is similar to the worker offering the employer a quantity discount. Although the worker has to increase his effort level if he is to receive the higher wage, he may obtain more utility from the additional income than he foregoes on the increase in effort. The employer obviously gains by the fact that the labour cost per unit of output is less as the wages go up. There is, of course, no suggestion that this relation exists for all possible variations in the wage rate. It is sufficient for our purposes that it exists for some range of wages.

We can decompose work into three components: (*a*) *activities*, (*b*) *pace of effort*, (*c*) *the quality of the way in which the activities are carried out*. For ease in presentation we consider work as composed of Activity Pace Quality (A.P.Q.) bundles. Each worker either chooses his own A.P.Q. bundle or has this bundle chosen for him by someone in the firm. A major distinction is between *pre-set* A.P.Q. bundles and partially free choice bundles. In the pre-set case all aspects of work performance are determined in advance and the employee simply agrees whether or not to perform in the pre-set mould. Our hypothesis is that some complete or partial free choice A.P.Q. bundles are likely to be more efficient than pre-set bundles. Although pre-set bundles are possible, they are likely to be far from optimal. For instance, some activities may be carried out with a greater degree of precision than others, or with more care, or with greater attention to details. The employer can choose to specify the required A.P.Q. bundle. However, if this is not to be done arbitrarily then the managerial capacity and knowledge of techniques would have to be of a very high order indeed for the specified A.P.Q. bundles to approximate an optimal bundle set. The alternative is to allow the workers to learn on the job and to choose an appropriate A.P.Q. bundle. Whether workers choose well or not will depend on their overall capacities and the incentives they face in the work context. It seems likely that in most circumstances the employer may, with various degrees of explicitness, offer some categories of workers a higher wage provided they learn and carry out, as well as choose, A.P.Q. bundles that are superior to the ones the employer could specify in advance. Employees who explicitly or tacitly accept this bargain receive a higher wage in return for which they agree to work more effectively.

It might be argued that if the employer could set the specifications of the job then there is no reason why he could not require the same pace and set of activities at the lower wage rate rather than the higher one. One of two situations may result: (*a*) there may be no workers who cay carry out these tasks as specified, or (*b*) if workers are available, the A.P.Q. bundles so determined might not be optimal. In other words, there may exist an A.P.Q. bundle functionally connected with a wage productivity system which yields a lower cost per unit of output. This is especially likely to be true under conditions of production that require the dovetailing of activities between workers, responsiveness to factory discipline, a fairly high degree of punctuality, a lack of direct, close, supervision. The result of such an arrangement is a psychological efficiency wage.

2. The Day Labour Wage and Migration

It is frequently reported in developing countries that even at relatively low skill levels at least two categories of labour (usually many more than two) characterise the industrial sector. These are a type of day labour who are hired either for short periods and who do not have any type of 'permanent' contractual relationship, and a second class of 'contractual workers' of whom a higher degree of punctuality, discipline, etc. is expected, and who have to some extent internalised the firm's production interests, and who believe they will be kept on if the output level of the firm continues and if their performance is relatively satisfactory. It is not that the second group have an explicit contractual arrangement, although they may, but they do have a set of expectations about their continuing relationship with the firm which is very different from a day labourer's. The extreme of this second type of arrangement is the Japanese industrial system where workers once hired expect to remain with the firm for the rest of their lives. The implicit expectation of this type of a contract and the related and usually implicit obligations undertaken by employees may help to explain the very high levels of productivity of the Japanese labour force. They are, in a sense, accepting a trade-off of employment security for an unusually high degree of internalisation of the firm's production objectives. Employment security implies a higher wage per year even if the day wage is the same.

There are, of course, a number of other aspects of normal managerial and industrial organisation that operate in the same direction. For example, the mere fact of a hierarchical system of authority and responsibility leads to a hierarchical wage structure which may not depend on initial differentials of the employees involved. Those who choose to show that they are capable of carrying out activities involving a higher degree of responsibility choose a tacit bargain in which they are paid a higher wage although their actual capacities may be no different than workers at a lower level. The mere fact that a firm uses a selection system for promotion may require that higher wages be associated with a higher level in a hierarchy. It is probably no accident that this is almost universally the case.

We will simply assume that there are two categories of labour, say (*a*) day labour and (*b*) contract labour; and that contract labour receives a significantly higher wage than day labour. However, the initial characteristics of the two groups are similar in terms of education, I.Q., and so on.

The opportunity cost of a day labourer in moving to the industrial sector is closely connected to his consumption standard in the agricultural sector. This may be above his marginal product. Even if the marginal product in the agricultural sector is zero the worker still has a consumption level which he obtains out of his family's income.

We assume that the consumption standard is above the marginal product in agriculture, and that the lower limit to the day labour wage level is the consumption standard in agriculture.

The consumption level in agriculture is not the only element involved in the opportunity cost. The cost of living in towns or cities may be higher than in the countryside. On the other hand workers may find town or city life more attractive than life in the country and to some degree this may be an offsetting element. All these elements enter in the determination of the price necessary to attract a day labourer from agriculture.

3. A Partial Model

To limit the exposition to the essential aspects of the problem, and to keep the argument simple, a number of simplifying assumptions will be made. The main assumptions are:

(*a*) Since problems of aggregate demand are not critical we assume that Say's law is operative, and that supply in the aggregate creates its own demand. Thus our focus is on the supply elements;

(*b*) while the labour force grows as a consequence of population growth, we assume that all labour force changes occur at the beginning of the period and are included in the labour force stock at the beginning of the period;

(*c*) entries and exits into the work force are functions of age;

(*d*) all prices are presumed to adjust very rapidly to other changes and do not depend on scale of output. The product of each sector is priced in accordance with the formula that price is equal to cost per unit of output.

The real wage in agriculture, W_a, depends on the number of workers in the agricultural sector, N_a. Formally

$$W_a = f_a(N_a) \tag{1}$$

By the wage in agriculture we have in mind the real income given up by an individual if he moves to the industrial sector. We have already discussed the possible interpretation of this as the consumption level he gives up. This in turn may be greater than his marginal product. As the work force increases in the agricultural sector the per capita consumption standard and the real wage are assumed to fall. Since the number of workers in agriculture is determined by net migration, we have

$$W_a = F_1(M) \tag{1a}$$

where M is migration to the urban sector. The next basic relation is

$$W_u = BW_a, \quad \text{and} \quad B \geq 1 \tag{2}$$

W_u is the average wage in the urban sector. We assume that it is normally larger by some factor than the wage in the agricultural sector. If $B = 1 + b$, and $b \geq 0$, then b measures the premium (in percentage terms) over the agricultural real wage paid to workers in the urban sector.

In the interest of simulating reality to a slight degree, it may be helpful if we view the urban labour sector as composed of day labourers and contract labourers. The wage in the urban sector is a weighted average of the wage for day labour and the wage for contract labour so that

$$W_u = \alpha W_d + (1 - \alpha)W_c \tag{3a}$$

$$\alpha = F_3(K_u, T_i) \tag{3b}$$

where α takes into account the ratio of day labourers to contract labourers and the relative number of days worked by the two labour groups. α depends on capital (K_u) and technique (T_i) in the urban sector. Part of the motivation for separating urban workers into two categories will become apparent later when we discuss the efficiency wage theory. It is quite likely that the theory is much more applicable to the contract labour sector rather than the day labour sector.

The amount of employment in the urban sector depends on the amount of capital in the urban sector, the nature of the technique used, the urban wage rate and the net migration, M, to the urban sector. Since for the time being we assume that there is (*a*) a given technique and (*b*) a given stock and type of capital in operation, hence

$$N_u = F_4(W_u, M) \tag{4}$$

where N_u is the amount of employment in the urban sector. The allocation of total manpower between the two sectors is determined by the amount of net migration to the urban sector, M. Given such an allocation we obtain the wage level in agriculture, the wage level in the urban sector (Equation 2), and if the allocated manpower in the urban sector is greater than N_u we get the amount of unemployment in the urban sector.

M in the argument of Equation (4) is a proxy for urban product demand. We assume that reallocations of labour take place between industries in each sector so that there is an equilibrium of supply and demand for each commodity within each sector. However, there is the problem of intersectoral equilibrium since there is intersectoral trade, and households in each sector want goods not produced in that sector. The demand in each sector is determined by its own output (that is, sectoral aggregate income), the output in the other sector, and the relative prices of commodities in the sector, P_a and P_u. Since output in the agricultural sector is determined by employment (N_a) and since migration determines N_a, it follows that the demand from the agricultural sector depends essentially on the rate of migration. Since population growth in each sector is given exogenously, then for given prices P_a and P_u the rate of migration is the basic independent variable that determines demand.

Normally, we would expect urban migration to vary directly with net migration. That is,

$$\frac{\partial N_u}{\partial M} > 0$$

Migration out of agriculture raises the marginal product of labour in agriculture and food per capita in agriculture, and hence the demand for urban goods, which in turn increases the demand for labour in the urban sector.

In the interest of brevity we leave markets for goods off stage, as it were. We shall assume that given the change in the value of B, we can determine the change in the related price of urban goods. Also we assume the usual relation that N_u varies inversely with W_u. The inverse relation does not change even if we include the indirect price effects of an increase in W_u (i.e. an increase in W_u raises cost per unit and hence the price as well as the wage). But the effect of an increase in price is to reduce the demand for urban goods. Hence N_u varies inversely with W_u even if indirect price effects are included.[1]

On migration supply we assume that an individual will move from the agricultural to the urban sector if his mathematically expected income in the urban sector is greater than his real wage in the agricultural sector, inclusive of adjustments for risk aversion, the relative probabilities (over time) of obtaining the more desired contract labour jobs, his assessment of these probabilities – and 'city lights' preferences, that is, the extent to which, if any, workers would prefer the city to the countryside even if the wage and employment conditions were equal. Our assumption of the motivations behind migration is similar to, but simpler than, the highly sophisticated models of migration supply developed earlier by Todaro and Harris.[2,3]

The essence of the argument at this point boils down to two

---

[1] If we write $N_u = f\left(\dfrac{W_u}{P_u}\right)$ and interpret W_u as a money wage when

$\left(\dfrac{W_u}{P_u}\right)$ is the real wage, the argument still holds since a change in the wage must result in a less than proportional change in the price P_u since the wage is only a portion of the price. Hence, the real wage cannot fall as W_u rises. In the extreme case where the good contains only labour as an input, prices and money wages rise proportionately and the real wage does not fall.

[2] When I wrote an earlier version of this paper I did not know of the important article by Todaro [4] which works out in considerable detail the migration supply theory in terms of the variables that determine the mathematically expected value of the urban wage rate.

[3] The paper by J. R. Harris and N. P. Todaro also contains the assumption that the flow of migration between the rural and urban sector depends on the mathematically expected value of the urban wage rate. However, my 'solution' to the problem differs from that presented by Harris and Todaro. Their solution depends on a politically determined urban minimum wage. This would not account for similar deviations between urban and rural wage levels and the persistence of urban unemployment in situations where politically determined minimum urban wages do not exist, or where there are well developed techniques for bypassing legal minimum wages [1] [4].

equations with three unknowns. These are

$$M_s = f_s(E, B); \quad E \le 1, \quad B \ge 1 \tag{5}$$

$$M_d = f_d(E, B) \tag{6}$$

M_s stands for the amount of migration supplied to the urban sector during the period, and M_d is a type of 'migration demand'.

Equation (6) is derived from Equation (4), which we restate below,

$$N_u = F_4(B, M) \tag{4a}$$

where M is a given amount of net migration per period and from the definition of the employment rate

$$E = \frac{N_u}{L_c + M} \tag{7}$$

where L_o is the labour force in the urban sector at the beginning of the period. Note that if M is given, then W_a is determined by Equation (1a). Hence, we can substitute appropriate values of B for given values of W_u, and vice versa, if M is given.

The 'migration demand' function has a slightly complex interpretation and depends on the demand for labour. In essence Equation (6) says that for every value of B and E there is a quantity of labour demanded in the urban sector, N_u, which in turn determines the employment rate E (through Equation 7) and the related consistent migration rate $\bar{M}$. In other words, for every given value of B and E there is a value of the migration rate, M_d, which is consistent with the functionally related amount of employment, N_u.

The nature of the analysis is illustrated in Figure 8.1 opposite. The curves M_{s1}, M_{s2}, M_{s3}, etc. are migration supply isoquants. Each point of M_{s1} indicates the various values of B and E that would yield the same migration rate.

The curves M_{d1}, M_{d2}, M_{d3}, etc. reflect the required migration consistent with the employment function in Equation (4). Each point on the curve M_{d1} is to be interpreted in the following way. For the given rate of migration M_{d1}, and a given value of B, we obtain a value of the derived employment level N_u from Equation (4a), and we then compute the related value of E from Equation (7).

Thus, the point marked x_2 indicates that for the migration level M_{d1} and the value of the wage multiplier B_2, the employment demanded that would result would lead to a related employment rate E_2. All other points on M_{d1} are obtained in a similar fashion. Of course, parallel procedures are used to obtain points on M_{d2}, M_{d3}, etc. and the locus of intersections between the isoquants M_{d1}, M_{d2}, etc. and the M_{s1}, M_{s2}, etc. form a set of

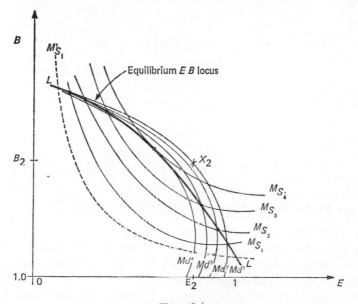

FIG. 8.1

potential migration equilibrium points. That is, each point is a pair of values for B and E for which the migration flow to the urban sector and the labour employed are consistent with each other and with the implicit mathematically expected value of the urban wage rate including adjustments for risk aversion, and other preferences.

In Figure 8.2 the locus of migration equilibrium points is redrawn apart from the isoquants that produced the locus. Looking at the equilibrium locus from the lower right to the upper left, note that at first migration rates increase and beyond some point, where the equilibrium migration rate is a maximum, the migration rates decline.

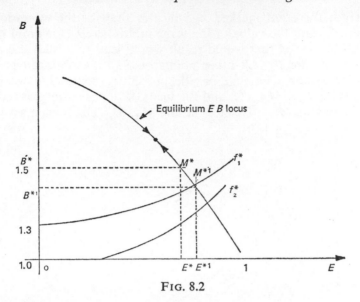

FIG. 8.2

4. Can There Be an Unemployment Equilibrium?

The critical question is whether unemployment in the urban sector can drive the urban wage BW_a below any value for $B > 1$. In the neoclassical mode of analysis we would presume that an unemployed individual would be willing to offer himself at a lower wage than the going wage, and that employers would be willing to recontract at this lower wage. This is part of the more general mode of analysis which says that an excess supply forces the price to fall, and that an equilibrium price can exist only when the excess supply is zero. But this is only one mode of analysis. Our purpose is to suggest alternative ways of looking at the matter.

In actual fairly competitive markets excess supplies frequently exist for long periods without affecting price. For example, in many instances hotels are never fully occupied but a given price range persists despite less than 100% occupancy. Similarly, in many types of transportation 100% occupancy is rarely achieved but price remains unaffected. Various forms of entertainment, such as cinemas, persist in the less than complete utilisation of all seats without price reductions. In a similar vein we can readily expect less than full utilisation of a labour force without prices necessarily falling. The question that has to be raised is whether there is really any impelling reason for any employer to lower the wage simply because unemployment exists.

(1) Under full employment we would expect the day wage to be above the agricultural wage in order to attract labour from the agricultural sector. But if unemployment exists a lower wage will suffice to attract labour since the unemployed labour is available.

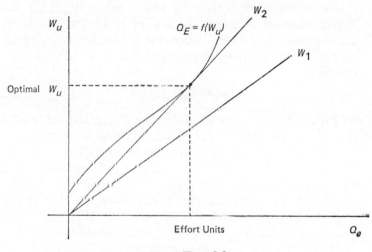

FIG. 8.3

(2) An alternative solution is to assume that the average urban wage is an efficiency wage. The efficiency wage could exist entirely apart from unemployment. While unemployment might affect the level of the efficiency wage, its impact might still be relatively minor. Thus we shall see that the interpretation of the urban wage as an efficiency wage is consistent with unemployment.

First let us consider the case in which the wage-effort relation is independent of the employment rate. A possible wage/effort relation in the urban sector is shown in Figure 8.3 above. Quality/effort units are shown on the ordinate and the wage in terms of values of B is shown on the abscissa. The rational employer wants to minimise the cost per effort unit and not the cost per man employed. In Figure 8.3 the minimum cost per effort unit is reached at the point at which the wage effort function Q_e is tangent to the lowest wage ray from the origin. In Figure 8.2 this is at the point where the value of $B = 1\cdot5$. $B = 1\cdot5$ becomes the equilibrium value of B irrespective of the rate of unemployment, and the related values of E and M become the equilibrium values of these variables. These values are indicated in Figure 8.2 as B^*, E^* and M^*.

Even if we assume that the urban wage W_u is an efficiency wage, it is not necessary to make the restrictive assumption that the rate of unemployment has no influence on the optimum urban wage multiplier B. Thus we have a relation

$$\text{opt. } B = f_1^*(E) \tag{8}$$

In Figure 8.2 the optimal multiplier B (i.e. the value of B that minimised the cost per effort unit) and E are related so that B falls as unemployment increases, but it falls to a lower bound which is greater than unity, say to $B = 1\cdot3$. In other words, the influence of unemployment on the optimal wage premium exists but it is not sufficiently important to wipe out the wage premium. If in this case a lower bound for $B > 1$ exists for successively lower values of E, then this lower bound could become the equilibrium value $B^{*\prime}$. Or, as illustrated in Figure 8.2, the intersection of f_1^* and the equilibrium EB locus determines $B^{*\prime}$ and the related equilibrium values $E^{*\prime}$ and $M^{*\prime}$.

Even if the relation between B and E does fall at a point so that for very low values of E we obtain a B equal to 1 as shown in Figure 8.2, for the function f_2^* we may still obtain an equilibrium value of $B > 1$. This could come about because the equilibrium EB locus in Figure 8.2 intersects f_2^* at a value of $B > 1$. Thus, even in this case there is the possibility of unemployment and an urban wage above the agricultural wage coexisting side by side.

One more wrinkle to be considered is the possible connection between the wage/effort relation and the shape of the equilibrium *EB* locus in Figure 8.2. On the basis of the wage/effort relation the equilibrium *EB* locus can have a range for which some values of *E* increase as values of *B* increase. The reason for this possibility is that as *B* increases the cost per effort unit falls, and the demand for effort units increases while the price per unit of product falls. It is possible that up to a point the elasticity of demand for the product, and the elasticity of substitution of labour for capital, are sufficiently high so that sufficiently more effort units are demanded (in proportion to the increase in efficiency) to require an absolute increase in demand for labour to produce these additional effort units. Beyond some point we would expect the elasticity of substitution and the product demand elasticity to fall so that the rising demand for labour is reversed.

(3) A final and perhaps most important possibility consistent with unemployment would be the introduction of inertial elements. In my *X*-efficiency theory the concept of an inert area is employed. An inert area is a set of bounds for the values of a variable within which decision makers do not change their decisions. In this particular case we would presume that the equilibrium wage W_u^* for a value of $B > 1$, say for $B = 1 \cdot 3$, falls within the inert wage range for every employer. In general the reason that an inert area exists is that any change within the inert bounds implies a gain (in utility terms) that is less than the cost (also ultimately in utility terms) necessary to introduce the change. Hence, potential changes for which the relative gains and losses fall within the inert area are not introduced. Behaviour of this type is by no means irrational. In the real world there is a considerable disruptive cost in changing the overall wage rate. The question is not whether an additional employee is hired at a lower wage than the existing employees, but whether the fact that an additional employee is willing to work for a lower wage will make it worthwhile for the employer to recontract the wage level to a lower level for all existing employees. In addition to the protests on the part of the employees, and the possible ill will generated by such a procedure, there may be other costly consequences. Some employees might seek other jobs. Costs of hiring and

training replacements have to be considered. More important, the remaining employees might choose to reduce their effort level as a form of silent protest against the wage reduction. Thus, all things considered it is reasonable to presume that there will exist an inert area so that for the existing wage level the employer will not attempt to recontract to a lower level. The expected advantage would not be worth the cost of doing so. Thus, an additional equilibrium condition is that W_u^* be in the inert areas of all existing or potential employers.

It may appear at first blush that new employers have an advantage since they can hire low wage labour and they do not have to recontract. But a similar argument to that which exists for old employers could still be invoked. The work standards in the industry would become known. The employees in the low wage firms would discover that they work as hard for less pay and (*a*) would either demand higher wages, or (*b*) reduce their effort standard to show their resentment for their mistreatment compared to those who work for higher-wage firms. The end result need be no different in effect than that which we attributed to existing employers. In other words, the new employers in a sense have to adopt the same inert area with respect to the going industry wage rate as the old employers.

There is nothing inconsistent between the efficiency wage idea of a psychological type and the inert area idea. They are, in fact, complementary ideas. If employers see the urban wage as an efficiency wage they will not reduce it despite the fact that workers appear to be offering themselves at a lower wage. They know from practical experience that this is an inefficient alternative. In fact, the psychological efficiency wage idea and the employers' inert area idea should be seen as two sides of the same coin – two possibilities based on similar psychological-economic processes.

Thus we end up with two alternative theories that attempt to explain why the urban wage should be above the rural wage despite the existence of unemployment. This is in essence a short-run analysis. We leave for another occasion the longer-range problems as to why labour saving technology is not introduced as capital is replaced so that the unemployed are gradually absorbed and the urban unemployment level reduced.

References

[1] HARRIS, J. R. and TODARO, M. P., 'Migration, Unemployment and Development: A Two Sector Analysis', *American Economic Review*, LX (March 1970), 126–142.

[2] LEIBENSTEIN, HARVEY, *Economic Backwardness and Economic Growth*, New York: J. Wiley and Sons, 1957.

[3] LEIBENSTEIN, HARVEY, 'Organisational or Frictional Equilibria, X-Efficiency and the Rate of Innovation', *Quarterly Journal of Economics*, LXXXIII (November 1969), 600–623.

[4] TODARO, M. P., 'A Model of Labor Migration and Urban Unemployment in Less Developed Countries', *American Economic Review*, LIX (March 1969), 138–148.

9 Dependent Monetary Systems and Economic Development: The Case of Sterling East Africa

JOHN M. LETICHE*

THE monetary systems of the former British territories have highly varied histories, but their fundamental features are the same. They have a common structural pattern because they all emerged from a larger currency and banking system of which the United Kingdom was the centre.

The currency history of each region reflects its more general politicoeconomic history, and the direction of its principal economic and trading relationships was the most important factor determining the larger monetary system to which it belonged. Each colonial territory tended to adopt the form of money actually belonging to or closely dependent on that of the country with which it conducted the greater part of its trade. As that trading relationship shifted, the territory's monetary association underwent a corresponding change.

On the technical side, there was a steady strengthening of conscious governmental control over the monetary systems. First, a variety of coins and other media of exchange circulated. These moneys were usually locally available and they appealed to the taste or convenience of the population. Then came a period of consolidation with the establishment of a single unit or series of coins as virtually the sole 'monetary standard' of the country.

* University of California at Berkeley. Aid from the Institute of International Studies, University of California, Berkeley, is gratefully acknowledged, particularly for the research assistance of K. Y. Amoako and Henri Vandendriessche. It is also a pleasure to acknowledge the intellectual stimulus and careful reading of this paper by the following friends and colleagues: Richard S. Eckaus, Howard S. Ellis, Robert A. Gordon, Sung Y. Kwack, Abba P. Lerner, Neil J. Smelser, Benjamin H. Ward and Paul Zarembka.

The third period witnessed the issue of private banknotes, or government paper money. These notes gradually displaced coins except for subsidiary use, although in some regions of Africa this process was (and still is) extremely slow. At first, the notes were convertible on demand into local legal tender; they were 'backed' by reserves containing a large portion of actual coin.

In the fourth period, notes further replaced coin except for small change, but in most cases the notes themselves were no longer convertible into local coin. With a few exceptions, they were only convertible into sterling in London.

The fifth or current period is distinguished by the fact that practically all the colonial territories have achieved their political independence. As a consequence, the former British territories in Africa established their own central banks and related financial institutions.[1]

These monetary systems, however, are still and will continue for many years to be subsidiary or dependent financial systems in the primarily nonpolitical sense that these countries have not as yet succeeded in developing truly independent monetary systems of their own; they are part of the larger sterling area system. An appraisal of the objectives and workings of these dependent monetary systems before independence is therefore indispensable for an understanding of the African reaction against monetary colonialism, as well as of the present structure and policies of the new central banks.

1. Operating Rules of Currency Boards

The key monetary institution of the colonial territories was the Currency Board. In West and East Africa the legal status of the authority was created by an executive act of the Colonial Secretary, with the Board's domicile originally situated in

[1] Kenya, Tanzania and Uganda established independent central banks in 1966, replacing the East African shilling by their national shillings. Tanganyika had achieved independence in 1961 and Zanzibar in 1963, combining to form Tanzania in 1964; Uganda gained independence in 1962, and Kenya in 1963. For surveys of these economies, see: [16, chaps 7–9].

London.[2] Although the institution varied in outward forms, in legal status, and in domicile in different colonial territories – and its constitution was revised with changes in circumstances – the essence of the system was the interchangeability of local currency with sterling at a fixed rate of exchange and the 'automaticity' of monetary adjustment to international disturbances.

As regards interchangeability, the Currency Boards had the responsibility of issuing coin and notes locally on demand against an equivalent amount of sterling paid to the relevant Board in London, and of redeeming coin and notes locally on demand against the Board's payment of an equivalent amount of sterling in London. The Board's obligation to issue or redeem applied to transactions at its currency centres, e.g. for East Africa in Dar es Salaam, Jinja, Nairobi, Aden, and Zanzibar.[3] The commission rates at which the Currency Boards operated governed the rates charged to the public by the banks. But the Currency Boards had no power to alter the rate of exchange between the local currency and sterling. In most instances, their rates were fixed long ago on the basis of the then prevailing metallic face values. With the exception of brief periods after the First World War, they remained stable in terms of sterling until the devaluation of the pound in November, 1967. Their

---

[2] The circumstances leading to the creation of these monetary systems are given in the original 'Report of the West African Currency Board' for the period ended 30th June, 1914, pp. 2–5, with Appendix I (p. 9), defining the Constitution, Duties, and Powers of the Board. For excellent discussions on the colonial period, see: [18], [21], [14], [20]. While my own formulation is based on primary data and owes much to consultations with African monetary officials during personal visits in 1962, 1964, and 1969 to almost every African country, I have greatly benefited from the literature cited above and from the following studies: [22], [24], [17], [4], [2], [10], and [19].

[3] This was unconditional apart from two minor qualifications: the Board was permitted to charge a small commission on transactions either way, but no higher than a fixed maximum, and it stipulated a minimum figure for currency issued or redemptions in which it dealt. This minimum assured that normal business transactions passed through the commercial banks. According to law, the Currency Board was obligated to deal with the public on demand for amounts over the prescribed minimum sums. In practice, it dealt almost entirely with the banks.

values in terms of other currencies had therefore changed only with changes in the international value of sterling.

Automaticity of the system was possible only because the Currency Board did not act as a central bank. When capital imports, domestic investment, production, and exports rose, businessmen in the territory required larger amounts of coin and notes. They obtained the additional currency from the local banks. The banks, in turn, got the currency from the Board. In effect, the Board expanded the quantity of local currency by telegraphic authorisation of the issue of coin and notes against the receipt of sterling balances in London. The sterling received may either have belonged to the banks – if they themselves were financing increased transactions – or have been transmitted on behalf of their customers.

Normally, the process of expansion took place during the export season when there was demand for more local currency due to local 'prosperity', and when the surplus in the Balance of Payments automatically provided additional sterling, which was then converted to local currency by the locally domiciled exporters. However, the economic expansion itself brought about an increase in local purchases of imported goods, as well as enlarged foreign remittances. The Balance of Payments surplus thus tended to be checked As the seasonal fall in production occurred, redemptions of currency would tend to exceed new issues as the demand for local currency declined, and as the Balance of Payments was reversed from surplus to deficit. The forces of monetary contraction, in turn, would tend to check the deficit and once again set into operation the mechanism of adjustment leading toward equilibration of the international accounts. This is reportedly how the payments mechanism normally worked, but after the Second World War It changed considerably.

Clearly, the currency board system had the task of rigidly relating changes in quantity of money in circulation to the Balance of Payments. It was believed that by keeping the territories 'in step' with their trading partners the system achieved a cardinal objective – external equilibrium through adjustment to disturbances in the level of exports and imports. But such a system precluded an active monetary policy on the part of the colonial government; Currency Boards had no responsibility whatsoever for carrying out a monetary policy directed at price stability, development, or growth. Each Currency Board maintained a Currency Reserve Fund in sterling. All sterling received by the Board was paid into this fund. The Crown Agents for Overseas Governments and Administrations normally acted as the Currency Board's agents in London.[4] A portion of the fund was held in bank balances and other assets of undoubted liquidity; practically the entire remainder was invested in sterling securities, mainly those of the United Kingdom. Also approved under the regulations were securities issued by other governments of countries in the Commonwealth – including, to a limited extent, those of the Currency Board countries themselves – and by United Kingdom municipalities and corporations. The assets of the fund could be used only to meet redemptions of currency, to purchase metal for minting into coin, to pay the fees of managers and currency agents, to meet incidental operating expenses, and to make authorised distributions to the member nations. The authorised distributions were made only when the assets in the fund exceeded a level sufficient to ensure full convertibility of the notes and coin issued and to provide a 'reasonable reserve' [*sic!*] against depreciation of securities and other contingencies. Disbursements were usually made only when the assets in the fund exceeded 110% of the liabilities! The portions paid to the participating governments were revised from time to time by agreements between them. In the last resort, the participating governments were jointly liable to meet the obligations of the Currency Board if at any time its assets should be inadequate to meet legal demands for conversion of local currency into sterling.

[4] In the field of trade and finance, the 'crown agents' have been a complex, controversial group. They have no formal constitution, are not a part of the United Kingdom Civil Service or of the United Kingdom Government machinery, but operate as a small number of individuals who have been appointed by the Secretary of State for Oversea Governments and Administrations on terms decided by him. The 'Office' serves as a nonprofit making institution, furnishing quotations and arranging deliveries throughout the commonwealth (and elsewhere) on hundreds of thousands of contracts ranging from aircraft and engineering installations to postage stamps and serums. See: [1, esp. pp. 1–4, 72, 83–94].

2. The Role of Commercial Banks

While the Currency Boards in Africa could not make any decisions of substance on monetary or banking policy before independence (and even up to their termination), the commercial banks played an indispensable role in the functioning of the Currency Boards and supplied the countries with the benefits of a well-developed banking organisation. Broadly speaking, they could be separated into two groups: (*a*) the overseas banks and (*b*) the indigenous banks.

The overseas banks consisted primarily of branches of United Kingdom banks with head offices in London. They did (and, in most cases, still do) the preponderant volume of banking business, as measured by deposits or by the value of loans and advances. Other overseas banks with head offices in India, the Netherlands, the United States, France, Belgium, and so forth were also represented. As a group, the overseas banks contributed greatly to the efficiency and stability of the banking business. They drew on non-African resources in periods of short-term financial strain and were important in financing and extending African trade through their world-wide connections. But their purely *local* banking business developed rather slowly. Whatever their nationality or seat of control, they were tied, with unimportant exceptions, to the United Kingdom system by the fact that they kept their main reserves invested in sterling assets.

The indigenous banks conducted only a small fraction of the total transactions; most were concerned primarily with domestic banking and were largely national and local in character.

3. The Working of the System

The monetary and banking systems of the African countries in the sterling area developed in a more complex manner than would be assumed from the rules of the Currency Boards. They did not work in accordance with many of the positive claims of their proponents or some of the negative criticisms of their critics. The record of the annual rate of increase, or decrease, of the total currency in circulation in East Africa – Kenya,

TABLE 9.1 *Compounded Annual Rate of Increase or Decrease (−) of Total Currency (Notes and Coin) in Circulation in East Africa; 1913–65**

Selected years – in percentages

Period	Compounded annual rate of increase or decrease
1913–61	8·5
1925–61	6·3
1925–38	0·8
1925–28	−4·1
1928–32	−8·5
1930–39	3·5
1932–38	10·5
1939–45	18·6
1946–61	6·3
1946–57	9·1
1957–61	−0·7
1961–65	5·5 (a)

Sources: Annual Reports of the East African Currency Board (E.A.C.B.), data for 1913, Archives of the E.A. Statistical Department; for 1925–32, Sir Sydney Caine, 'Monetary Systems of the Colonies', The Banker (1948), pp. 16–17; and the Bank of England. For 1953–62, Tanganyika's Statistical Abstract, 1963, p. 102 The figure for 1913 is based on an estimate of the East African Statistical Department.

(a) Official estimates of currency in circulation in East Africa were discontinued after 1962. The rate for 1961–65 is for the Currency Board Area as a whole, which in that period included Aden in addition to the three East African countries.

* East Africa for purposes of this Table comprises Kenya, Tanzania (Tanganyika and Zanzibar) and Uganda. East Africa currency circulated in Kenya, Tanganyika, Uganda, Zanzibar, British Somaliland, and the Aden Protectorate. The shilling currency was introduced into Kenya, Tanganyika, and Uganda in 1922; and into Zanzibar in 1935; and into Somalia, Eritrea, British Somaliland, and Ethiopia at various dates subsequent to 1941, and withdrawn from Ethiopia in 1945, and from Somalia and Eritrea during 1949 and 1950. In October 1951 it was made legal tender in the Aden Protectorate, and was withdrawn from former British Somaliland in April–June 1961. It was withdrawn from Aden in October 1964–December 1967. The E.A.C.B. notes, and coins, ceased to be legal tender in East Africa in 1967 and 1969, respectively. For conversion operations see East Africa Currency Board, *Report for the Year Ended 30th June 1966*. Nairobi: Printing and Packaging Corporation, Ltd., n.d.; *op. cit.* for the years 1969–70; the Southern Yemen (formerly Aden) Currency Authority, *Report for the Years 1967 and 1968*. London: Balbik Systems Ltd, n.d., pp. 26–30. See also *The Final Report of the East African Currency Board*, 1972.

Tanzania, and Uganda – is summarised in Table 9.1. Three conclusions are evident from the data.

(1) In the long run, the widespread view (including Keynes') to the contrary notwithstanding, the East African Currency Board system did not operate in a restrictive manner. From 1913 to 1961, the annual rate of increase of the total *currency* in circulation was 8·5%, and from 1946 to 1961 it was 6·3%.

(2) In shorter periods, the volume of currency fluctuated greatly, with perhaps a high rate of decrease from 1925 to 1928 and of increase from 1939 to 1945 – to say nothing of the 'great contraction' from 1928 to 1932. From 1925 to 1938, the annual rate of increase was 0·8% – definitely restrictive – and from 1939 to 1945 it was 18·6% – a wartime-induced phenomenon.

(3) The Currency Board system strongly reflected not only the expansions and contractions of East Africa's international payments resulting from fluctuations in the world and domestic economy, but also the instabilities related to the coming of independence. Thus, from 1957 to 1961, a period during which the rest of the world economy was expanding, there actually occurred an annual rate of *decrease* in the currency stock of 0·7%.

In the private sector, from 1957 until the achievement of independence (and, indeed, until the announced dissolution of the East African Currency Union in 1965), variations in the *total* stock of money – currency plus deposits – were inversely correlated with variations in the total external assets of the Currency Board *and* the commercial banks. This inverse relationship occurred in every year but one, 1959, a rise in the quantity of money being associated with a decline in external assets, and conversely. The two components of the stock of money behaved differently: variations in the quantity of currency in circulation were positively correlated, whereas variations in demand deposits were negatively correlated, with variations in total external assets. The only exception in regard to the positive correlation of changes in currency in circulation and changes in external assets occurred in 1964/1965, a year in which the Currency Board for the first time adopted countervailing measures. Fluctuations in the East African currency, but not in the total quantity of money, were therefore generally consistent with the rules of the Currency Board system – an orthodox mechanism of adjustment whereby *changes* in the volume of currency were directly brought about by the Balance of Payments and therefore positively correlated with it – a positive Balance of Payments increasing the currency and vice versa.

Variations in demand deposits, on the other hand, were not only negatively correlated with variations in external assets, but they were so large in magnitude that they overbalanced the fluctuations in the currency, thereby bringing about the overall negative correlation between changes in the total stock of money and changes in external assets. Private demand deposits, however, and government demand deposits behaved differently. From 1957 to 1965, both *private* demand deposits and overseas banks' balances in East Africa declined. This simultaneous decline was associated, in part, with capital flight. But the banks ran down their overseas balances to a much greater extent than private demand deposits were reduced. The difference in the banks' utilisation of their total external assets and the reduction in private demand deposits was approximately equal to the banks' net creation of credit through an increase in their loans, and advances, and bills discounted by the private sector of the economies. From 1957 to 1963, this expansion of credit exceeded the increase of private time and savings deposits by about £17 million. The ratio of the banks' private advances to private deposits rose from 72·2% in 1957 to 106·7% in 1965. Large increases in government deposits, on the other hand, found their immediate counterpart in banks' loans to governments. The important fact is that from 1957 until the dissolution of the Board in 1965, the total stock of money in East Africa increased while the sum of external assets of the Currency Board and commercial banks declined. This occurred before the governments of East Africa established their independent central banks. In effect, the East African monetary and banking system long consisted of a comparatively modern private banking structure which developed side by side with a comparatively orthodox 'dependent currency' structure. In a rudimentary way, the private banking structure acted like a central bank, i.e., like a monetary authority.

As shown in Table 9.2, the evidence demonstrates that for the

TABLE 9.2 *Regression Analysis: Logarithmic Relations
in Monetary Terms*
(Current Prices)
Symbols Used in Tables

E = East Africa
K = Kenya
T = Tanzania (Mainland)
U = Uganda
Y^i = G.D.P. (monetary and subsistence sectors) of ith region
X^i = Value of ith's exports
T^i = Terms of trade of ith's region
D^i = Demand deposits of ith's region
M^i = Value of ith's imports
 i = E, K, T, U
X_{-1} = Exports in the previous year

TABLE 9.2(*a*) *East Africa, 1954–63*

Dependent variables	Constant term	Regression coefficients of (and standard error)					
		X^E	X^E_{-1}	T^E	D^E	Y^E	R^2
Y^E	1·94	0·92* (0·14)					0·84
Y^E	1·92		0·91* (0·09)				0·91
Y^E	11·73			−1·23* (0·26)			0·73
Y^E	5·57				0·16 (0·47)		0·01
M^E	3·34					0·24 (0·20)	0·14
T^E	7·44	−0·64* (0·09)					0·86

* Variable significant at 5 % level. Many variables having been omitted, it should be expected that errors are correlated to each other. The D.W. statistics are, in effect, generally lower than hoped for, ranging from 0·6 to 2·1. In the presence of serial autocorrelations, the standard error of regression coefficients might, of course, be understated.

TABLE 9.2(b) *Kenya, 1954–63*

Dependent variables	Constant term	Regression coefficients of (and standard error)					
		X^K	X^K_{-1}	T^K	D^K	Y^K	R^2
Y^K	3·70	0·49* (0·05)					0·91
Y^K	3·66		0·49* (0·06)				0·87
Y^K	11·12			−1·30* (0·25)			0·76
Y^K	7·06				−0·45 (0·49)		0·09
M^K	2·94					0·23 (0·20)	0·13
T^K	5·45	−0·30* (0·05)					0·77

* Variable significant at 5 % level.

TABLE 9.2(c) *Tanzania (Mainland), 1954–63*

Dependent variables	Constant term	Regression coefficients of (and standard error)					
		X^T	X^T_{-1}	T^T	D^T	Y^T	R^2
Y^T	1·84	0·88* (0·16)					0·78
Y^T	2·13		0·79* (0·12)				0·83
Y^T	1·57			0·79 (1·01)			0·07
Y^T	3·65				0·52* (0·17)		0·52
M^T	2·44					0·23 (0·20)	0·13
T^T	4·38	0·04 (0·11)					0·01

* Variable significant at 5 % level.

TABLE 9.2(d) *Uganda, 1954–63*

Dependent variables	Constant term	Regression coefficients of (and standard error)					
		X^U	X^U_{-1}	T^U	D^U	Y^U	R^2
Y^U	4·39	0·16 (0·31)					0·03
Y^U	3·50		0·40 (0·28)				0·19
Y^U	6·79			−0·41* (0·08)			0·76
Y^U	5·53				−0·21 (0·14)		0·21
M^U	2·31					0·20 (0·40)	0·03
T^U	6·45	−0·57 (0·63)					0·09

* Variable significant at 5 % level.

period 1954 to 1963, variations in demand deposits were generally not an important source of variations in GDP. This result holds both for East Africa as a whole and for Kenya, and Uganda, considered separately (although not for Tanzania).[5] Moreover, variations in the total quantity of money – currency plus demand deposits – and variations in GDP were more highly correlated than variations only in deposits and GDP. This conclusion bears out, indirectly, the results to be expected from the operation of the Currency Board System.[6]

[5] In 1963, the termination of the Currency Board was announced. Furthermore, in 1964 there were expectations that the Board would soon be brought to an end, causing much uncertainty and capital flight. Thus the data for the regressions in Table 9.2 were used only until 1963. Regressions performed for data up to 1965, with a dummy variable for 1964 and 1965, yielded similar results.

[6] During the transitional period of independence, understandably, several indexes of monetisation declined, but thereafter they continued their upward trend. For the three countries, from 1960–1965, currency as a percentage of money supply (including time and savings deposits) fell from 38–33%, and currency plus demand deposits as a percentage of G.D.P. in the monetary sector rose from 17–18%. Further, e.g. in Kenya, money supply (including time and savings deposits) as a percentage of G.N.P. rose from 24·1% in 1967 to 26·9% in 1969. For compounded rates of growth in monetary, trade and G.D.P. variables in East Africa, selected periods, 1946–1965, see Table 9.4. See also [15], and for international comparative data (but not for East Africa), see: [11] and [12, pp. 168–171].

4. From Currency Board to Central Bank

From approximately 1955 to 1965, the East African Currency Board extended, to a very limited degree, its operations to include functions that are normally attributed to a central bank. This transition from a currency board to central bank was regarded by the Board as a means of assisting in the establishment of an East African Central Bank and in preserving one currency for the entire region.

£ E.A. Millions

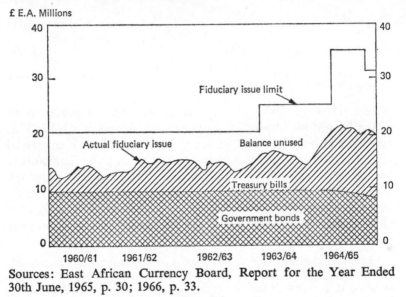

Sources: East African Currency Board, Report for the Year Ended 30th June, 1965, p. 30; 1966, p. 33.

FIG. 9.1

Consequently, in 1955, the Board's regulations were changed and it was permitted to include among its assets £E.A. 10 million of member-government securities and/or local securities guaranteed by the respective governments. In 1960, local treasury bills were also added to its portfolio. By the end of 1964, the Board was allowed to hold a maximum of £E.A. 35 million of all such securities (i.e. the limit of the fiduciary issue proper, excluding crop finance).[7] The Board was authorised to acquire these holdings by direct subscription to new issues, by

[7] See Figure 9.1.

purchasing government securities in the market, and/or by providing facilities for the rediscount of treasury bills. In these ways the Board began to serve the governments with respect to their financial requirements. Concomitantly, it furthered the aims of providing demand for liquid funds in East Africa and of taking initial steps toward establishing a local money market.

The Board also began to serve as banker to the banks by providing them with limited crop finance. It was empowered, in 1961, to discount commercial paper held by the banks and to make advances to them against security for a maximum of £E.A. 5 million! Many factors combined to restrict the use of these facilities: the Board's discount rate was initially set at 7%, in line with going United Kingdom crisis rates of the time; floods damaged crops, particularly in Uganda; and prohibitive *ad valorem* stamp duties on commercial bills existed in all the member countries and had to be replaced by a nominal fixed duty. Reluctance by the Board to grant loans against external means of payment or against assets expressed in external currencies also restricted the volume of collateral for crop finance. Further, the more costly long-established practice in East Africa of financing exportables by means of overdrafts rather than by firm commercial bills operated in this setting as a general restraint to modern banking methods.

Although this circumstance was primarily the result of an underdeveloped money market, its perseverance was also a cause of the slow development of an organised market for the rediscounting of commercial bills. As a result, during the fiscal year of 1961/1962, the Board granted the banks only £E.A. 1·3 million for crop finance, 26% of the permissible amount. Nevertheless, the Board's insistence upon maintaining lending standards in the private sector comparable to those of leading central banks and national discounting institutions doubtless served a useful purpose. The Board endeavoured to provide guidance and discipline with respect to the quantity and quality of negotiable instruments – an incontestable objective of central banking operations, the absence of which could not help but establish an undesirable precedent for formative years when many commercial banks would be more diversified, more national, more complex – and less experienced.

The Board tried to take into account the special conditions existing in East Africa. Frequently, the banks' customers had no valid title to the produce on which they wished to borrow: no fixed contract existed between grower, or intermediary, and the final customer to whom the goods were being shipped. A compromise was reached whereby the Board agreed to include among paper eligible for discount, or as security for advances, acceptances of the banks themselves. It maintained, however, that these acceptances or advances were to be strictly linked to the banks' lending for the marketing of specified crops.

In 1962, the Board lowered its discount rate for crop finance to 5·5%, and the banks simultaneously lowered their minimum overdraft rate from 8 to 7% – the first reduction since the 1960 crisis which was a spillover from British Balance of Payments strains. Many African officials complained that the circumstances in East Africa differed so strikingly from those in the United Kingdom that the Board should have lowered its rate before the Bank of England. But the Board acted on the premise that even if it had lowered its rate, the East African market would still have been overwhelmingly dependent on London. The consensus of the financial community was that crop financing availabilites were of such small volume, compared with the total excess of demand over supply of loanable funds, that even if the Board had lowered its rate, the expatriate banks would not have followed suit.

With improved economic conditions in East Africa during 1962, especially a better cotton crop in Tanzania (Mainland) and the coffee crop in Uganda, the Board raised the limit of its crop financing to £E.A. 10 million. Thereafter, and until the dissolution of the Board, the banks increased the use of this facility and the scheme worked reasonably well. As of June 30, 1965, the maximum amount of credit granted was, however, only £E.A. 3·4 million (December 1964). At all times the use of the facility was considerably below the Board's powers. Nevertheless, the record is noteworthy, both for the total credit granted and for the fact that, during the fiscal year 1964/65, borrowing occurred for the first time in all months of the year.

The Board also undertook the function of serving as a clearing agency for the banks. Throughout its previous history, if a banker needed more currency – say in Dar es Salaam – even for a short period of time, he was obliged to go through the process of handling notes and coin with respect to their issue and, later, redemption in Nairobi. It was a clumsy, inefficient, risk-laden operation. In May 1962, the Board expressed its willingness to maintain 'clearing settlement accounts' for the banks, initially only in Nairobi, Dar es Salaam, and Kampala. Although it was not made obligatory to open the accounts, the Board announced that it would not deal with the banks in the cities mentioned – e.g. for crop finance, security flotations, and so forth – unless they opened such accounts. No minimum balances were prescribed, and overdrafts were prohibited in any circumstances. This useful service, normally rendered by a central bank, greatly reduced the need for physical transfers of notes and coin among the three cities arising from not only currency issues and redemptions, but also from bank transfers among them and from interbank settlements.[8] By 1964, all banks operating on the East African mainland and in Zanzibar had opened clearing settlement accounts with the Board.

To improve its services to the public and the banks, the Board extended its network of currency subcentres. By 30 June, 1965, the system included not only the currency centres in Dar es Salaam, Jinja, Nairobi, Aden, and Zanzibar, but also subcentres in Tanzania at Mwanza, Tanga, and Moski; in Uganda at Kampala, Mbale, and Gulu; in Kenya at Mombasa and Kisumu; and in Aden at Mukalla (agency). In addition, the Board arranged for certain bank branches, particularly in Tanzania (Mainland), to hold limited amounts of coin in safe custody on its behalf. Seasonal needs were thereby met, and unnecessary expenditures related to transporting currency to and from outlying bank branches were avoided. As a result, the banks abolished the special levies previously imposed on the handling of bulk coin for their customers. Further, in May 1962, the Board altered the exchange commissions it charged on issues and redemptions of currency against sterling. The rate of commission previously was 0·25% each way; it was reduced to 0·125% for currency issues, and raised to 0·375% for currency redemptions. The banks, in turn, altered their minimum

---

[8] It is probably unnecessary to point out that the resulting economy in the need for currency was equivalent to an increase in its supply.

8

rates to the public. In making these revisions, the Board hoped to encourage the return of export proceeds to East Africa and to remove nominal impediments to the inflow of capital. Moreover, the Board announced that it would enter the exchange market at its discretion, since the widespread business in 'exchange compensations' throughout the region hindered the development of an orderly and broadly based exchange market. The Board's *unquestioned* objective was to supply the public with a uniform rate of exchange; it steadfastly pursued this aim by endeavouring to improve its currency service.

During the fiscal year 1964/65, an 'administrative office' for Tanzania (Mainland) was established in Dar es Salaam for the express purpose of enabling the Board to provide closer working contacts with the Government and the banks. This office took over a variety of functions which were previously carried out by the agent bank on the Board's behalf. A similar office for Uganda was also opened in Kampala. Special efforts were thus made by the Board to provide closer relations with the governments and the commercial banks, as well as to extend its relations with other national and international financial institutions and authorities.

The Board rightly felt that some of its surplus could properly be used for purposes designed to strengthen the independent position of the East African currency and to help develop the area's financial resources. Accordingly, in August 1962, it ruled that membership of these governments in the International Monetary Fund (I.M.F.) served a *currency* purpose, and it disbursed £E.A. 1,125,000 in sterling to what was then the Government of Tanganyika to pay its subscription in gold, free exchange, and East African currency as an independent member of the I.M.F., the International Bank for Reconstruction and Development (I.B.R.D.), and other international financial institutions. The Board set aside comparable amounts for Uganda and Kenya, which were transferred to them in 1963 when they, in turn, joined the I.M.F. and the I.B.R.D.

The total amount involved for all member governments (i.e. including Aden and Zanzibar) was £E.A. 3·99 million. In the fiscal year 1964/65, the Aden allocation was transferred to the Government of that territory after the Board's functions as an issuing authority there had ceased, and in anticipation of the

South Arabian Federation's membership in the I.M.F. and other international financial bodies. The Trust Fund set aside for this purpose was therefore reduced to the amount allocated for Zanzibar. In April 1964, however, Zanzibar became a member of the I.M.F. as part of the Republic of Tanzania, requiring no additional subscription. The Board ruled that since all member governments had joined the I.M.F. and related institutions, it would meet their remaining subscriptions in gold and free exchange when they fell due. This sum, including Aden's allocation, was expected to be approximately £E.A. 2·2 million. In effect, those distributions were based on the assumption that the Governments were shareholders of the Board, with the amount of capital subscribed by each – and therefore the proportional size of the dividend entitlement – being dependent on the amount of currency which each had in circulation. It is noteworthy that Tanzania (Mainland), Kenya, and Uganda received equal shares. Even the amounts distributed to them out of profits for the fifteen-year period 1950/51 to 1964/65 (inclusive) were remarkably close: £E.A. 4·74 million for Kenya and Uganda, £E.A. 4·67 million for Tanzania (Mainland). As regards the other members, Tanzania (Zanzibar) obtained £E.A. 600,528 and Aden £E.A. 1·69 million, while Somaliland (up to June 30, 1961 only) was allotted £E.A. 115,856 – comprising a grand total of £E.A. 16·55 million.

The formula representing equal 'bearer shares' of the Board for Kenya, Tanzania (Mainland), and Uganda was also applied in the early 1960s to determine each government's portion of the fiduciary issue. It was used, in turn, for setting quotas by the I.M.F. But it was not followed in establishing the capital stock subscriptions to the African Development Bank. In setting aside funds for this purpose, the Board provided each government with an equal sum to the amount of £E.A. 1,642,857; it was based on the smallest subscription of the three, that of Uganda. One of the reasons for this action was the Board's reassessment of its position regarding the distribution of profits and reserves. Facing dissolution, it required an estimate of the actual volume of notes and coin in circulation in each country. This estimate, together with other factors, formed the basis for calculating the Board's indebtedness in free exchange to each country.

Although the 'territorial circulation' represented the capital which each country had invested in 'bearer shares' of the Board, the precise division could not be simply calculated by reference to the net issue in each country. The position had been altered by the transfer of notes and coin from one country to another in payment for inter-regional trade and in response to other financial transactions. At times, therefore, the Board used the value of external trade to estimate the division of circulation. In October 1964, with the introduction of the new 'Lake Victoria' design of currency notes in the entire currency area except Aden, a new perspective was gained on this problem. The conversion of old notes into new suggested that, in the area as a whole, notes accounted for approximately 86·5% of total circulation. Net transfer of currency also appeared to have taken place from Kenya, Tanzania, and Uganda, as a group, to Aden – pointing to a tendency for the three countries to incur Balance of Payment deficits with Aden.

5. Toward Monetary Independence

One of the most instructive experiments in the Board's history occurred during the financial year 1964/65, at a time when the forces operating toward national central banking were well under way. In 1963, for the first time since the financial crisis of 1960, a substantial return of funds took place into East Africa. The Board's currency and other sight liabilities rose by 14·3%. The G.D.P. of the three countries combined regained the level it had attained before the severe economic setback of 1961. This resumption of expansion was achieved without substantial increase in the Board's holdings of local securities. On 30 June 1962 the Board's sterling assets comprised 96·4% of its total currency liabilities, and 82·4% of its total assets. The Board's East African assets comprised 20·6% of its total currency liabilities and 17·6% of its total assets. Exactly one year later, the Board's sterling assets still comprised 96·4% of its total currency liabilities and 85·7% of its total assets. The Board's East African assets comprised only 16·2% of its total currency liabilities and 14·4% of its total assets. The fiduciary issue clearly had been kept under strict control.

Considering the composition of the Board, it is not surprising that it had to protect itself from the charge of helping one government or territory rather than another. As late as 1963, the Board consisted of a Chairman (who was Secretary – General of the East African Common Services Organisation – E.A.C.S.O.), a banking member (who was adviser to the Bank of England) – both of whom were appointed 'in a personal capacity' by the governments of the member countries – and five other members who then comprised the three Permanent Secretaries of the Territories of Kenya, Tanganyika, and Uganda, and the two financial Secretaries of Aden and Zanzibar, all five of whom were *ex officio* members with the power to appoint alternates.

Even with respect to crop financing, the Board considered it necessary to proclaim that territorial (i.e. national) distinctions were to be avoided; that the operations were to serve as a means of relieving pressure on the banking system of the *whole currency area* and not 'merely' of the country whose produce was individually involved. However, with the initial list of crops representing the essentially diverse exports of all the countries – coffee, cotton, cloves, pyrethrum, sisal, tea, and tobacco – it was impossible in practice to meet the needs of the different peak harvest periods and to avoid territorial distinctions. On the contrary, in its very attempt not to impose a 'penalty rate' for crop finance, the Board found it necessary to maintain a close watch on the amount and nature of the credit it granted to each commercial bank. The Board allowed a small margin in the banks' favour to cover the cost of their work on business brought to the Board for refinance. But it proclaimed on several occasions that it was not the Board's function to provide units of the banking system with continuing *working capital*.[9]

Yet the Board had no real supervisory powers over the banks, to say nothing of more effective quantitative and qualitative

---

[9] 'It remains no part of the Board's function to provide units of the banking system with continuous working capital'. [7, p. 6]. 'To summarise the position, it can be said that East Africa has already acquired the vital attribute of sovereignty in monetary matters, *viz* the sole power to issue lawful money. It also possesses and enforces safeguards affecting the extension of this power to the granting of credit by the issuing authority. The further extension to bank credit is in practice contained but without formal apparatus. More formal controls will no doubt be introduced in time but their absence gives no immediate cause for concern' [sic]! [8, p. 6].

controls. Even regarding settlements between the Board and the banks, the Board declared that it was not its policy to establish automatic and compulsory clearing arrangements under extant conditions. With respect to government and private needs for medium-term and long-term credit, the Board ruled that the liquidity principles which governed the sterling portfolio also applied to local investments [*sic!*]. It pronounced that it would not wish to accept, say, 4·5% bonds of the governments for any development purposes. Nor could it become significantly associated with the activities of East African industrial development banks. In effect, the maintenance of the external value of the East African pound – and its free convertibility – remained the paramount objectives of the Board.

TABLE 9.3 *Compounded Annual per capita Growth Rates of G.D.P. in East Africa: Kenya, Tanzania (Mainland), and Uganda. Selected Periods, 1954–64, (%)*

Region	1954–58	1958–62	1962–64
East Africa	2·4	1·2	7·0
Kenya	3·9	0·7	4·4
Tanzania (Mainland)	2·4	2·9	6·2
Uganda	0·8	−1·1	11·8

Source: East Africa High Commission. *Economic and Statistical Review* (Annual Issues).

The conflicting aims of the Board and those of the three sovereign governments of Kenya, Tanzania, and Uganda came to a head in the financial year 1964/65. As can be seen from Table 9.3, the annual rise in G.D.P. for the East African nations from 1963 to 1965 was generally erratic but substantial. After correcting for changes in export prices, the rate of growth in the volume of production was approximately 5% for each of the three countries. In 1963, East Africa had a favourable export surplus; in 1964 it was exceptionally so. Weather conditions were good and productivity rose. Wage rates and prices were comparatively stable, especially in Kenya and Tanzania, while the cost-of-living indexes in Uganda showed only a limited rising trend. The development plans of the countries were progressing reasonably satisfactorily, with no visible inflationary strains on the economies (see Table 9.4). Indeed, with population growing by approximately 2·7% per year, it was unemployment and underemployment that the governments considered serious problems.

TABLE 9.4 *East Africa: Compounded Annual Rates of Growth in Monetary, Trade, G.D.P., and Cost of Living Variables Selected Periods, 1946–65 (%)*

	1946–53	1953–57	1957–61	1961–65
Estimated currency in hands of public in East Africa*	5·7ᵃ	11·8	0·4	6·1ᶜ
Demand deposits	11·3	−0·1	2·4	11·9
Interregional trade	16·8	8·7	7·4	15·7
Domestic exports	20·5	6·3	2·5	8·8
Total imports	24·0	7·2	−0·9	7·4
G.D.P. at factor cost	n.a.	6·3ᵇ	2·8	7·1
G.D.P. per capita	n.a.	3·7ᵇ	0·4	4·5
Cost of living (Nairobi: Europeans and Asians)	6·5ᵃ	3·8	0·9	3·3

Sources: Monetary data: East African Currency Board, *Annual Reports;* Banking and price data: East African Statistical Department, *Quarterly Economic and Statistical Bulletins;* Trade data: East African Customs and Excise Department, *Annual Trade Reports;* G.D.P. data: East Africa High Commission, *Economic and Statistical Review.*
* East Africa, as used here, comprises Kenya, Tanzania (Tanganyika and Zanzibar) and Uganda.
ᵃ 1947–53.
ᵇ 1954–57.
ᶜ Official estimates of 'currency in circulation' in East Africa were discontinued after 1962. The rate for 1961–65 is for the Currency Board area as a whole, which for that period included Aden in addition to the three East African countries.

But the commercial banks found themselves under severe strain at the close of this period. From the end of the financial year 1960/61 to that of 1964/65, while government deposits increased each year, private deposits declined steadily to a net overdrawn position throughout 1964/65. Furthermore, during the financial year 1964/65, the banks' private deposits declined by £E.A. 4·2 million, at a time when East Africa had recorded a large export surplus.[10] This resulted in a higher ratio of private

[10] See: [9, pp. 43, 46].

credit to private deposits in the banking system as a whole than at any other time during the period 1960 to 1965.[11] To a large extent, this phenomenon was caused by capital flight, primarily through the failure of enterprises to deposit their export receipts and other current earnings in the East African countries rather than in London.

Not only did the banks' private deposits in East Africa decline, but their resources from abroad also fell. In 1963/64, the commercial banks operating in East Africa increased their borrowing of overseas funds by £E.A. 9·2 million, whereas in 1964/65 they reduced their overseas indebtedness. The confidence of the financial and business community declined and it reacted accordingly. This decline in confidence was fully apparent by the close of the financial year 1963/64; political and economic forces operating toward the division of East Africa proved demonstrably more powerful than those operating toward unification.

With the failure of discussions regarding East African federation, the strictly national interests of each government understandably became paramount. Rumours about the breakup of the East African Currency Union spread, and the likelihood of the establishment of independent central banks approached certainty. In August 1963, the Currency Board finally obtained permission to increase its fiduciary issue of government paper from £E.A. 20 million to £E.A. 25 million. As noted, in 1962 the crop finance limit was enlarged from £E.A. 5 million to £E.A. 10 million, making a grand total of £E.A. 35 million! In September 1964 the Board requested and received authority to raise its limit for government paper by an additional £E.A. 10 million to £E.A. 35 million, thus raising the overall limit to £E.A. 45 million. Although individual quotas of the member countries were thereby increased, full use of them could not be made by the governments as a right without regard to the monetary conditions of the time as seen by the Board. Normally, no government was permitted to borrow more than its allocation. But the Board endeavoured to avoid undue rigidity. Therefore, through the banking system, it stood ready

[11] See: [9, pp. 46–49].

to rediscount treasury bills of any Government whose fiduciary share was fully used, provided that the total limit for all member countries was not exhausted. In July 1964, the Board agreed – exceptionally – that the Government of Uganda, which expected to exhaust its allocation, might borrow up to a specified maximum against part of the unused share of the two other members. This arrangement was soon made unnecessary by the increased total fiduciary limit for government paper to £E.A. 35 million.

But in November 1964, when crop harvesting, gathering, and marketing of East African goods raised the demand for bank credit within the region, the United Kingdom again tightened its monetary policy. It did so as a result of yet another United Kingdom Balance of Payments crisis. The Bank Rate in London was raised from 5% to 7%; the United Kingdom Treasury Bill Rate from $4\frac{3}{4}\%$ to $6\frac{5}{8}\%$. There was no reason – as there often had been none in the past – why credit contraction in London should necessarily induce credit contraction in the East African countries. At last, the Board decided to put particular emphasis on domestic objectives of East Africa and took countervailing measures.

It charged overseas banks operating in East Africa a penalty rate for borrowing in London. The disparity between this cost and the cost of credit from the Board widened when, on 25 November, 1964, the Board reduced its rediscount rate and advance rates on crop financing from 5·5% to 5%. The banks naturally turned in greater degree to the Board for financing. The Board responded by increasing the availability of credit and by maintaining the reduced rate throughout the financial year 1964/65. It insisted, however, on maintaining what it considered 'strict central banking principles' which underlay the crop-financing scheme, and, therefore, the maximum credit granted by the Board did not reach more than approximately one third of the permissible limit of £E.A. 10 million.

The Board's rediscount rate for treasury bills in Dar es Salaam, Kempala, and Zanzibar remained throughout 1964 at 0·5% above the tender rates in those centres. The treasury bill rates themselves showed, with the Board's support, important progress toward a distinctive East African pattern. The trend of money rates in London exerted a diminishing

influence on them; according to the Board's own pronounce-
ment, this trend was at no time a decisive influence.[12] As can be
seen in Figure 9.2, from February 1962 until February 1964 the
cost of treasury bill borrowing by the three governments in
East Africa remained approximately 4%, thereby widening the
current disparity to more than 0·25%. In November 1964,

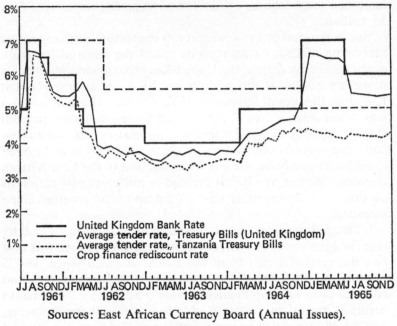

Sources: East African Currency Board (Annual Issues).

FIG. 9.2

when the United Kingdom Bank Rate and the Treasury Bill Rate
rose markedly, the Board held the East African rate to 4·4%.
This level receded slightly in May 1965, and was unaffected by
a 1% reduction of London Bank rates in June 1965.

The Board also pursued a more independent foreign exchange
rate policy. Throughout 1964 its official buying rate for sterling
was kept at £E.A. 99⅝ per £100 sterling. Its selling rate, however – which until 25 November, 1964, stood at £E.A. 100⅜ –
was raised to £E.A. 100½, and maintained at that level for the
rest of the year. This rise in the price of sterling constituted one

[12] See: [9, p. 28].

of several defensive measures against the effects of the 2% increase in the United Kingdom Bank Rate. It was expressly designed to offset the attraction of short-term funds flowing to London. But, under the circumstances, a 0·5% differential in exchange rates could hardly have much effect. At £E.A. 100½, the selling rate reached the maximum permitted under the Board's regulations, *viz.*, 0·5% either side of par – less flexibility than permitted under the I.M.F. rules! The Board realised the need for greater flexibility and sought approval to amend its regulations. After much delay, this approval was granted by the United Kingdom Government in March 1965: permission to alter the exchange rate 1% either side of par, which brought the Board's regulations into line with the range of fluctuation then permitted under the I.M.F. rules. No use was made of this change during the remaining months of the financial year 1964/65, although the Board employed still other means to discourage short-term capital flight.

The Board reduced its special cover facilities for its banking customers and saw to it that they in fact covered their sterling requirements with the Board at the increased official rate. This, in turn, led the banks to charge their customers the higher rate. All these measures notwithstanding, the financial year 1964/65 witnessed net telegraphic transfers from East Africa to London through the banking system. In the aggregate, the stock of currency in East Africa rose less rapidly than G.D.P. Indeed, from December 1962 to December 1964, bank loans and advances to the *private* industrial sector declined by 15%.

The Board recognised, albeit belatedly, the importance of giving assistance to both the member governments and the banking system. It increased its short-term lending to the governments through an expansion of its fiduciary assets. To a limited extent, this policy helped to counteract the deflationary tendencies in the industrial sector. The Board's position with respect to the banks, however, demonstrated the practical impossibility of reconciling its monetary objectives – not perceptively different from those of the Bank of England – with the diverse monetary objectives of the three independent East African governments. While the Board endeavoured to promote the development of an *East African* money market, its policies were not designed to undermine the interests of the overseas banks. It believed that the freedom of movement of funds within East Africa, and between East Africa and London, constituted the most efficient basis for commercial banking operations. The Board took the position that in a currency union with complete freedom of internal transfers, there might be seasonal or other variations in interest rates between different areas, but that there could be only one interest rate policy. This objective, it pointed out, simplified the movement of funds to centres where they were seasonally required. The basic identity between interest rates in the different centres, the Board emphasised, enabled firms and institutions to borrow in one place for the purpose of their operations in several.[13]

The Board warned that if the East African Currency Union were dissolved, the conditions for such uniformity might no longer exist. It even noted that under future currency systems the need for uniformity in basic interest rate patterns would no longer be compelling. It therefore advised the commercial banks to look still more closely at the territorial nature of their lending in order to be prepared for the new situation. Furthermore, the Board drew attention to the growing pressure for a closer identification of territorial assets and liabilities in the banking system; hence it suggested the need for a re-examination of the entire pattern of banking business in the different countries.

Although the Board adopted various traditional measures to discourage capital flight, it regarded the imposition of foreign exchange controls strictly in terms of their potentially deleterious effects on foreign trade and investment. No consideration was given to their short-term potentially stabilising effects on foreign reserves and domestic output. By the financial year 1964/65, however, capital flight took place in large volume through the unofficial compensation market. But the Board did not have the power even to obtain information on these deals. It was at this late stage that it notified the member governments that, if a new constitution were offered to it, the Board would seek authority to obtain such information.

On 10 June, 1965, the governments of Kenya, Tanzania, and Uganda individually announced their joint decision to

[13] See: [9, p. 29].

terminate the Currency Board system as of 10 June, 1966. As a result of this action, they not only put a terminal date on the existing basis of expatriate commercial banking operations in East Africa, but also put an immediate stop to the dealings in the compensation market. On 11 June, 1965, the three governments extended their foreign exchange controls to all external payments, making it illegal to remit funds even to sterling area destinations outside East Africa – or to enter into compensation deals – without official permission.[14]

The preparation and application of the foreign exchange controls owed much to the technical advice received by the three governments, both from the Board and from experts seconded by the Bank of England. The reasonable efficiency of their application – although rampant evasions later occurred – was, in large part, obtained through the assistance of the overseas banks to which were delegated powers to authorise and supervise. The record suggests that the short-term results of the exchange controls were effective. According to the Board, the volume of transactions passing through its centres immediately increased, the proportion of foreign exchange earnings deposited in East Africa rose, and the volume of bank loans and advances to industry substantially recovered. The Board was as surprised as it was pleased by these results; it now hoped that if the expansion in remittances were sustained, a more orderly market for foreign exchange might emerge, reducing the need for the 0·5% wider spread in official exchange rates.

The three new nations – still working under Currency Board supervision – therefore demonstrated the possibility of collaboratively conducting an independent monetary, banking, and

---

[14] See: [9, p. 17]. In a letter dated 20 July 1965, John B. de Loynes, Esq., C.M.G., member of the Board (who was Adviser to the Bank of England) wrote: 'I assume, by the way, that you are aware of the fateful (if this is not too strong an adjective) decision announced by the three East African Finance Ministers on 10 June last to set up their own central banks and issue their own currencies as soon as this can be arranged. I must say that the decision in large measure represents the failure of my efforts over the past five years to uphold the currency union'.

I am deeply indebted to the late Mr de Loynes for the generous and thoughtful consultations he gave me in his capacity as member of the Board, our differences in views notwithstanding.

exchange rate policy in East Africa. The Board conceded that a policy of monetary contraction in London – and some of its repercussions – need not be spread to East Africa. This view was confirmed by experience. It would be erroneous, however, to draw general and optimistic conclusions from this experiment. The policies were carried out within the framework of a long-established, conservatively managed currency union; a reasonably responsible and, for the most part, co-operative commercial banking system; and a common market which, it was believed, would not disintegrate. For the foreseeable future, however, there are imminent obstacles of an institutional, technical, political, and personal nature to the successful implementation of monetary sovereignty in Kenya, Tanzania, and Uganda.

6. Appraisal of Criticisms

The currency and banking systems of the African countries in the sterling area have been subject to much warranted criticism. Some of it stems from official and academic sources within the United Kingdom – from the Treasury, the Bank of England, the universities – as well as from a small number of United Kingdom currency agents and managers of overseas banks who have had an intensely human interest in Africa. But the most vigorous criticism has come from African officials who have taken over the financial responsibilities of their countries. This criticism falls into five categories:

(1) Criticism based on explanations of how the system worked before independence, or before termination of the Board, that lead to deprecatory predictions about the future;

(2) criticism based on the essential need for an independent central banking policy;

(3) criticism based on questionable ideas of the miracles that can be performed by having the central banks independent;

(4) criticism blaming the colonial training policies of the Board, but which apply to bad administration of *any* monetary system;

(5) criticism that does not question the desirability of having the independent central banks with independent monetary

policies, but emphasises dangers from faulty discretion, from subservience to foreign banks, international financial institutions, and to powerful national Treasuries.

6.1 *Criticism based on old vs new interpretation*

Before independence, the East African Currency Board was neither intended to have, nor did it assume, the responsibility of managing the currency and banking system in any meaningful interpretation of that term. Nor was it ever linked with the major operations of the commercial banking system. It was distinctly not a central bank nor in a real sense a monetary authority. The governments could borrow from the Board only by notifying it of their needs in advance and, of course, only within strictly defined limits. Until the Board's dissolution in 1965, and the attendant creation of the three independent central banks, the maintenance of the external value of the East African pound – and its free convertibility – was its paramount concern, or indeed duty. This is understandable in the light of its overall Commonwealth responsibilities. But this duty came increasingly into conflict with the domestic objectives of the East African countries. Emerging differences in these objectives among different countries, different government organs, different persons – and different objectives in the same countries at different periods of time – produced the conflict as to what constitutes an appropriate monetary system.

Practically all East African economists consulted believe that under the Currency Board system the virtual nonmanagement of the monetary situation in the proximate years preceding and following independence aborted the potential role of the Board as an instrument of transition from the Currency Board system to the establishment of central banking institutions. They claim that neither historic Currency Board arrangements nor their changes in the 1960s, provided sufficient flexibility for the African countries to manage their monetary affairs effectively. But they hold strikingly different explanations of how the monetary system actually worked and of the importance – or unimportance – of monetary policy for East African stability, development, and growth.

Two positions are often encountered. In certain cases, one is held by the treasury and the other by the central bank. The first position belittles the importance of monetary policy, maintaining that the international payments mechanism works in a manner rendering the role of money, and of the central bank, unimportant. The case is usually presented in the following terms:

The quantity of money of a small, open country with pegged exchange rates (e.g. in the East African Currency Board system) is determined by its Balance of Payments. A positive balance enlarges the quantity of money, and conversely. An expanded quantity of money, however, raises the country's relative prices, costs, and incomes. This worsens its Balance of Payments and reduces the stock of money. Under appropriate conditions, the resulting fall in local prices, costs and incomes balances its international accounts. Accordingly, the argument continues, the country cannot retain a larger stock of money than its relative prices can support and, at the same time, maintain the value of its trade in balance. After adjustment, the quantity of money the country (allegedly) can have is therefore determined by its Balance of Payments, regardless of monetary policy.

This analysis, although defensible under restrictive assumptions, does not fit the facts for the closing decade of the East African Currency Board's operations. Our analysis for the period 1954–1964 (and thereafter) shows that East African variations in G.D.P. were indeed highly correlated with variations in the value of its exports, but were not significantly correlated with variations in the stock of currency (or in demand deposits, or in the stock of money) or with variations in the Balance of Trade (or the Balance of Payments).[15] In the years immediately before and after independence (1957–1965), annual changes in the stock of currency generally took place in the same direction as annual changes in the Board's external assets, the important exceptions occurring in 1965/1966 when the Currency Board took countervailing measures. Demand

[15] See Table 9.2. The conclusions that follow in the text are based on data provided in East African Statistical Department, *Quarterly Economic and Statistical Bulletin* (Issues for 1957–1961), superseded in 1961 by *Economic Statistical Review* (issues for 1961–1965). They are presented in my forthcoming book on *Dependent Monetary Systems, Trade and Development*, where the problems resulting from neocolonialism *vs* the current African development process *per se* are further discussed.

deposits, however, constituted so large a fraction of the total stock of money – approximately 60% – that their fluctuations could, and did, counterbalance the fluctuations in the currency bringing about the *inverse* correlation of changes in the *total* supply of money in the private sector and changes in total external assets of the Board and the commercial banks. Manifestly, changes in the quantity of money were not determined by changes in the Balance of Trade, or in the current account, or even by *autonomous* changes in the basic Balance of Payments. These latter changes could not have produced, therefore, via the monetary variables, relative price and income effects in the mechanism of adjustment to bring about equilibration of East African international accounts.

The Currency Board system did bring about net changes in the stock of East African currency in accordance with private and governmental – endogenous as well as exogenous – net changes in the aggregate balance of goods, services, and capital movements. But it was private and government capital transfers that played the predominant role in the Balance of Payments. These transfers were channelled through the monetary and banking system which, in effect, developed into two distinct parts: a modern commercial banking structure engaged primarily in financing foreign trade and exchange transactions, and an antiquated currency board structure engaged primarily in telegraphic authorisations of the issue and redemption of notes on behalf of the commercial banks against the receipt from and payment to them of sterling in London. The two parts of the system complemented each other, with fixed exchange rates giving bankers and traders a risk premium. Although the entire analysis was based on the explicit assumption of price and wage flexibility and *related* labour mobility, in practice these elements of the international payments mechanism were displaced by large-scale capital movements.

There is no evidence to support the view that Balance of Payments automaticity made independent monetary policies unimportant for the East African countries. Even if considerable automaticity did exist, much harm would be caused by short term inflationary and deflationary pressures resulting from external imbalance. There is no reason why small and open developing countries cannot pursue countervailing monetary policies toward the achievement of reasonable price stability and rapid economic growth – particularly with a policy of standby reserves and substantial exchange-rate flexibility.

6.2 *Need for a central banking policy*

East African monetary officials realise that real economic development must be accompanied by a process of monetary development. They regard their independent central banks and attendant financial institutions as essential not only to regulate the level of production and income, but also to transform the unbalanced structure of their economies. Normally, as a country develops, the stock of money required rises. In time of crises, however, capital flight plays havoc with money supplies. It is therefore not surprising that in the final decade of the Currency Board's operations there was no significant correlation between changes in the monetary variables and changes in national output. Since the countries had no central banks to implement any banking policy whatsoever, capital flights and the uncertainty resulting from their possibility doubtless contributed to the economic instability.

To accelerate their growth, the East African countries must increase the proportion of G.N.P. invested and alter its distribution. In recent years, Uganda and Tanzania have found it difficult to borrow funds in private capital markets. Foreign aid also has been small compared to their desperate need. Therefore they have to rely predominantly on the expansion of their own investment and output – and the enlarged incomes, profits, and savings that it generates – to help develop their economies. Not only must they allocate more resources to agricultural extension, to technical training, to capital formation, and to liquid external assets, but they must do so at a time when traditional liquidity sources available to them are shrinking. A difficult choice has to be made between the proportion of saving directed to producing longer-term investment goods locally and the proportion to finance imported investment goods by increased output of exportables. The need is great in both directions, for in Africa they are joint instruments of modernisation. Their impact on economic development depends primarily on the extent to which the financial returns from the resources used in both the domestic and export industries are utilised to expand the supply of total reproducible investments: managerial, technical, and physical, but above all, investment in the African human agent. Indigenous central, agricultural, and other specialised banking institutions are important for the achievement of these objectives. They are necessary to help generate a more effective decentral- ised form of market organisation with strong material incen- tives in the domestic and export sectors of the commercial economy, and a more effective co-operative movement with increased social and educational facilities in the rural and sub- sistence sectors. The latter would tend to reduce the rate of migration from agriculture, which is swelling catastrophically the ranks of the urban unemployed.

To finance investment expenditures in industry and agri- culture, the federal and local governments, as well as private firms and cooperatives of East Africa, must issue a substantial volume of securities. Financial intermediaries – commercial, savings, investment, agricultural, and acceptance banks – are essential to purchase these securities. They perform the function of enabling owners of money to hold securities indirectly in the more attractive form of liabilities issued by the financial inter- mediaries, and thereby encourage an increase in the proportion of G.N.P. invested rather than consumed. For an effective money market to develop, however, the securities offered for sale must become sufficiently differentiated in form (i.e., risk) and adequate in volume to provide the owners of cash with a satisfactory choice of purchasable assets.

The East African Currency Board system, with its 'affiliates,' did not provide this choice. The area suffered from a lack of the kinds of institutions which convert demands for loanable funds into demand for local savings. This fact was an important reason for the growth of the sterling area in East Africa. It pro- vided the owners of cash with a liquidity center in London for the employment of their liquid funds. But this did nothing to promote development locally.

Even so, the system worked only reasonably well under normal market conditions. Whenever there was a sudden calling-in of bank loans in London, a shock was administered throughout the sterling area. East Africa suffered from several such shocks in the 1950's and 1960's. Tight monetary and credit policies of the Bank of England reduced the financial manoeuverability of the East African governments to the extent that they even complained of not being masters over their own fiscal policies. It was particularly during such periods that the fusion between the British and East African banking systems caused harsh criticism and charges of neocolonialism.

Like any other capital good, money itself is an asset, the demand for which (and growth of demand) in real terms depends primarily upon the level (and growth) of production and income. The development of monetary and financial institutions – designed to expand finance, production, and income – and real economic development are therefore inseparably connected. Further, the ratio of cash to deposits that the commercial banks maintain in East Africa is a pragmatic, behavioural relationship. The same is true of the ratio of cash to sales or income that the firms and households tend to hold. These ratios can be altered substantially by the operations of their central banks and financial intermediaries. The problem of monetary control involves, in large measure, the provision of assets primarily by way of a central bank for the possible adjustment of the actual to the desired stocks that the holders of funds may wish to maintain. The central bank acts more or less directly on the commercial banks and other financial intermediaries while they, in turn, influence the decisions of private firms and households. Just as the choice of assets and the pattern of interest rates are affected by the policies of the government and the central bank, the decisions of the financial intermediaries are affected by the relevant alternatives available to them within the context of the entire economy and their state of confidence in its future.

Most financial intermediaries in East Africa are still private institutions that attempt to maximise their expected returns. They follow economic behaviour patterns on which the central bank can, and must, operate if it is to control the money supply. To perform this function effectively, a sovereign nation with a central bank must at least determine the reserve requirements and the Bank Rate. Without such authority it would be unable to have much influence on the price level, production and income.

Moreover, a more balanced development in the structure of the East African economies would gradually make it more feasible to implement modern stabilisation policies, both to dampen and to counteract extreme fluctuations in the Balance of Payments. In all probability, for the East African countries, diversified economic development and diversification of foreign trade are dynamically interrelated. A more balanced development in the structure of production would bring about a greater geographical and structural diversification of their foreign trade; greater diversification of their foreign trade would probably bring about a more balanced and higher level of East African economic development. In these newly developing nations, it is particularly important to generate this cumulative causal process of modern advance.

The record suggests that although Kenya, Tanzania, and Uganda experience different economic conditions, they all appear to be able to expand their production to meet an increase in foreign and domestic demand at comparatively stable costs and prices over a considerable range. This provides their monetary authorities with substantial discretionary power in implementing their policies. But unfortunately, with the exception of Tanzania, an understandable tendency has persisted at the highest level of government in Kenya and Uganda to underestimate and to underutilise the central banking authority in all its primary functions: the maintenance of price stability, the promotion of Balance of Payments equilibrium, and the expansion of monetary supply in line with the economy's real capacity to grow. The governors of the central banks have been made unduly subordinate to the ministers of finance. This costly neglect is to be matched only by the danger, in the future, of inexperienced treasuries usurping and perverting the central banking authority.

6.3 *Monetary illusions*

Since foreign trade constitutes a large proportion of the East African countries' production – and must play an important role in their economic development – in the longer run, under prospective forms of mixed economies, the net basic Balance of Payments of these countries will substantially affect their foreign exchange reserves. A large, rapid, and persistent increase in their bank loans would undoubtedly raise their relative prices, costs, and income, produce a Balance of Payments deficit, and result in a loss of foreign exchange.

In East Africa, notes and coin still comprise two fifths of the total stock of money. Under such conditions, the central banks' power to control, and the commercial banks' ability to expand loans on the basis of newly acquired funds, are greatly reduced. Increased loans may lead to a rapid depletion of bank cash rather than a rise in deposits. Commercial banks would therefore be expected to hold reasonably high ratios (15–20%) of cash to deposits, and a central bank's power to control them by attempting to alter reserve requirements, would be correspondingly curtailed – unless the central bank exercised control by means, say, of providing a prescribed ratio of cash, including its own notes, to commercial deposits. For these reasons, and because of generally underdeveloped money markets, the East African countries can pursue independent monetary policies to a much smaller degree than the developed countries. It is an illusion, widely held in the African press and among extreme critics of the prevailing African monetary systems, that there exists some mysterious source of untapped economic energy which, if only liberated, could provide both for development and for other self-sustaining national goals. They fail to clarify between the need for (*a*) an expansion of productive resources for economic development; (*b*) an expansion of monetary demand in line with the country's real capacity to grow; and (*c*) a monetary policy to offset general insufficiency or excess of demand. Not surprisingly, monetary and fiscal policies are often regarded as the efficacious instrument, the Aladdin's lamp, for releasing their illusory economic potential.

6.4 Dependent currency and banking tradition
A more legitimate criticism of the colonial and neocolonial monetary and banking tradition stems from its not having been, and not being, a productive agency in training Africans for responsible positions in central or commercial banking. The system may even have militated against the establishment of high, uniform standards of safety and control over *all* the commercial banks. Moreover, the system encouraged the overseas banks and commercial firms to concentrate unduly on short-term, self-liquidating business and, especially, to look for investments abroad to the detriment of economic development in Africa. The overseas banks placed excessive emphasis on the

financing of foreign trade as compared with supporting (and even with assisting in creating) domestic, short-term – and particularly medium-term – productive business projects. The bulk of their non-reserve assets consisted of loans and advances which fluctuated widely according to the season; but the total of all their assets in the form of claims on borrowers in East Africa was much less than their deposit liabilities. There was thus a tendency for deposits made in East Africa not to be fully used in Africa, with the overseas banks employing the remainder of their resources in short-term funds in London.

This tendency of savings to be partially retransferred out of East Africa was intensified during the struggle for independence by overseas banks granting a larger volume of credit to their European customers who were preparing to leave the countries concerned or to expatriate their assets. The banks were more lenient than heretofore in accepting physical-property assets as security, thereby converting – from the viewpoint of the individual – illiquid wealth into liquid transferable form. African economists have rightly emphasised that monetary authorities, even of the Currency Board kind, have a responsibility to determine the causes and extent of such capital flight, as well as the possible means of its prevention. Although the currency board system was not intended to handle these problems, regrettably it took little initiative in dealing with them as they arose. Modern economics would recommend expansionary monetary and fiscal policies without inflation in the face of capital flight stemming from political uncertainty during transition to independence. Such expansionary policies would have the aim of minimising the fall in output due to reductions in local liquidity and restoring confidence; they would, of necessity, have to combine quantitative and selective monetary controls.

But the East African countries were subjected to deflationary pressures during the transition to independence. From a private business point of view, the decisions of the overseas commercial banks are entirely understandable: not only did they serve the interests of their clients, but they even resorted to assistance from their head offices to enable them to do so. From the viewpoint of African national interest, however, deflationary pressure brought about by capital flight is an unmitigated evil; to facilitate it is irresponsible.

More important, after suffering from such conditions at the turn of the 1960s, East Africa immediately faced intensification of currency contraction brought about by the recurrence of a crisis in the United Kingdom, forcing a sudden calling-in of loans. Periodic deflations of this sort obviously could not be tolerated by independent nations. But only central monetary authorities could counteract the actions of the Bank of England, or of the powerful expatriate banks, thereby helping to stabilise the economies of East Africa. In the early 1960s, such monetary authorities – quasi-independent central banks with comparatively impartial and expert supervision – were perceptively required, although their establishment by the United Kingdom was imperceptively deferred.

Even if the overseas banks were justified in remaining primarily concerned with their own field of expertise, they still had the responsibility, as leaders of the financial community, to help develop other specialised institutions to provide medium- and long-term finance for economic growth and development. As matters stand, they must share the blame for this manifest neglect.[16]

Neither past Currency Board arrangements nor their subsequent changes provided sufficient flexibility for the African countries to manage their monetary affairs effectively. They were kept in a financial straitjacket for too long. By using foreign-exchange earnings to ensure full or 'more than full' convertibility on that proportion of notes and coin in circulation which is customarily used for domestic purposes, the system, in effect,

[16] In this regard, the Currency Board and the commercial banks followed outworn traditions even as compared with the policies which the Bank of England had pursued in the more comparable period of its early history or in more recent times of crises (e.g. in the 1930s or 1940s). Thus, in 1946, the bank of England established the Industrial and Commercial Finance Corporation to facilitate the London clearing banks and the Scottish banks in providing credit for industrial and commercial enterprises. Although not generally known, during the depression of the 1930s the Bank of England gave financial assistance to key industries when private banks refused. For an account of the early history of the Bank of England, see: [6]. A critical reappraisal of the Bank's policies from 1750–1844 is given by Rondo Cameron in [5, pp. 15–59] (Chapters by Olga Crisp, Hugh T. Patrick and Richard Tilly). The modern policies and practices of the Bank of England are presented in [13, esp. pp. 123–129; 135–188; 273; 303–338] and [3].

utilised extremely scarce resources that could have been used more productively for purposes of economic development. In the postwar period, the returns from sterling assets (at times negative, in real terms) were often much lower than those attainable from a more diversified portfolio.

According to well informed Africans – members of the judiciary, parliament, business, and agriculture – the most damaging criticism of the system, and this unfortunately applied to practically all neocolonial business institutions in sub-Sahara Africa, is that the non-African managers of the Currency Board and of the commercial banks made an insufficient effort to acquaint themselves with the African people, their problems, and their fundamental need for black institutions in basic nation-building. Hence, they were unable to determine the creditworthiness of African businesses (a difficult task under the best of circumstances), with deleterious effects upon the development of small African enterprise. Nor did the banks pioneer in the establishment of branches in outlaying areas. They considered each case strictly on its merits, establishing branches only after profitable business was reasonably assured. As a consequence, the banking habit was developed very slowly, and the growth of savings was not stimulated. Without government control and direction, it is impractical and, indeed, foolhardy to expect private firms to provide costly social services in their attendant fields, even though in the longer term they might serve private as well as national interests.

To be sure, by the mid-1960s, the rigid rules of the Currency Board system were slowly tempered by its own developments toward central banking, by modest stabilisation measures of marketing boards, by emerging counter-cyclical taxation policies of the governments, by cushioning effects of the commercial banks, by direct investments of foreign firms, and by international aid. These advances notwithstanding, until the financial year 1964/65, the monetary and foreign exchange system in East Africa remained fundamentally unchanged during a period of ever-increasing need to cushion the effects of extreme fluctuations stemming from international and inter-regional disturbances. This passiveness revealed more than a failure to recognise in time the need for adaptability. The entire system was based on goals and policies which were not meant to serve primarily the interests of the East African countries. In practice, it was principally concerned with the economic interests of British firms and nationals. Nonetheless, East Africa would have been worse off without it.

Historically, the Currency Board and the British banks played an extremely important role in setting the environment for the economic development that occurred. They were an interdependent facet of the entire East African relationship, with the bulk of the East African market-oriented activity – including finance – fused into the industrial bloodstream of Europe. The men who established and developed the contacts; the primary products that fitted into the economic structure of Britain; the complementarity between African needs and United Kingdom supplies of managing-agents, goods, and capital; British habits, language, and tastes; commercial policy – all these factors linked the territorial economies to the metropolitan centres. The United Kingdom was East Africa's main stable market. The United Kingdom banks, within the framework of the Currency Board system, were clearly in the best position to finance the area's exports and imports. Even if there had been no colonial connection, much of this trade would have taken place. But the colonial relationship certainly strengthened these ties excessively.

Further, on the positive side, the Currency Board furnished expert management at very small cost with regard to both the handling of investments in London and the work of currency agents in East Africa. The Board's investment income, commissions, and receipts from other sources often greatly exceeded their expenditures. The system was therefore a source of substantial income to the governments concerned. It also provided currencies that were used with confidence in the most outlying parts of the vast and diversified areas it served. Not only did the banks and traders carry on their business on the foundations of financial security, but foreign capital was also attracted for local development. A trader in East Africa knew at all times how much local currency he would get from the sterling he earned. The importer who contracted to buy goods anywhere in the world for a sterling price had no concern about obtaining the sterling or about its cost in local currency when he came to pay his debt. The governments, their Common Services

Organisation, the government institutions, marketing boards, banks, businessmen, private individuals – all could operate freely in sterling and keep sterling reserves on the same secure basis. The entire system operated according to impersonal market forces in the sense that the benefits it conferred upon the recipients were not directly contingent upon political decisions of the United Kingdom regarding preferential arrangements in trade and aid.

7. Conclusions

(1) The system lost its politicoeconomic legitimacy not because it was a dependent monetary system *per se*, but because it did not adapt expeditiously and satisfactorily to changing conditions. In important respects, the Board was inherently inapplicable to newly independent countries striving to accelerate their economic development. But Africans resented it for deeper, more sensitive reasons: during almost three decades before independence it was practically impervious to change. This, in itself, marked it as a colonial institution uncongenial to national advance. The new governments felt constrained, therefore, to use it as a required tool of transition, not as a nation-building device.

(2) This experience has more general applicability. Any leader-follower monetary relationship cannot but produce unifying economic effects as well as divisive undercurrents. To Africans, the British Secretary of State for the Colonies often appeared to be following policies bordering on 'benign neglect'. As Professor Tinbergen has observed, important decisions of this nature should be determined in a manner that does not adversely affect the interests of areas which are outside the one whose authorities make the decisions:

> A rule which will then roughly correspond to the optimum set of decision-making levels is probably that decisions should be taken at a level high enough to make external effects of such decisions negligible; that is, make the influence on well-being of areas outside the one whose authorities take the decisions negligible.[17]

[17] See: [23, p. 130].

In practice, under prevailing conditions, this would entail the gradual adjustment from key metropolitan to multinational monetary decision making. While slow progress has been made among the powerful Western nations toward this end, it has a direct and important bearing on the developing nations – such as the African countries in the sterling area – which require stronger representation in this advance.

(3) The independent central banks of Kenya, Tanzania, and Uganda separately hold a substantial volume of liquid assets in readily convertible form. They believe that they must do so in order to meet expected and unexpected payments in foreign currencies and to assure investors and traders that their foreign exchange requirements can be met in time of emergency. Normally, it is most natural, convenient and economical to invest these funds in the liquidity centre with which the country conducts the largest volume of its business. In this sense, part of the East African dependent relationship – monetary but *not* political – must, in fact, continue to prevail. But dependence of this sort, be it upon London, Paris, or New York, does not and should not imply control over the monetary, fiscal, and exchange rate policies of the affected participants.

(4) Progress toward this end must rely on harmonising the policies and objectives of many politicoeconomic centres. But as regards East Africa and, indeed, all sterling Africa, our analysis leads to the following conclusions that appear applicable to many developing countries: (*a*) Capital movements, to a greater extent than wage flexibility and related labour mobility, have been responsible for the comparatively successful operation of the international payments mechanism of the East African countries; (*b*) independent monetary policies, with greater exchange rate flexibility, can play a substantially more important role in the economic diversification and stabilisation of developing countries than has been heretofore recognised.

(5) Under current world banking conditions, once an important dependent-monetary relationship is established, it cannot quickly be transformed. No existing liquidity centre can withstand a large withdrawal of liquid funds;

no central bank or treasury can meet this kind of run. If, in a short period of time, the African countries in the sterling area endeavoured to convert their sterling securities into gold or other convertible currencies, the sterling area would no longer be able to continue in its present form. This would have detrimental consequences to all concerned – unless joint arrangements were undertaken to strengthen the sterling area within an enlarged E.E.C. monetary union and/or to accelerate the development of the I.M.F. towards operating as a world central bank. The real problem with respect to the issues at hand is how to procure the genuine financial and trading advantages of one, or more liquidity centres without their maintaining political and economic control over the organisation and direction of the new developing nations.

(6) Given the excess demand for loanable funds in the United Kingdom and in other countries of the Commonwealth, the East African countries are competing for funds in London at a time in history – and especially during periodic United Kingdom Balance of Payments crises with 'stagflation' – when Britain cannot supply them with as large an amount of funds or at as reasonable rates of interest as their situation justifies on economic grounds. This applies to all the liquidity centres, making it essential for developing countries to expand the use of domestic monetary and financial institutions to canalise an increased proportion of G.N.P. for development purposes.

(7) Since in East Africa the dependent monetary system and most monetary activity were managed by non Africans, a satisfactory foundation was not laid for an *endogenous* monetary and banking structure in preparation for independence – notwithstanding the fact that Kenya, in particular, was already a monetarily sophisticated country and the banking system was comparatively developed in regard to foreign trade and investment even by international standards. Consequently, after independence, the new governments not only had to establish national central banks, but also to convert the foreign commercial banks into more national-serving institutions and to press ahead with new methods and instruments applicable to their

changing conditions. Anticipating the break-up of the East African Currency Union, the commercial banks in Kenya curtailed their activities as sub-head offices for branches in Tanzania and Uganda. Once established, the new central banks in fact directed them to maintain a closer relationship between their local deposit liabilities and commercial assets. This brought about a reduction in intra-African capital movements which, together with increasing trade restrictions and declining growth rates, greatly reduced in 1966 – 1968 the volume of East African interterritorial trade.

(8) The new nations also established or expanded their own commercial banks, savings and loan associations, co-operative banks, and stock exchanges. They did so to increase government control of, and participation in, commercial banking, and to provide the opportunity of making loans and advances for development purposes in fields which foreign commercial banks had avoided. Irrespective of government 'ideology', there was a growing need for increased control over, and expansion in, the activities of each country's monetary and banking system.[18] The more underdeveloped the economy and its markets at the time of the Currency Board's termination, the greater was the new nation's need and inclination to use government directives for the granting of medium-term and long-term credits to African manufacturing and mining firms, to farmers and co-operatives, to 'parastatal' organisations, and to the governments themselves.

(9) The structure of banking that developed under the dependent monetary system, as well as the pattern of captial and trade flows, has so far rendered traditional monetary policy ineffective in the new East African nations.

---

[18] Accordingly, in 1967, Tanzania nationalised all private commercial banks; their assets and liabilities were taken over by a newly created state-wide bank, the National Bank of Commerce. In 1968, Kenya founded a new commercial bank, the National Bank of Kenya, to compete directly with the existing commercial banks and, in 1970, jointly formed with 'Grindlays' both the Kenya Commercial Bank in which the Government holds 40% of the shares, National and Grindlays Bank in each case holding the remainder. In 1970, Uganda acquired 60% of the shares of all private banking, financial, and insurance companies.

Since the British banks regarded their London head offices as the final sources of liquidity, they held the minimum possible cash reserves (approximately 3%) in East Africa. This practice, combined with the high ratio of deposits to currency in circulation for African countries, made the monetary systems potentially volatile. Even a small increase in the banks' liquid position, brought about (e.g. by a net inflow of capital) could generate a large increase in the quantity of money. The nationalisation of commercial banks in Tanzania and Uganda, as well as the moderate expansion in their foreign assets, reduced but did not eliminate the seriousness of this problem. In Kenya, from 1966–1970, foreign assets rose by about the same amount as the quantity of money! Under such conditions exogenous factors could easily influence changes in the quantity of money to a greater extent than induced variations in domestic monetary policy. Even, or perhaps particularly, in the more socialised economies of Tanzania and Uganda, if the authorities wish to develop an efficient market sector – as they do – the importance of central bank control over the productive utilisation of commercial (and other) bank credit cannot be exaggerated. Regrettably, the substantial development of commercial banking under the dependent monetary system was not matched by any controls whatever either on the amount of long-term capital the banks should have been required to keep in East Africa or on the maintenance of minimum liquid asset ratios to say nothing of keeping with *some* monetary authority adequate deposits as a proportion of their deposit liabilities for reasonably effective monetary control.

(10) The sterling East African countries suffered from a variant of the general problem of fixed exchange rates. But in their circumstances they could do nothing about it. Indeed, the periodic changes in exchange rates that did occur were connected with the needs of the British economy, not those of East Africa. The theory itself was based on the assumption of general price flexibility, including wages. But even in these developing countries, there was less price flexibility than the theory assumed, resulting in the need of monetary policy.

(11) Fortunately, monetary policy developed in practice long before the authorities were in a pragmatic sense aware of the theory or possessed the power and institutions to implement it. Instead of adjustments taking place primarily through price flexibility, they occurred essentially through changes in the level of economic activity, moderated by capital movements. The actual evolution took the following form: (*a*) Firms required money for paying wages and other costs to produce, gather and ship exports. Money was also required by firms and households producing and consuming goods locally. Under the dependent monetary and banking system, capital movements were thus a response to the need of holding money: seasonally, cyclically and in conjunction with the long-term growth of economic activity. (*b*) Positive or negative Balance of Payments brought about changes in the quantity of money. But, since prices were not fully flexible, it was possible to get an insufficient, or excess, quantity of money. In the case of insufficiency, the result was falling prices, comparative reduction in output, and unemployment; in the case of excess, rising prices. Imperfect price flexibility and imperfect factor mobility therefore engendered conditions which were not consistent with the theory of an automatic international payments mechanism. (*c*) As a result, there evolved an unconscious movement from traditional commercial banking to a monetary policy of adjustment by the commercial banks. This entailed the rudimentary origins of central banking, the development from Currency Board rules to adjusting capital-monetary flows. (*d*) These origins, in turn, produced the recognition of the need for independent central banks to perform the tasks *inter alia*, of national monetary policy that have nothing to do with commercial banking *per se*.

These are the logical ingredients, the theoretical counterparts, to the complex of East African monetary experiences. But, as always, and in the new developing countries pervasively, the logical ingredients were also mixed up, in practice, with institutional ingredients. This phenomenon resulted primarily from the lack of developed market institutions to perform their essential tasks. In consequence, the central banks felt impelled to help establish and/or to nationalise commercial, and other, banks to do more thoroughly and more completely what the foreign commercial banks had begun. However, effective monetary controls necessitate that the commercial banks maintain with the central bank a sufficiently high ratio of deposits to their deposit liabilities to be 'in the Bank' on a semi-permanent basis. To date, in sterling East Africa, this has not been achieved.

Nor have the central banks devoted sufficient attention to channelling credit for the support of entrepreneurial activities. If the corrosive mass unemployment is to be reduced, the central banks will be required to assist, more than heretofore, in the supervised flow of funds, to investigate the possibilities of developing various sectors of the economies, mainly on the basis of productivity or profit criteria. They can – and should – provide the framework for their related commercial institutions to promote the establishment and expansion of enterprises in growth-oriented fields. There exist in these countries, however, powerful market-oriented as well as pre-market forms of economic organisation. The latter may also belong to potentially growth-oriented fields. Unfortunately, there appears to be no satisfactory alternative but to use decentralised price mechanisms *and* governmentally instituted co-operative directives for dealing with these diverse economic sectors. Central banks could assist in both areas by innovating with the use, e.g., of 'regional investment funds'.

The major function of these 'parastatals' should be creating new enterprises and undertaking various forms of development work on their own, thereby expanding investment and productive employment. The argument of insufficient effective demand for industrial credit in sterling East Africa (and other parts of Africa) is true but spurious: for such new financial institutions as 'regional investment funds', financed primarily from development budgets (e.g., lending a maximum of, say, 15% of total investment for as long as 20 years duration) but controlled and assisted by the central banks, could provide the specialisation in training and consulting activities for the development of managerial talent that they desperately need.

Clearly, these are not the tasks for dependent monetary systems. The new nations of sterling East Africa require steadfast leadership capable of courageous and innovative change. These nations possess strong complementary relationships in production, trade, money and exchange, complementarities that extend to the entire sterling area. With a greater degree of monetary independence and exchange rate flexibility, they would be able to achieve more rapid development, as well as greater economic flexibility, to benefit from rising interterritorial and overseas trade. The operation of their international payments mechanism with continued, but more balanced, capital inflow would benefit thereby. But this is contingent upon a definite and stable economic framework within and among the three countries. Such stability is even more important than professed ideology, be it of an enterprise or a socialist form. The evidence is incontrovertible: a precise set of priorities, both in the private and public spheres, realistically related to the resources at hand and implemented with the aid of a definite foreign investment policy which postulates the governments' decisions on the role of effective noncitizens in the development process would yield high returns. It is the credibility in the future economic performance of Africa that must be restored. For this the increased independent role of the central banks, both in policy formulation and in the responsible presentation of the record of economic performance, is indispensable.

References

[1] ABBOT, A. W., *A Short History of the Crown Agents and Their Office*, London: Eyre and Spottiswoode, Ltd., Her Majesty's Printers at the Chiswick Press, 1959.

[2] BALOGH, T., 'A Note on the Monetary Controversy in Malaya,' *The Malayan Economic Review*, IV (October 1959), 21–26.

[3] Bank of England, *Competition and Credit Control*, Consultative document, May 1971.

[4] CAINE, SIR SYDNEY, 'Malayan Monetary Problems'. *The Malayan Economic Review*, III (October 1968), 25–32.

[5] CAMERON, RONDO, *Banking in the Early Stages of Industrialization*, New York: Oxford University Press, 1967.

[6] CLAPHAM, SIR JOHN H., *The Bank of England, A History*, Cambridge: The University Press, 1944, Vols I and II.

[7] East African Currency Board, *Report for the Year ended 30th June 1962*, Nairobi: Government Printer, 1962.

[8] East African Currency Board, *Report for the Year Ended 30th June 1963*, Nairobi: Government Printer, 1963.

[9] East African Currency Board, *Report for the Year Ended 30th June 1965*, Nairobi: Government Printer, 1965.

[10] ENGBERG, H. L., 'Commercial Banking in East Africa', in: Whetman, Edith H. and Currie, Jean I., eds., *Readings in the Applied Economics of Africa*. Cambridge: The University Press, 1967, 48–69.

[11] GOLDSMITH, RAYMOND W., 'The Development of Financial Institutions During the Post-War Period', *Banca Nazionale del Lavoro Quarterly Review*, June 1971, 143–145.

[12] GOLDSMITH, RAYMOND W., *Financial Structure and Development*, New Haven: Yale University Press, 1969.

[13] Great Britain Parliament, *Committee on the Working of the Monetary System*, London: Her Majesty's Stationery Office, August 1959

[14] GREAVES, IDA, *Colonial Monetary Conditions*, London: Her Majesty's Stationery Office, 1953.

[15] International Monetary Fund, *International Financial Statistics*, Washington, D.C.: I.M.F.

[16] International Monetary Fund, *Surveys of African Economies*, Washington, D.C.: International Monetary Fund, 1969, Vol. II.

[17] KING, FRANK H. H., 'Notes on Malayan Monetary Problems', *The Malayan Economic Review*, III (April 1958), 30–41.

[18] *Monetary Systems of the Colonies*, London: F. J. Parsons, Ltd. Revised reprint of eight anonymous articles from *The Banker* which appeared between July 1948 and February 1949 (written by Sir Sydney Caine).

[19] NEWLYN, W. T., *Finance for Development: A Study of Sources of Finance in Uganda with Particular Reference to Credit Creation*, Nairobi: East African Publishing House, 1968.

[20] NEWLYN, W. T., and ROWAN, D. C., *Money and Banking in British Colonial Africa*, Oxford: The Clarendon Press, 1954.

[21] SHANNON, H. A., 'The Modern Colonial Sterling Exchange Standard', International Monetary Fund, *Staff Papers*, April 1952.

[22] SHERWOOD, P. W., 'The Watson-Caine Report on the Establishment of a Central Bank in Malaya', *The Malayan Economic Review*, II (April 1957), 23–34.

[23] TINBERGEN, JAN, 'Some Suggestions on a Modern Theory of the Optimum Regime', in: *Socialism, Capitalism and Economic Growth*, ed. by C. H. Feinstein. Cambridge: Cambridge University Press, 1967.

[24] WILSON, P. A., 'Money in Malaya', *The Malayan Economic Review*, II (October 1957), 53–66.

10 International Policies and their Effect on Employment

H. W. SINGER*

IT is notoriously difficult to measure unemployment in less developed countries (l.d.c.s hereafter) in terms which make it comparable with unemployment in the richer countries. Its forms and apparitions are too different, and I agree with Gunnar Myrdal, Michael Lipton, Paul Streeten and others that we must be wary of transferring uncritically Western concepts to the different Third World. However, we must be equally careful not to jump from the legitimate refusal to apply First World concepts – or Second World concepts for that matter – to Third World problems, to the illegitimate assumption that unemployment and underemployment in open and disguised forms do not exist, or are not serious, merely because they cannot be measured by familiar concepts and caught by familiar definitions, or because the data are lacking. Without labouring the point, for my present purposes I shall simply assert: (a) that unemployment is extremely serious in the l.d.c.s; (b) that it is much more serious at present in the l.d.c.s than in the richer countries; (c) that on reasonable definitions unemployment is of the order of magnitude of 25–30% in many l.d.c.s, and 20–25% in the overall picture; (d) that it is serious, more or less equally so, both in its rural and urban manifestations; (e) that unemployment has become increasingly serious in the last 10–20 years; (f) that on present indications it is bound to increase further, unless counter-influences appear (which must probably include a vigorous and balanced development of science and technology in directions more relevant to the l.d.c.s and their factor endowments, and in the longer run a slowing down of population growth).

All this amounts to saying that the present contest of relations between richer countries and l.d.c.s has been at least consistent

* The author works at the Institute for Economic Development Studies of the University of Sussex.

with a global disequilibrium in the incidence of unemployment in the two groups of countries; say 3–5% in the rich countries and 20–30% in the poor countries. The thesis of this paper is to suggest: (*a*) that the present relations between rich and poor countries are not only *consistent with*, but also *contributory to*, this disequilibrium, with heavy persistent unemployment in the l.d.c.s; and (*b*) that reforms in the present relations of the two groups of countries are among the counter-influences, mentioned in (*f*) above, which are required to improve the situation, or even to prevent it from worsening.

We shall consider the possible contribution of rich/poor countries' relations to l.d.c. unemployment under the headings of trade, aid, private investment, science and technology, and international liquidity.

1. Trade

It is no accident that trade has been placed first. As an economist I am bound to say that the main avenue along which one would look for a major contribution to the solution of the unemployment problem in developing countries lies in trade. Traditionally, in the thinking of economists, trade has been the method by which each country exports, through the commodities produced and traded, those factors of production which it has in relative abundance, while it imports, again through commodities, those factors of which it is relatively short. For the developing countries this would mean that through trade they would find an outlet for their abundant labour, and be enabled to remedy their deficiencies in capital through imports.

Unfortunately, trade has not in fact played this major role conceptually attributed to it. But it still remains true that potentially this could be the case. The developing countries, with a good deal of support from enlightened opinion within the industrial countries as well, are putting forward in UNCTAD and elsewhere requests that their labour-intensive manufactures should be admitted to the huge markets of industrial countries on a duty-free or preferential basis. Similarly, freer access of agricultural commodities and other raw materials is also under debate. When we think of the tremendous markets involved, and the tremendous rate of expansion of international trade as a whole, in which the developing countries have so conspicuously failed to participate, one cannot help being impressed by the vast potential improvement in the employment picture of the developing countries which expanded trade could produce.

It is not easy to quantify hypothetical situations which cannot be isolated from other events and trends. However, I am going to stick my neck out and risk the guess that if the share of l.d.c.s in world trade had been kept up since 1955 by a reduction of agricultural protectionism and trade barriers in the richer countries, the employment volume in the l.d.c.s could be about 10% higher than it is now. That would be, say, $82\frac{1}{2}\%$ of the labour force instead of 75%, and unemployment would be $17\frac{1}{2}\%$ instead of 25%. Moreover, if this hypothetical assumption of a fully maintained share in total world trade could be projected into the future, and if world trade should continue to expand as rapidly as in the past decade, the establishment of this condition might prevent unemployment in the l.d.c.s from rising in the next decade, even in the presence of a capital-intensive technology and a certain rapid increase in the labour force. But this is a big and extremely hopeful assumption to make. Notwithstanding favourable votes in UNO bodies and acceptance of global targets which really depend upon such action, are we in the richer countries really ready for it? No doubt we could ourselves benefit in the long run by concentrating on the more sophisticated lines of production (but by the same token perpetuate global dualism and technological colonialism). But the case of aid should warn us that demonstrations of long-run advantage do not seem to be particularly compelling in eliciting from taxpayers, parliaments, civil services and politicians of richer countries any great willingness to make what looks like one-sided 'concessions' even though the sacrifice may be more apparent than real, and transitional rather than lasting. Perhaps real sacrifices could be more readily elicited than the inconveniences of adjustment?

The trouble, of course, is that the burden of adjustment, if not properly handled, will tend to fall on vulnerable groups most directly in line of competition with the potential exports of the l.d.c.s – the elderly textile worker in Lancashire, the farmer, the older, more labour-intensive firms. The necessary adjustments and compensations should certainly be within the power of the richer countries, as well as being in their own interest. Nobody wants to solve the problems of the l.d.c.s on the backs of the poorer people within the richer countries – but then we should also stop trying to solve the problems of our poorer (or simply more vocal!) sectors on the backs of the even poorer l.d.c.s.

In this paper which deals with 'international policies' we naturally look at the action required by the richer countries, but let us remind ourselves that the l.d.c.s may also have to make painful and difficult adjustments in their present policies and outlook to take better advantage not only of the present, but also of any potentially larger future export opportunities. This requires outward-looking policies, willingness to take risks, to study foreign markets and tastes. It takes two to export, and perhaps it takes a dash of Japanese! And the mentioning of Japan could serve as a reminder that the development of a prosperous home market base has never yet hurt a country in developing its exports as well. But there is also a counter-lesson from Latin America: the building up of a pseudo-prosperous home market under the banner of import substitution may be more of a hindrance than help in export development.

Hal B. Lary of the National Bureau of Economic Research in New York has found that the following industries stand out as particularly labour-intensive in relation both to skills ('human capital') and to physical capital: apparel and related products; leather and leather products; lumber and wood products; textile mill products; furniture and fixtures; miscellaneous manufactures; rubber and plastic products. Trade concessions in these products (which I have listed in more or less descending order of employment-intensity in terms of unskilled labour) would have particularly strong employment impact in the l.d.c.s, and relieve wage pressures and tight labour markets in the richer countries. Is there not a ready-made agenda here for international action? If the l.d.c.s can only provide the skills, even while lacking the physical capital, a number of other industries could be added as being employment-intensive in the l.d.c.s: fabricated metal products; printing and publishing; electrical machinery; non-electrical machinery. This list of eleven employment-intensive industrial groups *prima facie* suited for export from the l.d.c.s would still leave the richer countries with nine industrial classes which are both skill- and capital-intensive, and *prima facie* suitable for *their* exports.

The case made here for international trade concessions to the l.d.c.s specifically directed towards employment promotion is of course additional to the more general case for trade development as a way of reducing their foreign exchange bottlenecks and speeding up their general rates of growth and investment. This more general case has been amply made in UNCTAD, the Pearson Report, and elsewhere, but by comparison perhaps not much attention has been given to how to obtain maximum employment impact through trade concessions. The scope is certainly enormous, considering that imports of labour-intensive products from the l.d.c.s are only a small fraction of rich countries' total imports of such products, and only a fraction of that fraction when related to their total consumption of such products. Even a target of say 10% of the total *increase in* the consumption of such products to be imported from the l.d.c.s would have highly important employment impact.

But all this is 'potential', i.e. pie in the sky. Meanwhile, the ugly skeleton of the scandalous international cotton 'agreement' rattles its bones to remind us of reality, and of *one* reason for 25% unemployment in the l.d.c.s! To this we should add, as equally misleading, the moderate-looking nominal tariff rates on processed and manufactured products from the l.d.c.s which conceal the real, and much higher, effective taxes on value added by employment.

2. Aid

Here, once again, we must distinguish between the general case for additional aid, as contributing to fuller employment in the l.d.c.s, and the specific case for adjusting the forms and methods of aid so that a given volume of aid becomes more 'employment-intensive' in its impact. The general case is no doubt valid (within certain limits and with certain qualifications): 1·0% and 0·7% of G.N.P. for total financial flows and public aid, would increase the rate of investment and growth, and *ceteris paribus* increase employment.[1] Improvements in the terms of aid,

[1] This would be questioned by some, either on more general grounds that aid is 'bad' for l.d.c.s, or on more specific grounds such as by A. Qayum in [2].

untying, more grants and anything that leads to more effective use of aid would have the same presumptive favourable effect on employment. The limits and qualifications mentioned include a possibility such as the following: if the additional growth and employment created by more aid are in the urban/modern sector, then the increase in the number of urban jobs created might swell the flood of migration to the cities to such an extent that unemployment, at least in its open and urban forms, could actually increase. This possibility, based on East African conditions, is inherent in Michael Todaro's much-discussed model [3]. Another possibility would be that the higher growth rate and investment rate in the urban/modern (and capital-intensive) sector could be accompanied by such a change in the overall *composition* of investment, by drawing complementary domestic resources out of the rural/traditional/service sector (largely labour-intensive), that overall employment is diminished rather than increased. The possibility of this applying to Colombia has been pointed out by the ILO mission under the World Employment Programme, led by Dudley Seers [4]. However, broadly speaking, more aid, or more effective aid equals more employment, although the conventional aid/employment ratio is almost certainly unimpressive.

How can the aid/employment ratio be improved? This is the special relationship between international aid policies and employment with which we are concerned here. Space limits us to an enumeration of changes in international aid policies which could improve the employment impact of a given volume of aid.

(1) Aid is now available predominantly for the *import component* of projects, largely equipment. This puts an artificial premium, as far as the l.d.c.s are concerned, on preferring capital-intensive projects to more labour-intensive ones, or for any given project preferring a more capital-intensive (import-intensive) to a more labour-intensive technology. Both these effects reduce (or possibly pervert) the employment effect on projects (including local equipment). This could be done either by giving aid as a fixed percentage of total *project costs*, whether 100% or 50% or 25% of the total cost, or alternatively by giving aid on a programme or general budgetary basis. The Pearson Commission has recommended that aid givers remove regulations which

limit or prevent contributions to the local cost of projects, and made a greater effort to encourage local procurement wherever economically justified [1, p. 177]. This recommendation deserves full support. In particular, it is to be hoped that the multilateral aid sources will pay full attention to it; so far they have been more in the rear than in the van of the faint movement in this direction.

(2) Aid is more readily available for investment in the urban/modern sector than in the rural/traditional sector. This has the dual effect of raising the overall capital/output ratios by changing the investment mix in the direction of the more capital-intensive urban/modern sector; and of intensifying differential and the job attractions of the towns. Both these effects tend to reduce the employment impact of aid. The aid/employment ratio could be improved (lowered) if more aid were available for the rural/traditional sector (not necessarily agricultural but inevitably much of it directly agricultural and most of it agriculture related). Here again, we are pushing at an open door in so far as most aid programmes, especially the World Bank, have announced an intention to shift more aid into the agricultural sector, and into rural development. However, the implementation of such a policy will be more difficult than the policy-framers realise. Often the aid would have to be on a programme or budgetary basis, and channelled through local financial institutions in order to overcome the logistic difficulties of channelling aid into a multitude of small widely dispersed projects conducted under unfamiliar and unsophisticated conditions of bookkeeping, expenditure control, etc.

(3) Aid is more readily available for a few large projects rather than for a variety of smaller projects. Smaller projects however are both more likely to be employment-intensive and also more likely to be found in rural or small town locations where they reduce migration to the cities and consequently urban unemployment. There is, of course, a certain fungibility in that external aid for large projects may release local resources for smaller-scale projects (or vice versa). This fungibility however may work in reverse if the external aid covers only a relatively small part of the total cost of the large-scale project while the rest may have

to be covered from complementary local resources. The best approach would be either to channel aid through local financial institutions or to place it on a programme or budgetary basis.

It will be seen that the policy prescriptions under (1), (2), and (3) above coincide quite closely. In fact, it may be said that present aid practices form an anti-employment syndrome, while the corrective measures required also form a single syndrome.

(4) The employment impact of aid also suffers from a confusion within the present aid system of promoting new growth or development as distinct from promoting new development *projects*. It is a great deal easier to obtain aid for a new project rather than for the expansion of an existing project, or the repair and maintenance parts needed to keep existing projects going, or the import of raw materials required for their operation, or the additional expenditures (largely local wages) which would be needed to utilise existing plant more fully by multiple shift work. There has been some improvement particularly in the direction of providing aid for the import of required raw materials, but the statement is still broadly true. As a result we have the extraordinary spectacle of scarce capital standing idle or under utilised although no doubt deficiencies in management, income distribution, planning etc. also play a large part in this. Aid given for the more effective utilisation of existing capital would nearly always be much more employment-intensive than aid given for the introduction of new capital. In fact the kind of aid here advocated would represent the best kind of intermediate technology – capital saving yet without arousing the antagonisms conjured up by the idea of a 'different' technology.

(5) Aid for the financing of public works, and especially of rural public works, is almost impossible to obtain, partly because there is no single project and partly because the expenditure involved is local. Food aid is a form of aid particularly useful for the financing of public works and labour-intensive development in general. No doubt food aid can be harmful if it depresses prices for local farmers or

leads to a slackening of domestic effort in food production. But it would be throwing out the baby with the bathwater to go slow on food aid rather than administer it in such a way that it has no undesirable side effects. It is to be hoped, of course, that food aid, which essentially does not impose any real sacrifice on the donor of the surplus food, would be considered as additional to other aid rather than competitive with it. Perhaps for this reason it should not be counted within the 1% and 0·7% Pearson targets.

3. Private Foreign Investment

The present employment impact of private foreign investment is reduced by a number of factors and could be increased by changing them. A bare list must suffice here:

(1) A foreign firm, particularly a multinational firm, will almost automatically fall back on the capital-intensive technology available to it internally through the research products, know-how, patents, etc. of the head office or parent company;

(2) a foreign firm will not wish to be troubled with the incomprehensible and politically-charged problems of handling large masses of local labour, deciding who should be employed and who should be refused employment, etc. The employment of capital is the line of least resistance;

(3) a foreign firm will be faced with a demand for wages much higher than the prevailing local labour situation and the resource endowment of the country would justify. To push up wages against foreign firms is almost a patriotic duty, and will understandably be supported by the local government as one way of keeping the money in the country and reducing the repatriation of profits;

(4) where one of the original motives of the foreign investment was to use the local subsidiary or licencing agreement as a foothold for selling equipment, spare parts, operational raw material, etc. the provision of secondary local employment by ordering locally will be absent or greatly reduced.

This is by no means a full list, and no doubt there are also countervailing factors at work – including deliberate policies of a number of foreign firms – but it will help to indicate some of the changes in foreign investment policies which might be needed if we are to increase its impact on local employment.

4. Science and Technology

Although problems of science and technology are less discussed (at least by economists and politicians) than trade, aid or investment, in fact this is the area in which the rich countries have perhaps the most powerful impact – for better or worse – on employment in the l.d.c.s. The dominant fact of international life is that it is the richer countries, with one third or less of the world's population, which account for 99% of the world's scientific and technological innovation. Admittedly, R & D expenditures (on which the 99% figure is based) are a less than satisfactory input proxy for the output of innovation, and in addition it covers only one segment of the relevant inputs; but it is the best we have. In some ways, it even understates the dominance of the richer countries: such is this dominance that even the R & D expenditures of the l.d.c.s are largely devoted to making a marginal contribution towards 'extending the frontiers of knowledge', in ways and in directions automatically determined by the conditions and factor proportions of the richer countries.

In the Sussex Manifesto – prepared by a group of consultants to the UNO Advisory Committee on Science and Technology meeting at the University of Sussex last year [5], we described this phenomenon as the 'internal brain drain', and as perhaps more important and dangerous to the l.d.c.s than the external brain drain (visible geographical movement of highly qualified people) which has attracted so much more attention. It is on account of this internal brain drain as well as on account of the low efficiency of small and scattered R & D expenditures without adequate infrastructure and equipment (also discussed in the Sussex Manifesto), that one must be rather sceptical of the value of any targets of increasing the local R & D expenditures of l.d.c.s from 0·2% of their G.N.P. to 0·5% or any other figure, when such proposals are made in isolation.

It is only within the context of planned global change in the composition and direction of scientific and technological progress that such a target assumes a constructive meaning.

And it is again because of the dominance of rich-country technology which not only dominates the R & D inputs and controls the R & D infrastructure, but also sets the tone and determines what is considered as 'progress' or 'modern' or 'efficient' even within the l.d.c.s – however contrary to their true interests – that any such planned global change must include a restructuring of the R & D priorities within the richer countries. It is they who must redefine what constitutes 'progress' and where the 'frontiers of knowledge' lie. This they must do in such a way as to include more of the things which are useful to the l.d.c.s (production on a smaller scale, simpler product design, tropical product improvement, protein foods for young children, etc.), and fewer of the things which are directly harmful to them (certain developments in synthetics, automation, machinery with extremely high repair and maintenance requirements, etc.). The target of the Pearson Report that the richer countries should shift $2\frac{1}{2}\%$ of their R & D expenditures in this direction is an important, if modest, beginning.

For the purposes of our present discussion it should be noted that any such change in direction would be bound to give much higher priority to employment intensity, capital-saving and reduction of sophisticated skill requirements in operation, maintenance, etc. And let us not hear too much of the old canard that capital-intensity is good for l.d.c.s because it economises in skills. All the evidence is to the contrary; and the landscape of the l.d.c.s is strewn with the evidence of this fallacy in the form of under-utilised, broken down, idle, high-cost 'modern' capital equipment.

Hopefully, in later years those after us will shake their heads incredulously at how we set about this business. We take technologists and other experts involved away from their familiar environment and drop them in another country (usually with insufficient briefing), leave them to find houses to live in and schools for their children, to find local counterparts, to find their ways in unfamiliar surroundings, and all too often whisk them back just when they become effective. If this reads like a parody, few with experience would deny that it contains elements of truth.

Surely, the first step in a global partnership must be to use the wonderful and dreadful machinery of science and technology where it is and where it can operate most effectively, and realise its potential blessing for world economic development. The sending of experts abroad and the building up of an indigenous scientific and technological capacity within the l.d.c.s must take place simultaneously, and in alignment with a change of direction of progress within the dominant richer countries. The $2\frac{1}{2}\%$ suggested by the Pearson Report is less than one-twentieth of what is now spent on military, space and atomic technology, less than what the richer countries will have *added to* their R & D expenditures between the June day in 1970 when this is written and the end of the same year.

And once again, as with trade and aid, the thinking within the l.d.c.s will have to change as much as the thinking in the richer countries. Feasibility studies of projects will have to be based on spectra of technology and on pricing systems which reflect the real resources and needs of the l.d.c.s. At present, any such movement is only too easily resisted as evidence of technological colonialism, on the grounds that the l.d.c.s are permanently to be fobbed off with an inferior second-class technology. Tragically, exactly the opposite is true: the present dominance of a technology appropriate for the rich countries, a dominance obtaining within the l.d.c.s no less than without, ensures a continued handicap for the l.d.c.s. The present rates of population increase, the present capital-intensive trend of technology, and productive full employment are three things which simply cannot coexist. Something has to give – and at present it is employment.

5. International Liquidity

Here, of course, attention should be paid to the great step forward taken by the world community by the creation of the special drawing rights (s.d.r.)s. A little of that progress has rubbed off on development even at present, in that the l.d.c.s, contrary to the original intentions, at least participate in the s.d.r.s to the extent of their I.M.F. quotas. Perhaps more important is the widespread conviction which has emerged that now the s.d.r.s have been safely – and one hopes irrevocably – established, their potential for world development can be safely utilised without damage to their original and primary purpose. The technique for doing this is less important than the decision itself, although the opportunity to strengthen multilateral channels seems too good to miss – killing three birds with one stone!

The Balance of Payments objection to increased aid to the l.d.c.s was never too convincing, except possibly as a question of redistributing the overall burden of aid among the richer countries. It could always be pointed out that as long as the l.d.c.s did not use aid to increase their foreign exchange reserves – and with exceptions the main criticism of their policies was exactly the opposite – there was never a valid Balance of Payments argument against increases in overall aid. Now, with the creation of the s.d.r.s we can go a step further. The richer countries, taken together, will not only not have a Balance of Payments deficit, but they will in fact have a positive Balance of Payments surplus. The case for linking this new progress in international relations with a step forward in development assistance seems very strong – but what better direction than to link this even more specifically with the objective of providing constructive employment for the young in the l.d.c.s?

References

[1] The Commission on International Development, *Partners in Development*, New York, Washington, London: Praeger, 1969.

[2] QAYUM, A., 'Long-Term Economic Criteria for Foreign Loans', *Economic Journal*, LXXVI (June 1966), 358–369.

[3] TODARO, M., 'A Model of Labor Migration and Urban Unemployment in Less Developed Countries', *American Economic Review*, LIX (March 1969), 138–148.

[4] *Towards Full Employment*, A Programme for Colombia Prepared by an Inter-Agency Team organised by the International Labour Office. I.L.O., Geneva, 1970.

[5] *World Plan of Action for the Application of Science and Technology to Development*, United Nations Document E/AC.52/L.68 of 19 October 1969.

Appendix: Bibliography of Jan Tinbergen

MANY of Jan Tinbergen's articles were published in Dutch, German, Danish, French and other languages. The selected bibliography in this Festschrift covers only Tinbergen's work originally published in English and some translations from other languages into English. This means that a large number of his important publications will not be listed. The reader can find an extensive bibliography of Jan Tinbergen in his *Selected Papers*, edited by L. H. Klaassen, L. M. Koyck and H. J. Witteveen (Amsterdam: North Holland Publishing Co., 1959). A short supplement to that bibliography was published in *De Economist*, CVII (1959) 798–9, written by J. B. D. Derksen. Finally, J. P. Pronk wrote the most up-to-date bibliography of Jan Tinbergen, covering the period 1959–69 in *De Economist*, CXVIII (1970) 156–73. The selected bibliography presented here is ordered chronologically and includes the following areas: international trade and finance, long-term economic development and planning, econometrics and economic theory. The section on economic theory also includes publications on the theory of economic policy and miscellaneous topics in economics.

1. International Trade

[1] *International Economic Co-operation*, (Amsterdam: Elsevier Economische Bibliotheek, 1945). Translated into English by P. H. Breitenstein and E. Inglis Arkell.

[2] *Some Remarks on the Problem of Dollar Scarcity*, (Washington: Congress Econometric Society, 1946).

[3] 'Unstable Equilibria in the Balance of Payments', in: *Economic Research and the Development of Economic Science and Public Policy*, (New York, 1946).

[4] International Economic Co-operation, *Erasmus Speculum Scientiarum*, Aarau, Switzerland, I, 1 (1947).

[5] 'The Equalization of Factor Prices between Free-Trade Areas', *Metroeconomica*, I, (April 1949) 38–47.

[6] 'Long-Term Foreign Trade Elasticities', *Metroeconomica*, I, (December 1949) 174–85.

[7] 'Some Remarks on the Problem of Dollar Scarcity', *Econometrica*, XVII, (July 1949) Supplement 73–97.

[8] 'The Possibility of Price and Exchange Adaptation', in: *Tracing a New International Balance*, (Leiden: Stenfert Kroese, 1950).

[9] 'On the Theory of Economic Integration', *Les Cahiers de Bruges*, 4 (1952) 292–303.

[10] 'The Relation between Internal Inflation and the Balance of Payments', *Banca Nazionale del Lavoro Quarterly Review*, V, (1952) 187–94.

[11] TINBERGEN, J. and VAN DER WERFF, H. M. A. 'Four Alternative Policies to Restore the Balance of Payments Equilibrium: A Comment and an Extension', *Econometrica*, XXI, (February 1953) 332–5.

[12] 'Customs Unions: Influence of Their Size on Their Effect,' *Zeitschrift für die Gesamte Staatswissenschaft*, CXIII, (1957) 404–14.

[13] 'An International Economic Policy', *Indian Journal of Economics*, XXXVIII, (1957) 11–16.

[14] 'Heavy Industry in the Latin American Common Market', *Economic Bulletin for Latin America*, V, (January 1960) 1–5.

[15] 'The Impact of the European Economic Community on Third Countries', in: *Sciences Humaines et Intégration Européenne*, (Leiden: A. W. Sythoff, 1960), 386–98.

[16] TINBERGEN, J., RIJKEN VAN OLST, H., HARTOG, F. *et al.*, *Shaping the World Economy: Suggestions for an International Economic Policy*, (New York: The Twentieth Century Fund, 1962).

[17] 'The European Economic Community: Conservative or Progressive?', in *Wicksell Lectures 1963.* (Stockholm/ Gøteborg/Uppsala: Almqvist and Wiksell, 1963), 38ff.

[18] *Lessons from the Past*, (Amsterdam: Elsevier, 1963).

[19] TINBERGEN, J., HART, A. G. and KALDOR, N. *The Case for an International Commodity Reserve Currency; A memorandum submitted to the United Nations Conference on Trade and Development, 1964.*

[20] 'The Evolution in Communist Views on International Trade', *World Justice*, VI, (January 1964) 5–8.

[21] *International Economic Integration*, 2nd revised edition, (Amsterdam/New York: Elsevier, 1965).

[22] 'International, National Regional and Local Industries', in *Trade, Growth and the Balance of Payments; Essays in Honor of Gottfried Haberler on the Occasion of his 65th Birthday*, ed. by R. E. Caves, H. G. Johnson and P. B. Kenen, (Amsterdam: North Holland, 1965), 116–25.

[23] 'Trade between Western and Communist Countries', *Cronache Economiche della CCIA di Torino*, (1965) 266–7.

[24] TINBERGEN, J. *et al. Terms of Trade and the Concept of Import Purchasing Power of the Exports of Developing Countries;* UNCTAD, Trade and Development Board, Permanent Subcommittee on Commodities, First Session (TB/BIC 1/PSC/5), Geneva, 1966.

[25] 'Balance of Payments and Project Appraisal', *Development Planning Problems and Techniques Series*, No. 1, African Institute for Economic Development and Planning, 1967, 5–10.

[26] 'Shaping the World Economy', in: *World Peace Through World Economy*, Youth and Student Division of the World Association of World Federalists, 6th International Study Conference, (Assen, Netherlands: Van Gorcum, 1968).

2. Long-Term Economic Development and Economic Planning

[1] 'Central Planning in the Netherlands', *Review of Economic Studies*, xv, (1947/48) 70–7.

[2] 'The Netherlands' Central Economic Plan for 1947' *Revue Suisse d'Economie Politique et de Statistique*, LXXXIII (January 1947) 19–29.

[3] 'Problems of Central Economic Planning in the Netherlands', *National Økonomisk Tidskrift*, LXXXV, (1947) 96ff.

[4] 'Government Budget and Central Economic Plan', *Public Finance: Openbare Financiën*, XLII, (March 1949) 195–205.

[5] 'Planning for Viability', *The Way Ahead*, II (1949) 38–61.

[6] 'Capital Formation and the Five-Year Plan', *Indian Economic Journal*, I (January 1953) 1–5.

[7] 'Problems Concerning India's Second Five-Year Plan', *Public Finance: Openbare Financiën*, XI, (February 1956) 103–10.

[8] The appraisal of Road Construction, two Calculation Schemes', *Review of Economics and Statistics*, XXXIX, (August 1957) 241-9.

[9] 'The Optimum Choice of Technology', *Pakistan Economic Journal*, VII, (February 1957) 1-7.

[10] 'The Use of a Short-Term Econometric Model for Indian Economic Policy', *Sankhyā; The Indian Journal of Statistics*, XVII, (April 1957) 337-44.

[11] 'Choice of Technology in Industrial Planning', *Industrialization and Productivity; Bulletin of the United Nations*, I, (January 1958) 24-33.

[12] 'International Co-ordination of Stabilization and Development Policies', *Kyklos*, XII, (March 1959) 283-9.

[13] 'Problems of Planning Economic Policy', *UNESCO International Social Science Journal*, XI, (March 1959) 351-60.

[14] 'Fundamental and Derived Aims of Economic Development', *The Punjab University Economist*, I, (February 1960) 1-6.

[15] *Programming Techniques for Economic Development*, (Co-author) (Bangkok: U.N. Economic Commission for Asia and the Far East, 1960).

[16] 'The Appraisal of Investment Projects: the Semi-Input-Output Method', *Industrial India*, 1961, 25-6.

[17] 'Development Theory, and Econometrist's View', in: *Money, Growth and Methodology, and Other Essays in Economics in Honor of Johan Åkerman*, ed. by H. Hegeland, (Lund: Gleerup, 1961, 49-58).

[18] TINBERGEN, J. and Bos, H. C. 'The Global Demand for Higher and Secondary Education in the Underdeveloped Countries in the Next Decade', *Policy Conference on Economic Growth and Investment Education;* Washington, D.C., (O.E.C.D., 1961), Vol. III.

[19] 'The Spatial Dispersion of Production: A Hypothesis', *Schweizerische Zeitschrift für Volkswirtschaft und Statistik*, XCVII, (April 1961) 1-8.

[20] 'Again – The Development Issue', *The Ecumenical Review*, XIX, (February 1962) 226-8.

[21] 'Planning in Stages', *Statsøkonomisk Tidskrift*, (January 1962) 1-20.

[22] TINBERGEN, J. and CORREA, H. 'Quantitative Adaptation of Education to Accelerated Growth' *Kyklos*, xv, (April 1962) 768–86.

[23] TINBERGEN, J. and BOS, H. C. 'The Financing of Higher Education in Africa', *The Development of Higher Education in Africa*, Report of the Conference on the Development of Higher Education in Africa, Tananarive, 3–12 September 1962. (Paris: UNESCO, 1963, 155–212).

[24] 'Project Criteria', in: *Economic Planning*, ed. by L. J. Zimmerman, (The Hague: Mouten, 1963, 7–19).

[25] 'Projections of Economic Data in Development Planning' *Planning for Economic Development in the Caribbean*, (Caribbean Organization, Hato Rey, Puerto Rico, 1963), 26–51.

[26] 'A World Development Policy', *World, Nations and Groups in Development*, (The Hague: Mouten, 1963), 39–55.

[27] *Central Planning*, (New Haven/London: Yale University Press 1964), 1964.

[28] *Development Planning*, (New York, Toronto: McGraw-Hill, 1966).

[29] *Development Planning: The Sector Phase, with Different Gestation Periods* (Nederlands Economisch Instituut, Publication 26/64, Rotterdam, 1964).

[30] 'Educational Assessments', *Economic and Social Aspect of Educational Planning*, (UNESCO, Paris, 1964, 165–222).

[31] *Essays in Regional and World Planning*, (New Delhi: National Council of Applied Economic Research, 1964).

[32] TINBERGEN, J. and BOS, H. C. 'A Planning Model for the Educational Requirements of Economic Development', *The Residual Factor and Economic Growth*, (Paris: O.E.C.D., 1964, 147–69).

[33] 'Possibilities for Application of Operational Research to Problems of Development', *Management Science*, x, (February 1963) 193–6.

[34] 'Project Appraisal: A Traditional Approach', *Essays on Econometrics and Planning, Presented to Professor P. C. Mahalanobis on the Occasion of his 70th Birthday*. (Calcutta: Pergamon, 1964), 295–300.

[35] 'Reply', to T. Balogh, 'Education and Economic Growth', *Kyklos*, xvii, (February 1964) 261–75.

[36] 'Discussion on the Organization of Coexistence', *Review of International Affairs*, xvi, (October 1965) 13–14.

[37] 'Economic Development and Investment Indivisibilities', *Problems of Economic Dynamics and Planning; Essays in Honor of Michal Kalecki*, ed. T. Kowalik, (Warsaw: P.W.N. Polish Scientific, 1965), 455–67.

[38] 'The Economic Framework of Regional Planning', *Semaine d'Etude sur le Rôle de l'Analyse Econométrique dans la Formulation de Plans de Développement*, Pontificiae Academiae Scientarium, Scripta Varia, No. 28, (Rome, 1965), 1233–64.

[39] 'Ideologies and Scientific Development: The Optimal Order', *Review of International Affairs*, xvi, (October 1965) 6–7.

[40] 'Improving International Development Policies', *Review of International Affairs*, xvi, (September 1965) 10–12.

[41] 'Simple Devices for Development Planning', in: *Problems in Economic Development*, ed. by E. A. G. Robinson. (London/New York: Macmillan, 1965).

[42] *Some Principles of Regional Planning*, (Rotterdam: Nederlands Economisch Instituut, Publication 29/65), 1965.

[43] 'The Concept of Unbalanced Growth', in: *Economic Development: Issues and Policies*, Dr P. S. Lokanathan 72nd Birthday, Commemoration Volume, ed. P. H. Butani and P. Singh. (Bombay 1966) 14–17.

[44] 'Economic Growth Plans and Their Impact on Business Management', *United Malayan Banking Corporation Economic Review*, xi, (February 1966) 20–6.

[45] 'International Economic Planning', *Daedalus Journal of the American Academy of Arts and Sciences*, 1966 issue: 'Conditions of World Order', 530–57.

[46] 'Some Refinements of the Semi-Input-Output Method', *Pakistan Development Review*, vi, (February 1966) 243–247.

[47] 'Concluding Remarks', in: *Towards a Strategy for Development Co-operation*, ed. H. B. Chenery *et al.* (Rotterdam: Rotterdam University Press, 1967), 93–101.

[48] 'The Hierarchy Model of the Size Distribution of Centers', *Regional Science Association: Papers*, xx, (1967) 65–68.

[49] 'Links between National Planning and Town and Country Planning', paper presented at the *Symposium on Urbanization of the International Union of Local Authorities*, (The Hague, 1967).

[50] 'Planning in the Common Market', *Sosialøkonomen*, XXI, (June 1967) 14–16.

[51] 'Chenery: Efficient Development Research', *Economisch Statistische Berichten*, LIII, (November 1968) 1013–14.

[52] 'Myrdal's Asian Drama', *Pakistan Development Review*, VIII, (April 1968) 618–25.

[53] 'The Optimal International Division of Labour', *Acta Oeconomica Academiae Scientarium Hungaricae*, III, (March 1968) 257–82.

[54] 'Optimalization – of What?' *Co-Existence*, V, (1968) 1–5.

[55] TINBERGEN, J. and BOUWMEESTER, J. 'The Role of Social Security as Seen by the Development Planner', in: *The Role of Social Security in Economic Development*, ed. E. M. Kassalow. (Washington, 1968), 39–50.

[56] 'The Significance of Science for the Developing Countries', *Higher Education and Research in the Netherlands*, XII, (March 1968) 24–9.

[57] 'Similarities and Differences between the Social Problem and the Development Problem', *Mens en Maatschappij*, XLIII, (January 1968) 120–7.

[58] 'Wanted: A World Development Plan', *International Organization*, XXII, (January 1968) 417–31.

[59] *Gunnar Myrdal on Planning Models*, U.N. Asian Institute for Economic Development and Planning, Institute Monograph No. 11, (Bangkok, 1969), 13ff.

3. Econometrics

[1] *An Econometric Approach to Business Cycles Problems*, (Paris: Hermann and Cie, 1937).

[2] 'Statistical Evidence on the Acceleration Principle', *Economica*, New Series V (1938) 164–76.

[3] *Business Cycles in the United States of America, 1919–1932*, (Geneva: League of Nations, 1939).

[4] 'Econometric Business Cycle Research', *Review of Economic Studies*, (1939/40) 73–90.

[5] *A Method and its Application to Investment Activity*, (Geneva: League of Nations, 1939).

[6] TINBERGEN, J. and DE WOLFF, P. 'A Simplified model of the Causation of Technological Unemployment', *Econometrica*, VII, (July 1939) 193–207.

[7] 'An Acceleration Principle for Commodity Stockholding and a Short Cycle Resulting from It', in: *Studies in Mathematical Economics and Econometrics*, ed. by Lange *et al.*, (Chicago: University of Chicago Press, 1942), 255–267.

[8] 'Some Measurements of Elasticities of Substitution', *Review of Economics and Statistics*, XXVIII, (August 1946) 109–16.

[9] 'The Use of Correlation Analysis in Economic Research', *Ekonomisk Tidskrift*, XLIX, (March 1947) 173–92.

[10] TINBERGEN, J. and DERKSEN, J. B. D. 'Recent Experiments in Social Accounting: Flexible and Dynamic Budgets', in: The Econometric Society Meeting, September 1947, Washington, 1949.

[11] *Business Cycles in the United Kingdom, 1870–1914*, (Amsterdam: North Holland, 1951).

[12] 'Schumpeter and Quantitative Research in Economics', *Review of Economics and Statistics*, XXXIII, (May 1951) 111–19.

[13] 'Some Neglected Points in Demand Research', *Metroeconomica*, III, (February 1951) 49–54.

[14] 'Comments' on: ORCUTT, GUY H. 'Toward Partial Redirection of Econometrics', *Review of Economics and Statistics*, XXXIV, (March 1952) 205ff.

[15] 'Import and Export Elasticities: Some Remarks', *International Statistical Institute, Bulletin*, XXXIII, (1953) 215–26.

[16] 'The Functions of Mathematical Treatment: Mathematics in Economics, Discussion of Mr. Novicks' Article', *Review of Economics and Statistics*, XXXVI, (November 1954) 365–9.

[17] 'Quantitative Economics in the Netherlands Model Building for Economic Policy', *Higher Education and Research in the Netherlands*, II, (March 1958) 3–7.

4. Economic Theory (and Miscellaneous)

[1] 'Annual Survey of Significant Developments in General Economic Theory', *Econometrica*, II, (1934) 13–36.

[2] 'On the Theory of Business Cycle Control', *Econometrica*, VI, (January 1938) 22–39.

[3] 'The Dynamics of Share-Price Formation', *Review of Economics and Statistics*, XXI, (November 1939) 153–60.

[4] 'On a Method of Statistical Business Cycle Research: A Reply', *The Economic Journal*, L, (March 1940) 141–54.

[5] 'Unstable and Indifferent Equilibria in Economic Systems', *Revue de l'Institut International de Statistique*, IX, (1941) 36–50.

[6] 'Critical Remarks on Some Business Cycle Theories', *Econometrica*, X, (April 1942) 129–46.

[7] 'Does Consumption Lag Behind Incomes?', *Review of Economics and Statistics*, XXIV, (February 1942) 1–8.

[8] 'Professor Douglas' Production Function', *Revue de l'Institut International de Statistique*, X, (1942) 37–48.

[9] 'Some Problems in the Explanation of Interest Rates', *Quarterly Journal of Economics*, LXI, (1947) 397–438.

[10] 'The Reformulation of Current Business Cycle Theories as Refutable Hypotheses', in: *Conference on Business Cycles*, National Bureau of Economic Research, 1949.

[11] 'Economic Policy in the Netherlands', *Statsøkonomisk Tidsskrift*, LXIV, (1950) 70–80.

[12] *On the Theory of Economic Policy*, (Amsterdam: North Holland, 1952).

[13] 'The Influence of Productivity on Economic Welfare', *The Economic Journal*, LXII, (1952) 68–86.

[14] 'Financing Social Insurance out of Premiums or out of Income Tax', *Archive of Economic and Social Sciences*, XXXII, (1952) 71–7.

[15] 'Efficiency and Future of Economic Research', *Kyklos*, V, (April 1952) 309–19.

[16] *Centralization and Decentralization in Economic Policy*, (Amsterdam: North Holland, 1954).

[17] *Economic Policy: Principles and Design*, (Amsterdam: North Holland, 1956).

[18] 'On the Theory of Income Distribution', *Weltwirtschaft-liches Archiv*, LXXVII, (January 1956) 10–31.

[19] 'The Optimum Rate of Savings', *The Economic Journal*, LXVI, (1956) 603–9.

[20] TINBERGEN, J. *et al.* 'Comments on the Economics of Governor Stevenson's Program Paper: Where is the Money Coming From?', *Review of Economics and Statistics*, (May 1957) 134–42.

[21] 'Welfare Economics and Income Distribution', *American Economic Review, Papers and Proceedings*, XLVII, (February 1957) 490–503.

[22] 'The Economic Principles for an Optimum Use of Space', *Les Cahiers de Bruges*, XI, (1958) 15–18.

[23] 'Should the Income Tax be Among the Means of Economic Policy?', *Festskrift til Frederick Zeuthen*, (København, 1958), 351–62.

[24] *Selected Papers*, (Amsterdam: North Holland, 1959).

[25] 'The Theory of the Optimum Regime', *Selected Papers*, (Amsterdam: North Holland, 1959, 264–304).

[26] 'Economic Models of the Explanation of Inflation', in: *Stabile Preise in Wachsender Wirtschaft. Erich Schneider zum 60 Geburtstag*, ed. by G. Bomback, (Tübingen: J. C. B. Mohr, 1960, 115–24).

[27] 'Optimum Savings and Utility Maximization over Time', *Econometrica*, XXVIII, (February 1960) 481–90.

[28] TINBERGEN, J. and BOS, H. C. *Mathematical Models of Economic Growth*, (New York: McGraw-Hill, 1962).

[29] 'Do Communist and Free Societies Show a Converging Pattern?', *Soviet Studies*, XII, (April 1961) 333–41.

[30] 'The Significance of Welfare Economics for Socialism', *On Political Economy and Econometrics, Essays in Honour of Oskar Lange*, (Warsaw: P.W.N. Polish Scientific Publishers, 1965).

[31] 'On the Optimal Social Order and a World Economic Policy', (A discussion with Professor L. Leontiev), *Oost-West*, V, (October 1966) 242–4.

[32] TINBERGEN, J. and BOS, H. C. 'A Planning Model for the Educational Requirements of Economic Development', *The Residual Factor and Economic Growth*, (Paris: O.E.C.D., 1964, 147–69).

[33] 'A Model for a Flow of Funds Analysis of an Open Country', in *Essays in Honour of Marco Fano*, (Padova, 1966), 688–92.

[34] 'Some Suggestions on a Modern Theory of the Optimum Regime', in *Socialism, Capitalism and Economic Growth, Essays Presented to Maurice Dobb*, ed. by C. H. Feinstein, (London: Cambridge University Press, 1967), 125–32.

[35] TINBERGEN, J., LINNEMANN, H. and PRONK, J. P. 'Convergence of Economic Systems in East and West', in *Disarmament and World Economic Interdependence*, ed. by E. Benoit, (Oslo: Universitestsforlaget, 1967), 246–60.

[36] 'A Few Comments on Professor Lev Leontiev's Answer', *Oost-West*, VI, (May 1967) 49ff.

[37] 'Development Strategy and Welfare Economics', *Co-Existence*, VI, (July 1969) 119–26.

[38] 'Future Relations Between the Countries of Eastern and Western Europe', *Oost-West*, VIII, (May 1969) 165–6.

[39] 'Ideology and Coexistence', *Review of International Affairs*, XX, (1969) 1–2.

Index